OF PENGUINS AND POLAR BEARS

OF PENGUINS AND POLAR BEARS

A HISTORY OF COLD WATER CRUISING

CHRISTOPHER WRIGHT

The book has been written with help from Kevin Griffin, Managing Director, The Cruise People Ltd, London (UK)

Cover illustrations:
Front: Poster advertising travel to Spitzberg, Norway, *c.*1931 by Albert Sébille. (Christie's Images)
Front Flap: Magellanic penguin. (Courtesy Falkland Islands Tourism)
Back: OneOcean vessel (David Sinclair, courtesy OneOcean Expeditions)
Black Flap: Polar bear. (Roger Pimenta, courtesy OneOcean Expeditions)

First published 2020

The History Press
97 St George's Place, Cheltenham,
Gloucestershire, GL50 3QB
www.thehistorypress.co.uk

British Library Cataloguing in Publication Data.
A catalogue record for this book is available from the British Library.

ISBN 978 0 7509 9057 8

Typesetting and origination by The History Press
Printed in Turkey by Imak

CONTENTS

FOREWORD

Robert Headland, Scott Polar Research Institute, University of Cambridge

Of the several ways people present in either polar region may be described, those visiting as tourists are a major division. Considered in absolute numbers in any year, mainly during a summer (boreal or austral), they form the largest number of people in Antarctic regions and become a major component of the Arctic population. In contrast, their proportion of time measured in person days is minimal, barely reaching 1 per cent in the Antarctic and far less in the Arctic. This book presents a detailed and comparative study with analysis of tourism in the regions of polar bears and penguins. It coordinates aspects of the many subjects involved: history, geography, navigation, companies and commerce, and even anthropology (but only for the Arctic). While ships transport the majority of tourists, attention is also given to aircraft and, in some circumstances, a combination.

From the late 1990s, tourist visits to both polar regions have vastly increased, resulting from several factors. Those that might have been expected include: improved accessibility, much better public awareness and information, environmental concerns, and their being regarded as 'safe places' compared with many more politically unstable regions of the Earth. Unexpected factors also had strong influences on polar tourism, notably the abrupt availability of Russian ice-class vessels and removal of restricted areas in the Arctic rapidly following the dissolution of the Soviet Union in 1991. Things deemed almost incredible only a year previously became practicable. Trade and commerce reacted promptly to the supply and demand fluctuations.

One of the several contemporary coincidences was the formation of the International Association of Antarctic Tour Operators (IAATO) in 1991, which progressively developed procedures, regulations and guidelines for that region. A dozen years later, in 2003, the Association of Arctic Expedition Cruise Operators was founded that similarly introduced principles for member operators throughout the more frequently visited parts of the Arctic. From their establishment both organisations had rapidly increasing numbers of members (many belonged to both) and became coordinated, although informally, with governance of the polar regions. The objects of these organisations included not only coordinating shipping schedules to avoid encounters at the same location, but also preparing codes of conduct for avoiding adverse environmental effects and encouragement of favourable interaction with settlements, bases or similar habitations. Many principles are comparable but the political differences between national Arctic territories and the Antarctic Treaty region necessitate distinctions.

Details and discussion of these substantial and recent developments, with their historical precedents, form the subject of this very comprehensive book. Such a study is timely when polar tourism is evolving rapidly at a period when demand is strong, resulting in the construction of many new polar vessels. As well as changes from climatic variation and reduction of ice cover generally there are things considered appropriate such as fuel, engine design, victualling, passenger access ports and other facilities to analyse and estimate what future constraints they might impose. Increasing maritime traffic in Arctic regions is similarly to be anticipated, noting that tourist vessels are but one of several components.

Obtaining details of such a diverse industry involving many countries, companies and locations is a difficult task. This is achieved by the author by including a large range of information in appendices giving details of vessels, companies, voyages to specific locations and a compilation of noteworthy incidents. These include data from the earliest days of polar cruise tourism until present circumstances.

The reason why tourists are increasingly enthusiastic to visit both polar regions are several, general and particular for individuals. The magnificent scenery, highly adapted flora and fauna, historical remains, and stations and settlements appeal to virtually everyone, but personal acquaintance, political aspects, souvenirs (notably philatelic) and having been personally present in some of the most remote parts of the planet are additional factors.

Tourism to both polar regions continues to flourish and this book provides a very practical basis with which to understand its origin and development, thus providing basic data for assessment of its probable future.

Robert Headland,
Cambridge, August 2019

FOREWORD

Philip Dawson, AssocRINA

This is a fascinating book that in effect takes us around the world vertically from pole to pole in an extensive and varied look at cruising in the globe's Arctic and Antarctic waters. Steamship excursions into polar waters and to their surrounding lands first gained popularity early in the liner era during the latter decades of the nineteenth century. The compelling natural beauty of these oft-intemperate regions, themselves polarised by their own sharply contrasting seasons of formidable winter darkness (save for the phenomenal beauty of the Northern Lights) and the summer season's languid around-the-clock lightness, are ever a source of great fascination to those of a scientific turn of mind as well as to the curiously minded and adventurous world traveller.

For the great majority of us, those without the credentials, or indeed the opportunity, to join any sort of academic or scientific excursion into Earth's polar regions, a scheduled commercial shipboard voyage continues, even now, to be our only practical way to see these otherwise largely inaccessible regions, their unique geography, fauna and flora, for ourselves.

Thankfully, the great beauty of our polar regions still remains largely unspoiled, or at least more so than many other holiday and cruise destinations. As a fellow passenger said to me during a cruise to Spitsbergen aboard *Europa* a number of years ago, 'This is one of the few chances we still have to know something of the world's natural beauty as God created it.' Yet, on the other hand, climate change has now made the Northwest and Northeast Passages more open to navigation in the Arctic summer months. As the author explains, polar cruising has now become a distinct speciality in the global cruise industry, with purpose-built modern ships specifically designed for service in polar seas with ice-strengthened hulls and equipped to land passengers in places where there are no piers or landing stages. A number of former Soviet Arctic icebreakers have also been adapted for polar cruising. Beyond the basic home comforts of early ships such as *Nascopie* and *St Sunniva*, today's polar seas cruise passenger now also enjoys much the same luxury and service of larger cruise ships in mainstream Mediterranean, Caribbean and worldwide cruise markets. Polar expedition cruising is now considered by many to be a last frontier of cruise holiday development.

This book, to the best of my knowledge, is a unique treatment of passenger shipping in the domain of polar bears and penguins, as a literary travelling companion; a historical guide, gazetteer, companion and general reference resource. The story of expedition cruising from 1869 to the present day tells of a great diversity of ships, their owners and operators, of places and people, some well known and others far less so, that have influenced travel in these waters.

There is a comprehensive gazetteer of places in the polar regions where cruise ships call, with geographical information including climate, fauna and flora. There are also sections covering cruise operators, ships and fleet lists past and present, and future ships as of 2019, fares, regulations, safety and even a list of cruise ship incidents in polar waters. While one hopes that incidents such as these are less likely to be repeated, it is perhaps good to remind ourselves that there are still risks in these waters – perhaps in reality that's all still part of the adventure.

If, like the author, you are involved in the shipping industry, or perhaps you are planning to travel in polar waters or to relive past excursions, or perhaps like me, you are now an armchair traveller, relax and enjoy the voyage of your dreams by way of this fascinating book.

Philip Dawson, AssocRINA
Toronto, June 2019

INTRODUCTION

This book is about cruising in the Arctic and Antarctic regions, how and where it developed, and what has attracted people to these remote parts of the world. It starts with William Bradford's cruise to Greenland in the Newfoundland sealer *Panther* in 1869 and traces polar cruise activity from the first North Cape cruise by Thomas Cook in the *President Christie* in 1875 through the interwar period to the present day, with a chapter on where expedition cruising is going in the future. While polar cruising was sustained by large vessels up until the 1990s, largely on a sightseeing basis, the availability of Russian research ships as expedition cruise ships enabled this sector of the industry to offer a wide range of experiential cruises. In terms of destinations and activities, north of 60°N and south of 60°S are considered as being of a polar nature. The history of each region is reviewed, and up-to-date and comprehensive statistics are provided for each destination.

In brief, the Arctic can be considered as an ocean surrounded by land, while the Antarctic is a continent surrounded by an ocean. Each has different attributes, with the Antarctic 'brand' being penguins, while that of the Arctic is the polar bear.

The Arctic

Indigenous peoples have occupied almost all the lands that surround the Arctic Ocean, and the North Pole, for thousands of years and sovereignty is well established. The region also has a strong European history associated with sealing, whaling, resource extraction and attempts to use Arctic passages as a shortcut between the Atlantic and the Pacific Oceans.

The climate varies between the relative harshness of the Canadian Arctic islands, except during the short northern summer, to much milder temperatures in Iceland, Scandinavia and northern islands due to the influence of the Gulf Stream. This difference affects the flora and fauna of the different regions, as well as the history of cruise tourism. Depending on location, in north polar destinations the shipping season is generally between May and October, although Norwegian fjords are moving to a year-round cruise presence.

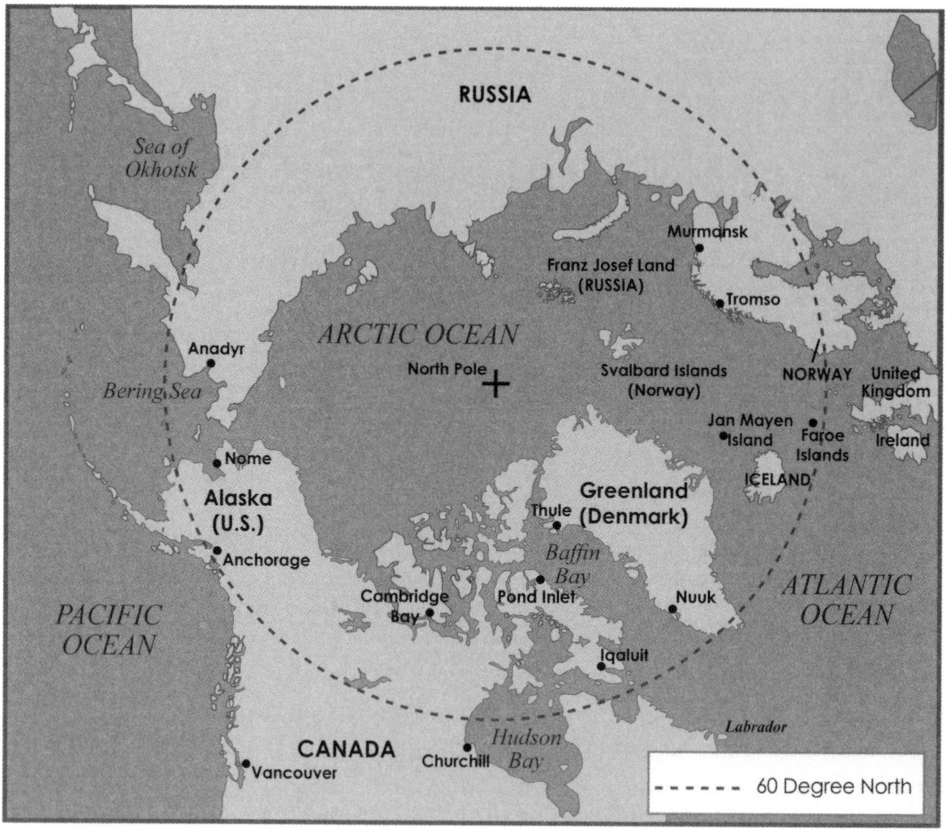

⬆ Map of the Arctic region.

⬇ Polar bears. (Robert Serrini, courtesy OneOcean Expeditions)

Different parts of the Arctic region have different attractions. For the Canadian Arctic Islands and the Northwest Passage, it is mainly the history associated with Franklin and his two ships, *Erebus* and *Terror*. Greenland is the home of ancient Norse settlement, while Svalbard markets itself as the home of polar bears, although its early attraction was for hunting reindeer. Iceland offers extraordinary scenery due to its volcanic nature. Nordkapp, at the northern tip of Norway, attracted early cruise passengers because it was seen as the end of the Earth, and they could travel there to see the midnight sun.

Because of the climate, there is a wide range of land animals, birds, whales and seals. While some are panarctic relative to their habitat, many have specific regions where they can be found during the cruise season. The Canadian Arctic Islands and Greenland and intervening straits are particularly prolific in terms of different species.

The Antarctic

This is a region where there has never been settlement, until Europeans arrived seeking seals and whales. The Antarctic continent is a forbidding area with an ice cap up to 4km thick, together with many associated islands. The region is under international agreement relative to access, exploitation and long-term residence. Mainly, the continent itself and islands in the Southern Ocean have research stations that date back to the International Geophysical Year of 1957, which had a focus on the Antarctic; cruise tourism is a relatively recent phenomenon.

Apart from a short period during the southern summer, which is generally taken as mid November to early March,[1] the region ranges from cold to very cold; there is no ameliorating influence like the Gulf Stream. The island groups that surround Antarctica are, generally, the tops of submerged mountains, and only the Falkland Islands have a permanent population. Historical locations are limited and mainly associated with expeditions to the South Pole by explorers such as Shackleton. However, much of this history is inaccessible to visitors from ships, although Shackleton's grave in Grytviken on South Georgia is frequently visited. Unlike the Arctic, fauna is almost exclusively avian and marine, and dependent on the ocean resources; the flora is also much less diverse.

Wildlife, typically visits to penguin colonies, is a major draw for visitors. There are five penguin species that make their homes on the Antarctic continent and immediate islands; another four nest on neighbouring islands, while one species – the Royal – is limited to Macquarie Island. See chapters on different destinations for more details. There are estimated to be about 100 million birds of many different species that make their homes in the Antarctic islands, the most notable being the albatross on South Georgia, and the southern giant petrel, with breeding pairs on many of the islands. After being hunted almost to extinction, fur and elephant seals have made dramatic recoveries and while whales are far from numerous, numbers are slowly increasing and blue, sperm and humpback sightings are more frequent, as are the ubiquitous orca.

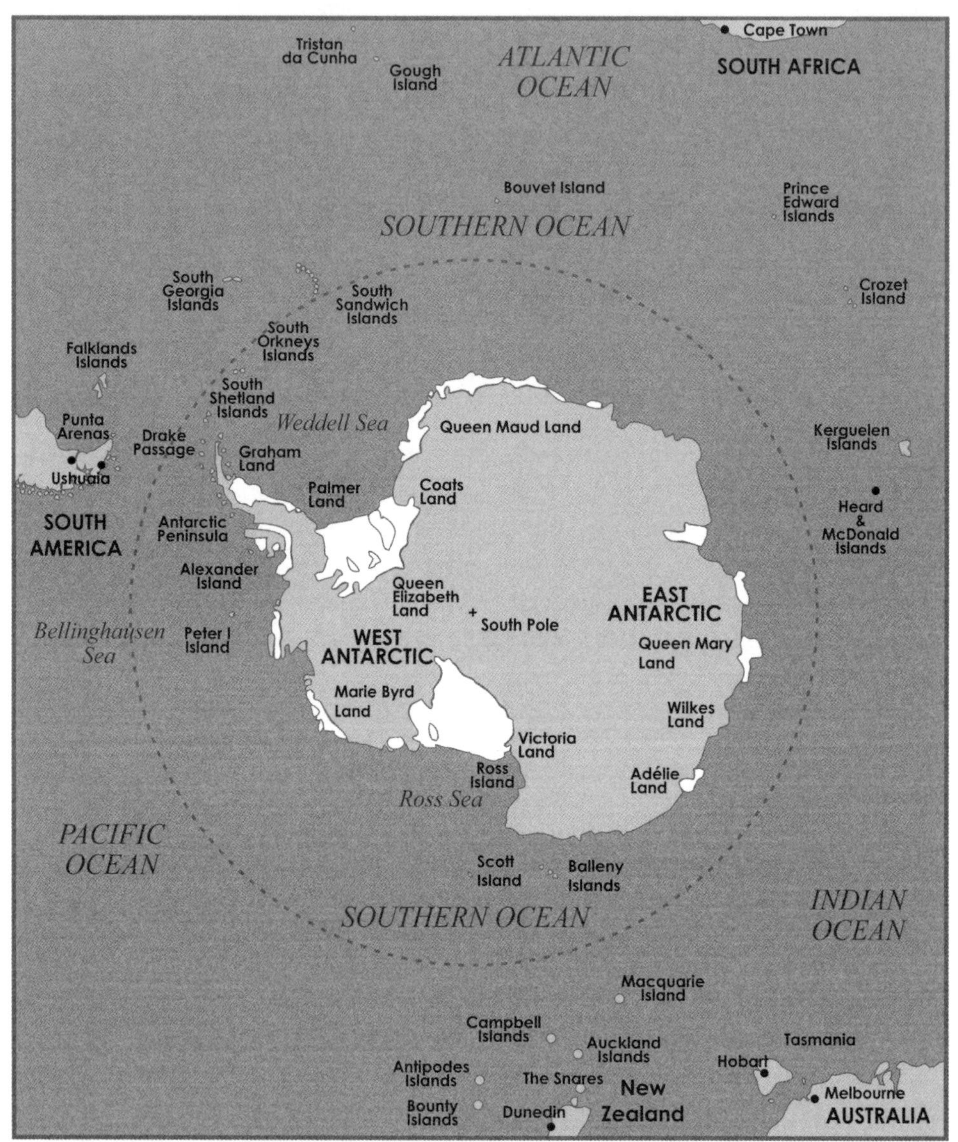

Map of the Antarctic region.

Penguins. (Ben Hagar, courtesy OneOcean Expeditions)

Polar and Expedition Cruise Ships

Prior to the arrival of the first true expedition cruise vessels in the 1970s, most ships that cruised to polar destinations were deployed from other routes for off-season travel. Up to the Second World War, accommodation on these ships was typically first, second and third class, and/or steerage, which was dormitories for emigrants. Passage for emigrants[2] from Europe to the Americas and Australasia was a major part of the business for ocean liners, but it did present some problems regarding ship occupancy. Although demand was strong through the 1920s, it occurred primarily in the spring on the North Atlantic on east to west sailings, and winter heading to the Antipodes. There was almost no use for steerage from west to east on the Atlantic, or at other times of the year. To compound shipping company occupancy problems, first class on the North Atlantic was, typically, booked by wealthy Americans heading to Europe in the spring for a summer of touring, then returning in the autumn. Thus occupancy was low during the summer period and to maintain revenue ships were often deployed on cruises. However, the strictly segregated classes, which had separate facilities and areas of the ship, made them less than ideal for such a role. Also, the optics of second class created issues for some lines in selling the cabins.

⬆ *Montclare* in the Norwegian Fjords, 1930s. (© National Maritime Museum, Greenwich, London)

⬇ Hamburg-Amerika Linie *Meteor* in a Norwegian fjord. (Courtesy Hapag-Lloyd AG, Hamburg)

After the First World War, some lines, of which Canadian Pacific (CP) was an early adopter, introduced cabin class, which combined first and second class into a single class that was priced slightly higher than the old second class, but provided first-class service. The next class was usually tourist, and then third class (which never had the same connotation as second class). As an example, the 1921-built CP liner *Montclare* had accommodation for 520 cabin, 278 tourist and 850 third-class passengers. The Compagnie Générale Transatlantique (CGT) liner *Lafayette* delivered in 1930 had accommodation for 583 cabin, 388 tourist and 108 third-class passengers. Both of these ships cruised to the Norwegian fjords and Spitsbergen.

As can be appreciated, these ships were relatively large, and it was such vessels that dominated polar cruising for a century. It was not until the 1990s, when the repurposed Russian research ships became available, that polar expedition cruising, as it is understood today, became a recognisable component of the growing cruise industry.

From the 1890s onwards, the equivalent of expedition cruising was yachting cruises. For example, the Thomas Cook publication *Excursionist and Tourist Advertiser* contained a yachting cruise section with advertisements such as: 'Orient Company's Yachting Cruises to Norway' and 'SS *Victoria* Yachting Cruises'. P&O promoted the *Vectis* with the tag line: 'Summer Cruises to Norway, Spitsbergen and Baltic Capitals by the P&O Cruising Yacht *Vectis*'.

Even as late as the 1950s, Cunard referred to the *Caronia* as having a yacht-like atmosphere, despite being 34,000grt. Expedition ships, some of which continue to promote their yachting ambience, have not yet reached that size, but Ponant's *Le Commandant Charcot* ice-breaking expedition ship, at 30,000grt, will be close.

The opening chapter of Philip Dawson's magisterial *Cruise Ships, an Evolution in Design*, published in 2000, discusses the early cruise yachts, while the penultimate chapter is subtitled 'Ascending Towards the 20,000 ton Yacht'. In his examination of future developments, Dawson quotes Wartsila's Kai Levander from a 1982 paper:

> The cruise market today shows an evident gap and demand for high class cruise vessels for 50–200 passengers. Some people find the existing bigger cruise liners too crowded, or the ports visited uninteresting and spoiled by excessive touristic exploitation.[3] On the other hand, the yachts that can be chartered and taken to unspoiled islands do not offer the comfort, service and safety that many passengers wish to have. Today there is great interest in both sailing and motor cruise liners in this gap between the big and the small.

These comments are as appropriate today as they were nearly forty years ago, and while some ships that can be considered as cruise yachts have been delivered since 1982, it has taken until the recent explosion in polar expedition cruise ship orders for the predicted 20,000grt cruise yacht to emerge. The 200-passenger, 19,800grt *Crystal*

Endeavour class and the 264-passenger, 23,000grt *Seabourn Venture* class may represent the realisation of Dawson's expectations.

Hamburg-Amerika Line's *Meteor* demonstrates the classic yacht lines, but until the arrival of the *Lindblad Explorer* in 1969, only four ships, the *St Sunniva* (1887), *Prinzessin Victoria Luise* (1900), *Meteor* (1904) and *Stella Polaris* (1927), had been built specifically as small cruise ships. Three other ships were converted to similar yacht-style cruise ships; these were *St Rognvald* (1888), *Prins Olaf* (1926) and *Ariadne* (1957). A decade later, the *Italia*, later *Ocean Princess*, was a somewhat larger cruise ship that still demonstrated a yacht-like profile. They offered itineraries similar to larger vessels, such as Norwegian fjords, Spitsbergen, the Mediterranean, the Caribbean and the Atlantic Islands. Some did undertake the occasional longer northern cruise that included Iceland and they did have tenders to take passengers ashore, but unlike today's expedition ships they did not offer unique destinations that could be considered equivalent to today's itineraries. Their role was to offer a yacht-like cruising ambience and, except for the *Ariadne*, were very successful. The *Ariadne* may just have come to market too early, and might have succeeded if the focus had been on the American market, as Europeans, in the late 1950s, were still recovering from the aftermath of the Second World War, and those that did have the money to cruise were more interested in southern destinations. The *Ocean Princess* did undertake both northern and southern cruises during its short life, taking advantage of tenders installed after its 1983 refit.

Early Yacht-Style Cruise Ships

Ship	Built	GRT	Cabins	Guests Single Class	Crew	Dimensions, metres Length x Breadth
St Sunniva	1887	807		142		71.62 × 9.14
Prinzessin Victoria Luise[4]	1900	4,409	120	192	161	124.2 × 15
Meteor	1904	3,718		220		105.5 × 13.5
Stella Polaris	1927	5,020		198[5]	130	127.1 × 15.5
Ariadne	1951	7,764	159	293	193	134.7 × 17
Ocean Princess	1967	12,200	251	587	252	150 × 20.7
Lindblad Explorer	1969	2,398		104	54	76.2 × 14

The impact of Russian research ships on expedition cruising can be judged by ship visits to Antarctica, where there has been a concerted effort to track activity. Through the period from 1950, passenger numbers were minor, except for the 1974/75 season when several large ships sailed through the region. During the late 1970s and until the 1986/87 season, when the *Illiria* joined them, there were just two ships offering Antarctic cruises, the *Lindblad Explorer* (after 1985 *Society Explorer*) and the 1975-built *World Discoverer*. Then in the 1988/89 season, Lindblad chartered the Soviet passenger ship *Antonina Nedzhanova*, and that season five ships undertook twenty-one cruises, with an average of 117 passengers per trip. A decade later twenty-one ships carried out 154 cruises. By the 2017/18 season, thirty ships had carried out more than 300 cruises where passengers were landed, and large ship activity, where passengers are purely sightseers, was a well-established annual event after being an occasional activity.

Large ships have continued to be the major participants in northern polar regions, dominating calls at the North Cape, Spitsbergen, Faroe Islands and Greenland. Expedition-style ships participate, but are relatively few in number. There is some expedition-style cruising within the Svalbard Islands, as well as Iceland circumnavigation itineraries. Falkland Islands fees favour expedition ships that call at one or more of the many islands that make up the archipelago, although Stanley does see a good number of large ships on both Antarctic and non-polar voyages. The Canadian Arctic, probably because of a time-consuming permitting process, only receives around ten ships per year offering about twenty cruises, including two to three Northwest Passages each season, although these numbers do depend on ice conditions. The region is ideal for expedition cruising, and may develop further if a resolution can be found to the complex permitting process. Numbers and activity to all destinations will probably change in the future as there are thirty-eight ice-classed expedition ships on order and due for delivery between 2019 and 2022. Most ships are under 300-passenger capacity, and range in size from 5,000grt to a remarkable 30,000grt.

In looking at expedition cruising as a component of polar activity, we have adopted the convention that expedition ships carry 30-500 passengers.[6] This is done to distinguish such ships from mega yachts, which may carry up to twenty-five persons all told. Vessels over 500 passengers are considered cruise-only and generally do not land passengers. Historically, the upper limit of expedition ships was probably established by the *Ocean Princess*,[7] which at the time IAATO was established was the largest ship to tender passengers ashore in the Antarctic. Chapter 1 traces the development of polar cruising from large liners on summer duty to the smaller dedicated expedition ships today. Details of ships known to have cruised to polar destinations are provided in the Appendices.

1

DEVELOPMENT OF POLAR CRUISING

Introduction

In 1856, Lord Dufferin (who was later to be a major figure in the British colonial service) took his schooner yacht *Foam*[1] on a trip from Oban, Scotland, via Stornoway in the Orkney Islands, Iceland, Jan Mayen Island, Spitsbergen to Copenhagen. The light-hearted account of his three-month voyage was published in at least five editions, some of which were illustrated, and translated into French and German.

↑ The *Panther* off Greenland in 1869. (Courtesy New Bedford Whaling Museum)

The account had a major impact on the perception of the Arctic, changing it from the forbidding ice-bound region suggested by Sir John Franklin's ill-fated voyage of 1845, to something much more benign. The gentleman travellers of the late nineteenth century now saw it as quite accessible, and many took their yachts to Spitsbergen on exploration and hunting trips.

In 1869, William Bradford, a Boston artist with a keen interest in the north (he had spent six summers sailing the Labrador coast) determined to go much further into the Arctic. In the foreword to his remarkable book *The Arctic Regions*, he states:

> In this connection, a perusal of the *History of the Grinnell Expedition* by Dr. Kane and Lord Dufferin's 'Letters from High Latitudes' made so powerful an impression that I was seized with the desire, which became uncontrollable, to visit the scenes they described and study nature under the terrible aspects of the frigid zone …

However, he estimated that he needed some $20,000 to mount such a trip to Greenland, and as an artist he did not have that kind of ready money. One of his patrons, LeGrand Lockwood, offered to provide the funding, but Bradford went further and advertised for gentlemen to join his voyage; some did at $1,000 each. Bradford retained the Arctic explorer Isaac Hayes to advise on the trip, and join the ship as an on-board expert, for a fee of $1,500.

The voyage had the sole goal of sightseeing for art's sake. The company took excursions to places such as the Viking remains at Hvalsey, had a picnic on a glacier and made other side trips. It can reasonably be considered the progenitor of both polar and expedition cruising. In fact, as a result of a letter from Isaac Hayes to James Gordon Bennett Jr, publisher of the *New York Herald*, the paper published an editorial on 8 September 1869 that stated: 'We do not see why the project of Mr. Bradford and his friend Dr. Hayes to inaugurate regular summer excursions to the Arctic Regions may not become practical and popular, with steamers properly equipped for the purpose.'

The ship that Bradford chartered was the New Brunswick-built, but Newfoundland-owned, ice-strengthened sealer *Panther*, part owned by John Bartlett, its captain. The ship departed St John's at 10 a.m. on 3 July 1869 and called at Julianhavn, Sermitsialik Glacier, Ivigtut, Upernavik and Tasiusaq, managing to get to 75° N before being stopped by ice. They returned via Melville Bay, Disko Island and Godhavn, then back to St John's, some three months later.

Expedition cruising then moved across the Arctic to Nordkapp in Norway in 1875, when Thomas Cook took twenty-one excursionists on the *President Christie*[2] to view the midnight sun. Then one Henry Clodius chartered the *Pallas* in 1881 and embarked about thirty intrepid vacationers for Spitsbergen after they had answered advertisements in hunting magazines, including *The Field*, that promised polar bear, seal, walrus and reindeer hunting.

These, and later voyages by smaller ships on unique voyages, set the tone for polar expedition cruising. Today, such ships still carry a relatively small number of passengers, but range from quite simple accommodation, sometimes with shared facilities, to opulent suites on some of the forthcoming polar expedition ships.

Polar Cruising Before the First World War

The Antarctic of this period was the Svalbard Islands, and polar cruising focused on Spitsbergen and seeing how far into the pack ice the ship could go. Cruise itineraries varied in length, with the longer ones incorporating Nordkapp and Iceland. German, British, French and Norwegian companies participated in the trade, as well as a number of independent charterers. In this respect, it is interesting to consider the language used in P&O's Spitsbergen itinerary for the *Vectis*.

In 1905, the ship's itinerary listed Merok, followed by the statement: 'Time devoted to steaming to the ice pack and Recherche Bay (Spitzbergen), stay in port and return to North Cape, 8 days.' In following brochures there is no mention of the ice pack and the time is steadily reduced. Then in 1911, the following statement is included: 'From Tromsø, conditions being favourable, the *Vectis* will steam north to Recherche Bay Spitzbergen, the time allotted for the stay there being about 48 hours.' One might speculate that the *Ile de France* incident in 1906, when it grounded on rocks, had spooked the underwriters, and insurance costs had gone up, necessitating cruises to go only as far as Recherche Bay and avoid the ice pack.

At this time, cruising as a vacation concept was only just developing and there were few purpose-built or specially converted ships. Most of the ships deployed to the north pre-First World War (as in later years) were regular passenger ships on summer assignments. While Thomas Cook had started interest in northern Norway in 1875 with a cruise for twenty-one excursionists on the *President Christie* to Nordkapp, the chartering of the ship was not planned. Because of a misunderstanding over cabin accommodation on the ships that provided coastal sailings prior to the introduction of the Hurtigruten service, the company was forced to charter to fulfil its obligations to the tourists on the trip.

One of the earliest companies to enter the market, although initially only to the Norwegian fjords, was the North of Scotland, Orkney and Shetland Shipping Company (The North Company), which sent its *St Rognvald* on a single cruise to Bergen and 'some of the principal fjords and places of interest on the west coast of Norway' in 1886. The success of similar cruises offered by the *Ceylon* in 1884 may have encouraged the venture. The trip, at £10 for ten days, was a resounding success and the company dispatched a second cruise that same season. It then built one of the very first dedicated cruise ships – *St Sunniva* – for the 1887 season. Interestingly, the accommodation was essentially one class, a precursor of other expedition cruise ships.

⬆ *St Sunniva* rigging plan. (© Aberdeen City Council (Art Gallery and Museums Collection))

Accommodation on the *St Sunniva* was for 142 passengers in a combination of two-berth cabins on the main deck and multi-berth cabins on a lower deck. An unusual feature was a twelve-berth ladies cabin on the main deck that had its own bathroom and two toilets, as well as two washbasins. This provision may have been a response to the keen interest of Victorian ladies in travelling to out of the way destinations. However, a feature of early cruise ships, extending into the interwar period, was the large number of single cabins provided. The upper deck cabins all had washbasins, but as was common at the time, shared bathrooms and toilets. The lower deck cabins did not have en suite washbasins and shared a bathroom and two washbasins, but did not have toilets; these were all on the upper deck. The main saloon could seat 132 persons, and there was a smoking room as well as a ladies room aft.

Pricing for the *St Sunniva* was as follows:

Cabin on Upper Deck for one person: £15
Cabin for two persons: £12.12.0 each
In Ladies cabin and in a cabin holding more than two persons: £10.10.0
A Four-Berth Cabin, when taken by a party not exceeding four persons: £34.00.0

The passage money included:

Tea and Coffee from 7 to 8 a.m.
Breakfast at 9 a.m.
Lunch at 1 p.m.
Tea at 4 p.m.
Dinner at 7 p.m.
Tea and coffee afterwards.

Tea at 4 p.m. was said to include 'substantials', which means that it was high tea; that is tea, sandwiches, cakes and pastries.

The *St Sunniva* cruises sold out and the *St Rognvald* had to be brought in for an additional two cruises, which were limited to fifty passengers in order that guests should have the same level of accommodation as on the new vessel. The success of the *St Sunniva* programme persuaded The North Company to upgrade the *St Rognvald*, and in 1887 she was given twenty-two new midship cabins. Further modified in 1894 and 1898, she eventually offered 100 berths and a dining room that could seat eighty. The *St Rognvald* also went to the North Cape on a twenty-one-day cruise in 1888. Competition for the British market started immediately, with the Wilson Line offering a cruise with the *Domino*, after the perceived success of the first cruise by *St Rognvald*, and then Orient Line entered the market in 1889 with *Chimborozo* and *Garonne*. Ultimately, competition became too much, and The North Company exited the market after the 1908 season, converting the *St Sunniva* into a ferry.

Despite the success of The North Company, Captain Wilhelm Bade is often considered to be the father of polar cruising. Reports state that his company, Nordische Hochseefischerei Gesellschaft, was established in 1892 to undertake fishing, whaling, mining and tourism in Spitsbergen. Interestingly, the first Bade cruise to Spitsbergen was on the *Amely*, which Lloyd's Register notes was an iron screw trawler built that year and owned by a German deep-sea fishing company. It sailed from Tromsø with a small group of hunters and prospectors. As part of company business, a whale catcher, *Glukhauf*, was built, and it was intended that tourists could board the ship to participate in a whaling trip. The first three of the intended activities of the company failed after the 1892 season, but Bade, in today's parlance, 'found his passion' with tourism and went on to develop a successful business that was continued by his son after his death in 1903. Bade Senior chartered small, but well-appointed ships, focused on offering good food as well as interesting activities. The cruises were so well thought of that the passengers created a house flag for the company, and the Baedecker travel guide of the period recommended them. It would appear, from register details for the ships he chartered, that he took on ships that met the probable passenger numbers expected. For 1897–99 he chartered the *Kong Harald*, a small but well-appointed ship from Nordenfjeldske D/S. However, for 1900, he selected the *Herthe*, a 253grt wood steam auxiliary vessel, for a hunting trip to Franz Josef Land. Ice prevented them getting to their chosen destination, but they were able to take some polar bears and seals from Spitsbergen. Along with most operators, he did not charter in 1901, but for the next five years the *Oihonna* was the ship of choice, and on the 1903 cruise she carried forty-five passengers, of which thirty-seven were German.

The leading German liner company offering northern cruises was Hamburg-Amerika Line (the precursor to today's Hapag-Lloyd), which started cruising with the *Columbia* in 1893. Subsequent twenty-day cruises were offered in 1895 and 1896 from Hamburg, usually with a thirty-six-hour stopover in Spitsbergen, visiting Belsund and Isfjorden, then returning to Cuxhaven. The ships the company deployed into Spitsbergen were mainly used on its transatlantic service, which, as with

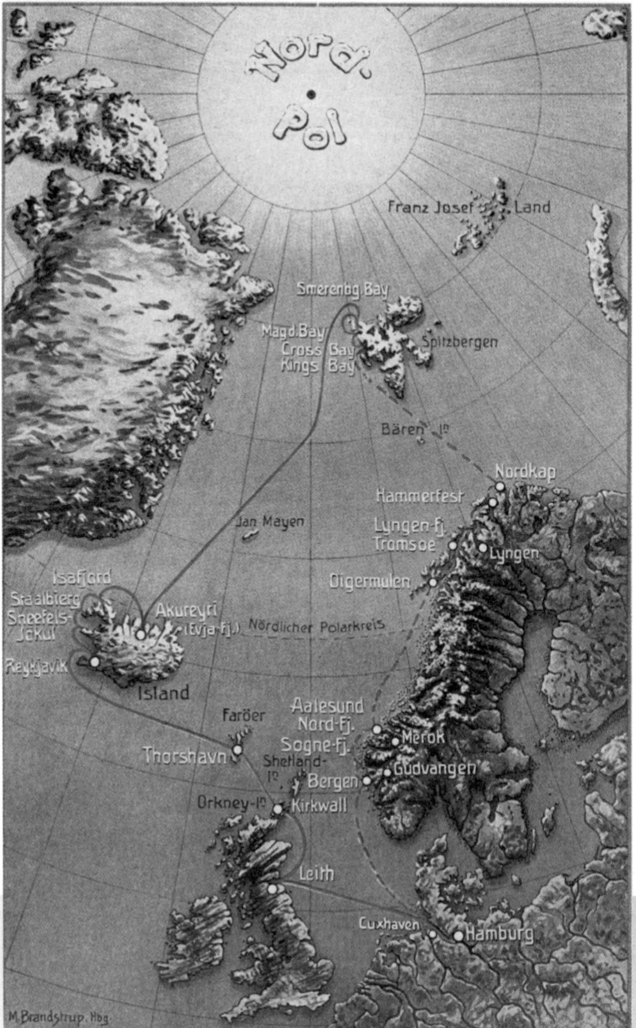

← Northern itinerary for *Victoria Luise* in 1912. (Courtesy Hapag-Lloyd AG Hamburg)

Zweite Nordlandfahrt mit dem Doppelschrauben-Postdampfer **„Victoria Luise"**
nach Island und Spitzbergen, ab Hamburg am 2. Juli 1912.

Fahrplan.

Datum	Zeit		Ungefährer Aufenthalt Stund.
2. Juli	Mittgs.	Abfahrt von **Hamburg.**	
4. „	Morgs.	Ankunft in **Leith (Edinburgh)** . .	41
5. „	Abends	Abfahrt von **Leith.**	
6. „	Nachm.	Ankunft in **Kirkwall (Orkney-Inseln)**	4
6. „	„	Abfahrt von **Kirkwall.**	
7. „	Morgs.	Ankunft in **Thorshavn (Farör)** .	5
7. „	Nachm.	Abfahrt von **Thorshavn.**	
9. „	Morgs.	Ankunft in **Reykjavik (Island)** . .	21
10. „	„	Abfahrt von **Reykjavik** (Fahrt längs der **isländischen Küste,** vorbei an **Sneefels-Jökull, Staalbierg,** dann in den **Isafjord,** am folgenden Tage in den **Evjafjord***) bis nach **Akureyri.**)	
11. „	Vorm.	Ankunft in **Akureyri**	7
11. „	Nachm.	Abfahrt von **Akureyri**	
		nach Spitzbergen:	
14. „	Morgs.	Ankunft in **Smerenberg-Bai** . .	12
14. „	Abends	Abfahrt von **Smerenberg-Bai.**	
14. „	„	Ankunft in **Magdalenen-Bai** . .	15
15. „	Nachm.	Abfahrt von **Magdalenen-Bai.**	
15. „	Abends	Ankunft in **Croß-Bai**	18
16. „	Nachm.	Abfahrt von **Croß-Bai.**	
16. „	„	Ankunft in **Kings-Bai**	7
16. „	Abends	Abfahrt von **Kings-Bai**	

Datum	Zeit	**nach Norwegen:**	Ungefährer Aufenthalt Stund.
18. Juli	Morgs.	Ankunft am **Nordkap**	5
18. „	Nachm.	Abfahrt vom **Nordkap.**	
18. „	„	Ankunft in **Hammerfest**	5
18. „	Abends	Abfahrt von **Hammerfest.**	
19. „	Morgs.	Ankunft in **Tromsö**	8
19. „	Nachm.	Abfahrt von **Tromsö.**	
20. „	Vorm.	Ankunft in **Digermulen**	8
20. „	Abends	Abfahrt von **Digermulen.** (Fahrt durch den **Vestfjord,** dann bei **Aalesund** in den **Storfjord,** durch den **Slyngs- u. Sunelvfjord** in den **Geirangerfjord** bis **Merok.**)	
22. „	Morgs.	Ankunft in **Merok**	7
22. „	Nachm.	Abfahrt von **Merok.** (Zurück auf dems. Wege, dann in den **Jörundfjord,** endlich in den **Sognefjord,** durch **Fjaerlands- u. Näröfjord** bis **Gudvangen [Dördal].**)	
23. „	Morgs.	Ankunft in **Gudvangen (Dördal)** (Überlandreise via **Stalheim** und **Vossevangen** nach **Bergen.**)	14
23. „	Abends	Abfahrt von **Gudvangen (Dördal).**	
24. „	Morgs.	Ankunft in **Bergen**	35
25. „	Abends	Abfahrt von **Bergen.**	
27. „	Vorm.	Ankunft in **Hamburg.**	

*) Die Fahrt in diese Fjorde kann nur bei günstiger Witterung ausgeführt werden.
Dem Kapitän bleiben Änderungen des Fahrplans, soweit sie durch besondere Umstände gerechtfertigt sind, vorbehalten.

Reisedauer 25 Tage.

Fahrpreise.

Kammer Nr.	ℳ
Zimmer für 2 Personen:	p. Platz
A-Deck:	
A 1, 2, 7, 8, 9, 10, 11, 12, 14, 15 .	1400
A 25, 26	1300
A 5, 6	1700
A 16	1300
A 17	1600
B-Deck:	
B 73, 74, Staatszimmer, besteh. aus Wohn-, Schlaf- und Badezimmer nebst Toilette, für 1 bis 2 Personen	pro Zimm. 6000
B 89, 90, Luxuszimmer, mit Bad und Toilette, für 1 bis 2 Personen .	4600
	p. Platz
B 50, 51, 69, 70, 77, 78, 79, 80, 85, 86	1400
B 52, 53	1200
B 61, 62	1400
B 54, 55	900
B 63, 64, 65, 66, 67, 68 . . .	1500
B 71, 72	1300
C-Deck	
C 150, 151, 153, 173, 175, 192, 194, 196, 198, Luxuszimmer, mit Bad und Toilette, für 1 bis 2 Personen	pro Zimm. 4000
C 155, 157, Luxuszimmer, mit Bad und Toilette, für 1 bis 2 Personen	4800
C 159, Staatszimmer, besteh. aus Wohn-, Schlaf- und Badezimmer nebst Toilette, für 1 bis 2 Personen	5200
C 177, Staatszimmer, besteh. aus Wohn-, Schlaf- und Badezimmer nebst Toilette, für 1 bis 2 Personen	5400
C 200, Luxuszimmer, mit Bad und Toilette, für 1 bis 2 Personen	4200
C 213, Luxuszimmer, mit Bad und Toilette, für 1 bis 2 Personen	3200
C 215, Luxuszimmer, mit Bad und Toilette, für 1 bis 2 Personen	3000
	p. Platz
C 110, 111, 126, 127, 128, 129 .	1400
C 114, 115	900
C 118, 119, 124, 125	1000
C 130, 131, 136, 137, 144, 145, 146, 147	1200

Kammer Nr.	ℳ
C-Deck (Fortsetzung):	p. Platz
C 132, 133, 134, 135, 142, 143, 148, 149	950
C 152, 158, 160, 163, 165, 166, 168, 171, 176, 182, 184, 190 . . .	1400
C 172, 178	1000
C 174	1600
C 211, 217, 219	750
C 212	950
C 216, 221	780
C 218, 220, 223, 225	850
C 222, 227	800
C 279, 281, 282	800
C 283, 284	700
C 270, 271	750
D-Deck:	pro Zimm.
D 361, Luxuszimmer, mit Bad und Toilette, für 1 bis 2 Personen	3000
D 370, 371, Luxuszimmer, mit Bad und Toilette, für 1 bis 2 Personen	3000
	p. Platz
D 300	750
D 304, 305	800
D 306, 307	900
D 310, 311, 316, 317	950
D 340, 341, 346, 347	1000
D 365, 367	1100
D 372, 373	1100
D 380, 381	1000
D 382, 383	900
D 397	700
E-Deck:	
E 402, 405, 410, 413	550
E 416, 419	600
E 422, 423, 440, 441	550
Zimmer für 1 Person:	pro Zimm.
A-Deck:	
A 3, 4, 22, 23, 24	1200
A 18	1700
A 20, 21	1600
B-Deck:	
B 56	950
B 57, 58, 59, 60, 87, 88	1700

Kammer Nr.	ℳ
B-Deck (Fortsetzung):	p. Zim.
B 75, 76, 81, 82, 83, 84	1200
C-Deck:	
C 100, 101, 102	1300
C 106, 107	1300
C 108, 109, 116, 117	1300
C 120, 121, 122, 123, 140, 141 . .	1000
C 138, 139	1300
C 154, 156	1200
C 161	1000
C 162, 164, 167, 169, 170, 186, 188	1200
C 210, 224, 229	800
C 250, 251, 256, 257, 258, 259 . .	750
C 252, 253, 254, 255, 260, 261, 262, 263, 272, 273, 274, 275 . . .	850
C 264, 265, 266, 267, 276, 277, 278	750
C 280	850
C 285, 286	750
C 287, 288	850
C 289, 290	800
C 291, 292	700
D-Deck:	
D 301	700
D 308, 309, 318, 319	1000
D 320, 321, 326, 327, 328, 329 .	950
D 322, 323, 324, 325, 330, 331, 332, 333, 338, 339	900
D 334, 335, 336, 337	1000
D 342, 343, 344, 345	950
D 348, 349	1200
D 363, 369	800
D 350, 351, 374, 375, 376, 377, 378, 379	700
D 384, 385, 386, 387	750
D 390, 393, 395, 396, 398 . . .	650
D 388, 389, 391, 392, 394 . . .	750
E-Deck:	
E 404, 406, 407, 409, 414, 417 . .	600
E 408, 411, 412, 415	550
E 424, 425, 446, 447, 448, 449 . .	580
E 426, 427, 432, 433, 434, 435 . .	600
E 428, 429, 430, 431, 436, 437, 439, 444, 445, 450, 451	550

21

⬆ *Victoria Luise* itinerary and passage prices for her twenty-seven-day northern cruise in 1912. (Courtesy Hapag-Lloyd AG Hamburg)

many other companies over the years (see *Caronia* later), were pulled during the summer to offer northern cruises.

Columbia's 1896 brochure shows that the ship departed Hamburg on 15 July, was at Nordkapp on 22 July, Spitsbergen on 24 July, then on 29 July at Alesund and Bergen on 2 August, finishing at Cuxhaven on 5 August. Prices ranged from 600 to 1,500 marks for a twin cabin. Hamburg-Amerika's *Auguste Victoria* made annual visits between 1897 and 1903 on twenty-two-day cruises from Hamburg. On the 1898 cruise only 100 of the 360 prospective climbers made it to the top of Nordkapp because of a snowstorm, but the passenger complement took full advantage of the Hornvik post office, with 400 passengers sending 4,000 postcards.

Hamburg-Amerika advertised its cruises in the American market offering 'Special Summer Cruises to Norway, Spitsbergen, North Cape, Iceland, Scotland, Orkney, Faroe Islands and Northern Capitals during June, July and August. 14–24 days starting from Hamburg in *Oceana*, *Meteor* and *Koenig Wilhelm II*.' The date of the advertisement is not known, but a similar advertisement appeared in 1907, without ship names, and the 1911 route of the company's ship *Cincinnati* started in Hamburg, then proceeded to Bergen, Nordkapp, Spitsbergen, five ports in Iceland including Akureyri

⬆ *Prinzessin Victoria Luise*. (Courtesy Library of Congress)

and Reykjavik, Faroe Islands, Orkney, Leith and back to Hamburg. The *Victoria Luise* followed the same itinerary after its conversion to cruising in 1911. Prices ranged from an astronomical 6,000 marks for a stateroom with a sitting room, bedroom together with bathroom with toilet (there were just two of these suites) to a more manageable 700 marks for an inside cabin.

Hamburg-Amerika's *Prinzessin Victoria Luise* was built specifically for cruising in 1900; she made regular cruises to the North Cape until wrecked off Jamaica in 1906. The *Meteor*, built in 1904, also cruised to the Fjords and Spitsbergen. Itineraries for both ships included Iceland. The *Victoria Luise* was originally the *Deutschland* on Hamburg-Amerika's transatlantic service, and briefly held the Blue Riband[3] in 1900 and 1903, but ongoing engine problems persuaded the company to down rate the engines and convert the ship to cruising.

Another German company that offered cruises to Spitsbergen was Nordeutscher Lloyd, with annual cruises on the *Grosser Kurfurst* in 1908–13. The cruise included Iceland, although again the ship's primary role was on the North Atlantic. The ship frequently included Reyardneset, a small beach at the head of Mollerfjorden where the crew erected beer tents and ran barbecues for passenger beach parties. The ship's band also went ashore to entertain the guests. Hamburg-Amerika offered similar excursions and the tradition continued after cruising started up again after the First World War. In 1926 a permanent hut was erected, which became known as the Lloyd Hotel.

The French *Ile-de-France* called at Spitsbergen in 1906 on a cruise sponsored by Revue Generale de Sciences, and carried a Swedish geologist and geographer – Nils Otto Nordenskjold – as tour leader. The ship reportedly could carry 214 guests in roomy cabins (forty-one single, seventy-one double and sixteen triple berths), each with a large washbasin, chest of drawers, cupboard, clothes pegs, shelves, a desk, a sizeable mirror, a caned bench and a chair for each person. There was also an electric ventilator, an adjustable heater and two electric lamps. The ship boasted seven bathrooms, each with a shower, as well as two saloons on the upper deck. One of these could hold 184 persons for dinner, the other was a smaller one for the ladies, and there was a spacious smoking room. There were two darkrooms on board, and for those passengers who went hunting, the ship carried a taxidermist as well. The *Ile-de-France* departed Dunkirk in July with 184 passengers, arrived at the Lofoten Islands on Bastille Day, and Recherchefjorden two days later, where it met several Norwegian whalers and Hamburg-Amerika's *Oceana*.

Perhaps lulled by the excellence of the weather, the captain took the ship further north to Raudfjorden, where it suffered perhaps the second recorded polar cruise ship incident when it grounded on a rock, and the passengers had to be evacuated. All ended well, and the ship returned to Spitsbergen in 1910, again sponsored by the General Review of Sciences, but this time they chartered a small steamship, *Viking*, to

The *Ceylon*. (© P&O Heritage Collections, www.poheritage.com)

accompany the ship for safety. Dense ice blocked Raudfjorden, so passengers boarded the *Viking* and this sailed north and reached 80° 5'N.

The *Ceylon*,[4] of the Ocean Steam Yachting Company, appears to have been the first excursion by a British company into the Northern fjords, with a cruise to Spitsbergen in 1884. The ship was described as a 'stately ship of 2,200 tons with powerful engines and fully rigged as a barque'. On a cruise to the Mediterranean in February 1884, twenty-four gentlemen and three ladies sat down to dinner with the captain; this was presumably at the captain's table. The ship was sold in 1896 to the Polytechnic Touring Association, which started offering tours to the Norwegian fjords as early as 1891, but using other vessels.

Another early company to offer northern cruises was the Wilson Line, and in Thomas Cook's *Excursionist and Tourist Advertiser* of 1 June 1888, under 'Yachting Cruises', it advertised the steamer *Domino*[5] with four departures between June and September on twenty-one-day cruises from Hull to the North Cape. The ship was noted as carrying a steam launch for the benefit of the passengers. The Wilson Line offered regular sailings to Scandinavian ports from Britain, and reportedly offered summer cruises to the Norwegian fjords from 1885. However, information is lacking on whether they continued beyond 1891, until restarting Fjord cruises during the 1920s.

Orient Steam Navigation entered the market in 1890 as a means of finding employment for its older ships from the Australian trade during the summer lull (peak season was October to February). Also, Australia entered a severe depression in the early 1890s due to drought and trade with Britain was much reduced. Orient moved several vessels into cruising, starting in 1890. Its older ships were apparently well suited for the trade with extensive first- and second-class accommodation and electric light.

One guinea[6] per day appears to have been the general passage figure for cruising to the Fjords; Orient's rates were higher, with a bed in a two-berth cabin running at 40–50 guineas for a twenty-seven-day cruise in 1892. In justifying its prices, Orient stressed the size, strength and power of its ships; excellent fittings including electric light, bells and first-class cuisine with wine and beer. The company pointed out that the ships carried experienced surgeons, musicians, stewards and stewardesses, and it also offered high-quality tour guides. In 1890, one of its published guides was *Pleasure Cruises to the Land of the Midnight Sun by the Orient Line SS Garonne and Chimborozo.* Orient seemed to appreciate the need for forward advertising, and the complete 1891 programme was available by November 1890. However, this still seems remarkably short notice by today's standards, when cruises are booked a year or more ahead. Another Orient Line ship involved in occasional northern cruises was the *Ophir*, which in 1899 was advertised as departing London on 11 July for a twenty-nine-day cruise to the Fjords, Spitsbergen and Iceland.

In 1896 there was a total eclipse of the sun on 9 August and the lines that offered cruises to the Norwegian fjords had special sailings. Orient Line's *Garonne* left London on 22 July and called at Vadsø on the morning of 8 August, departing the next day after the eclipse. The passage fee was 50 guineas including shore excursions at Odde,

⬆ P&O *Vectis*. (© P&O Heritage Collections, www.poheritage.com)

CRUISE No. 9, 1906.

S.Y. "VECTIS."

LONDON TO THE NORWEGIAN FJORDS, THE NORTH CAPE, SPITZBERGEN, &c.

July 11th to August 7th. 28 Days' Cruise.

Fares from 30 Guineas.

RATES OF PASSAGE MONEY.

55 Guineas—161, 164, 165, 168, 169, 170, 171, 174, 175, 176, 177, 180.

50 Guineas—9–10, 11, 14–15, 18–20, 21–23, 29, 68–70, 71–73, 76–77, 144, 149, 166–167, 172, 173, 178–179.

45 Guineas—12–13, 16–17, 24–25, 26–28, 30–32, 36, 59, 63–65, 66–67, 74–75, 78–79, 162, 163.

42 Guineas—33–35, 60–62, 146, 147, 148, 151, 152, 153, 154, 155, 156, 157, 158, 159, 160.

40 Guineas—5–6, 7–8, 37–38, 57–58, 80–81, 82–83, 84–85, 86–87, 134–135, 136–137, 138–139, 140–141, 142–143, 201–202, 203–204, 209–210, 211–212.

38 Guineas—1–2, 3–4, 39–41, 54–56, 88–89, 90–91, 197–198, 199–200, 205–206, 207–208.

35 Guineas—42–43, 52–53, 94–95, 96–97, 100–101, 102–103, 106–107, 108–109, 110–111, 113, 114–115, 118, 123, 126–127, 128, 130–131, 132–133.

32 Guineas—112, 116–117, 124–125, 129.

30 Guineas—44–45, 46–47, 50–51, 92, 93, 98, 99, 104, 105, 119–120, 121–122.

5

← Passage money table by berth for P&O *Vectis*. (© P&O Heritage Collections, www.poheritage.com)

↓ Deck plan for the *Vectis* showing berth numbers. (© P&O Heritage Collections, www.poheritage.com)

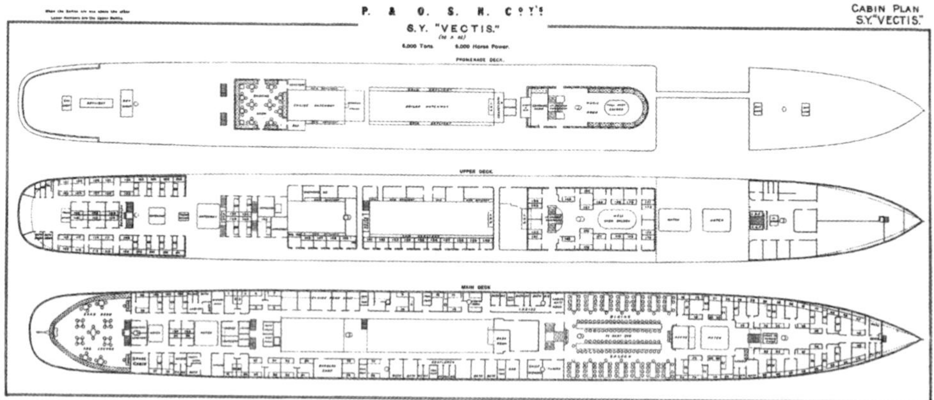

Bergen and Trondheim. The ship returned to London on 18 August. The *Lusitania* offered a similar cruise, but for the enthusiastic observer. It left London on 24 July, arriving at the Varangerfjord on 3 August and remaining until 10 August 'in order to allow observers to erect their instruments and prepare for their observations'. This was part of the five-cruise programme that year by *Lusitania* and *Garonne* to the Fjords, North Cape and Spitsbergen. Prices ranged from 35 guineas for a twenty-two-day cruise to 60 guineas for the twenty-nine-day cruise departing on 25 August.

In 1898, Thomas Cook advertised Land of the Midnight Sun cruises to 'Scotland, Norway, Sweden, Denmark, Holland and England' from New York on Anchor Line's *City of Rome* and from Boston on the Dominion Line's *Canada*. The fifty-one-day cruise cost $450 with seventeen ports of call, including the North Cape. Also in the same edition of the *Excursionist and Tourist Advertiser*, North Cape cruises on four ships of Berganske D/S and Nordenfjeldske D/S were offered. However, these were most likely Hurtigruten sailings as the coastal service had been started in 1893 and these two companies introduced ships on the route from Trondheim to northern ports in 1894.

Typically, Thomas Cook did not charter ships, but as a tour operator booked space on other company vessels. For example, in 1896 it offered three conducted tours of Iceland, which also visited the Faroe Islands. The ship was not mentioned, but prices ranged from 21 guineas for twenty days to 49 guineas for fifty days. There were well-established passenger cargo ship links between Britain and Iceland at the time.

P&O entered the northern cruise trade with a conversion. In 1903 it withdrew the *Rome* from its Australia service and converted her to cruising as the *Vectis*. All second-class accommodation was removed and first class extended to 150 guests. From 1904

⬆ A single stateroom on the *Prinzessin Victoria Luise*. (Courtesy Library of Congress)

to 1913 she undertook twenty-eight-day summer cruises to the Norwegian fjords, North Cape and Spitsbergen.

It is interesting to note that, while the *Victoria Luise* was sold by cabin number, the *Vectis* was sold by berth number. For ships of this period, accommodation was typically a cabin, or stateroom, that might have a washbasin. Baths and toilet facilities were elsewhere on the ship; see the descriptions of the *St Sunniva* and the *Ile-de-France*. This type of accommodation was also common ashore, even in grand hotels, so it wasn't seen as a negative by the cruise passenger. In fact, ship designers endeavoured to make the passengers feel as if they were in a hotel, rather than a ship. Hamburg-Amerika's *Prinzessin Victoria Luise* was unusual as an all-suite ship. Each suite had two rooms and bathroom, although toilet facilities were elsewhere; only the two 'Regal Suites' had full en suite facilities.

During this period companies often stressed the yacht-like features of the ship, and Thomas Cook had a section of its *Excursionist and Tourist Advertiser* headed 'Yachting Cruises'. Some Expedition companies today, 180 years later, also promote their ships as yacht-like and, as in the early years, some have 'Yachting' in their company name, such as Seadream Yacht Club and Norwegian Yacht Voyages.

The Interwar Years

The world changed in many ways after the First World War, and the easy Edwardian affluence of the pre-war period disappeared. In terms of shipping, the Allies focused on re-establishing line service on the North Atlantic; for Britain this also meant the colonies. The trend to ever-larger, faster ships before the war gave way, at least initially, to more modest vessels. Germany, a leader in liner service before the war, had an even more difficult time and Hamburg-Amerika, in particular, only operated cargo passenger ships.

The Fjords, North Cape and Spitsbergen were still the primary polar destinations during the 1920s and '30s, although other destinations were emerging. In 1922, the Canadian company Alberta and Arctic Transportation Company (AATC) offered its new steamer service with the stern wheel riverboat *Distributor* on the Mackenzie River,[7] with a special round-trip fare of $240[8] excluding berth and meals between Waterways, Alberta, and Aklavik, Northwest Territories. The Hudson's Bay Company (HBC) followed suit with the *Mackenzie River*, and by 1928 reportedly could not keep up with demand.

In 1933, the Hudson's Bay Company entered the ocean cruise business with eastern Arctic cruises on the 1912-built *Nascopie*. Trips were offered from Montreal, Quebec, to Churchill, Manitoba, or vice versa, or a round-trip passage could be booked by no more than ten 'carefully selected' passengers. Cruises were continued until 1941, when

⬆ SS *Grahame*. (Courtesy Peace River Museum Archives and Mackenzie Centre – Weaver family fonds F033-PRMA, 87.1506.007)[9]

⬇ SS *Nascopie* departing Montreal, probably 1936. (Courtesy Hudson's Bay Company Archives HBCA 1987/363-N-7/42)

they stopped,[10] probably for security reasons. Mackenzie River cruises also continued to be offered by the HBC until 1941.

The first passenger trips to Antarctica also took place during the 1920s and '30s, with the *Fleurus*[11] from Stanley in the Falkland Islands to South Georgia and Deception Island in the Antarctic Peninsula. Then in February 1933, the Argentinean cargo vessel *Pampa* sailed to the Argentine base on Laurie Island in the South Orkneys, with members of the University Club of Buenos Aires on board to help defray the cost of the trip. The ship undertook another trip in February 1937, also to the Laurie Island base. Passenger numbers were limited because the ship only had forty-two berths. It was noted that there were four ladies among the tourists.

Germany had financed the First World War through debt (expecting to win and reap benefits from the vanquished). It lost and as well as having to repay its debts, the Treaty of Versailles effectively stripped it of its maritime assets. Debt and reparations had to be in hard currency, which paper marks were not, as Germany had abandoned the gold standard at the outset of the war. The Weimar Republic's efforts to solve its financial difficulties eventually led to hyperinflation in 1921–23. As a consequence of these economic issues, Hamburg-Amerika did not return to the north until 1927 with the 15,982grt cargo/passenger ship *Reliance.*[12] Nordeutscher Lloyd was there two years earlier with the 13,325grt *Munchen,*[13] although after 1930 cruising only with 484 first-class passengers as the *General von Steuben*. The company included Iceland in its northern itineraries, as the ship was photographed in Reykjavik some time in the 1930s.

The *Reliance* was followed in 1928 and 1929 by the Hamburg South America Line *Monte Cervantes*, although the 1928 Spitsbergen cruise resulted in a near sinking. However, the focus of the German lines was not on the Norwegian coast, which had largely sold into the domestic market, but cruises out of New York. These earned much-needed hard currency from the emerging American cruise market, which was more interested in the Caribbean and Mediterranean than northern destinations.

In 1924, the Hamburg South America Line delivered the *Monte Sarmiento*; the first of five nearly identical ships[14] for the South American emigrant trade. After the trade did not materialise, the company decided to focus on offering inexpensive cruises, and the ships were reconfigured accordingly. Cruises were offered in South America, as well as to the Mediterranean, Atlantic Islands and the Norwegian coast. The *Monte Cervantes* cruise to Svalbard in 1929 offers a window into German budget cruising of the 1920s. For this cruise she operated as a one-class ship, carrying 1,800 passengers, their passage rate depending solely on the type of cabin. A berth in a 120-bed dormitory (steerage) on F Deck could be had for 240 Reichmarks. A bed in a two-berth cabin on A Deck cost 630 Reichmarks; these cabins had hot and cold running water. Passengers in the dormitories had access to 'white-tiled' men's and women's bathrooms. The ship had a promenade deck, two dining rooms, a large smoking room, theatre, post office, beauty salon and a barbershop. Food was also relatively simple. The menu for 29 May 1929 reportedly offered the following:

Breakfast: Cooked eggs, pancakes with apple sauce, oatmeal with milk
Lunch: Broth with Tyrolean dumplings, roast veal, young peas, potatoes, California apricots
Afternoon Tea: Cakes
Dinner: Milan-style schnitzel

While water was free, liquor, wines, beer and mineral water was extra (no mention of tea and coffee). The style and menu gave a sense of what was to come in the next decade with the Kraft durch Freude[15] (KdF) cruises.

A poster for 1931 cruises by the the Hamburg South America Line shows four northern cruises that year: Fjords 3–11 July, Nordkapp 13–28 July, Spitsbergen 5–23 August, and a special educational (Deutscher Akademika) cruise 4–23 July that sailed to the Fjords, Spitsbergen, Iceland, Faroes, Scotland before returning to Hamburg. The ships listed were *Monte Cervantes*, which had actually sunk in South America in 1930, and the *Monte Rosa*. Presumably one of the other five sisters was substituted. These seasonal cruises probably continued through 1934 as the *Monte Rosa*[16] reportedly grounded in the Faroe Islands on 23 July 1934.

In 1934, the German Strength Through Joy (KdF) organisation began building up a fleet of cruise ships by initially chartering or purchasing ships from existing lines, and then with new construction. One of its goals was to restore the moribund German tourism market and by 1939 the organisation had an eight-ship cruise fleet[17] offering bargain price cruises for German workers. It isn't known which of the ships went north, but Norwegian fjords and Spitsbergen were specific destinations for their ships. The cruise of the *Monte Sarmiento* on 10–16 July 1936 was reportedly the company's twenty-ninth Norwegian cruise. Following delivery in 1937, the *Wilhelm Gutsloff* undertook an inaugural Norwegian cruise with Adolf Hitler occupying a special sixteen-room suite.

Although there is little information about the ship, and Royal Holland Line cruise operations, its *Gelria* cruised to the Norwegian coast in 1925 and may have operated there in other years after re-entering service in 1919. She was laid up after the 1931 cruising season.

Norway also entered the cruise market in 1921 when Bergen Line purchased the 1904-built, Hamburg-Amerika *Meteor* from Royal Mail Line for cruises out of British ports. The ship had been ceded to Britain after the war, then sold by the British Government to Royal Mail. Building on the success of the *Meteor*, Bergen Line then built the *Stella Polaris* in 1927. Both of these yachts were dedicated to cruising, and are the nearest equivalent to today's expedition ships. The *Stella Polaris* had accommodation for 198 passengers. This included four deluxe double suites, each of which

Monte Sarmiento

Auszug aus dem Schiffstagebuch

29. „Kraft durch Freude" Norwegenreise

Kapitän C. Lübbe

Freitag, den 10. Juli 1936

10,00—12,00 Uhr Einschiffung von 1905 Passagieren.

Sonnabend, den 11. Juli 1936

13,00 Uhr Abfahrt Hamburg. 18,30 Uhr passierten Cuxhaven. 19,20 Uhr Elbe 3 Feuerschiff; Elblotse ging von Bord. 20,00 Uhr erreichten die offene See. 21,30 Uhr passierten Helgoland, Wind SW., Windstärke 3, mäßig bewegte See.

Sonntag, den 12. Juli 1936

4,20 Uhr passierten Horns Rev Feuerschiff. 9,00 Uhr begegneten dem „K. d. F."-Urlauberschiff „Monte Olivia". 12,00 Uhr: 57 Grad 08 Min. Nord, 6 Grad 34 Min. Ost. Wind: Süd, Windstärke 3; mäßig bewegte See. 15,30 Uhr kam die norwegische Küste in Sicht. 22,00 Uhr erreichten Kopervik, hier Uebernahme 2 norwegischer Fjordlotsen.

Montag, den 13. Juli 1936

Fuhren durch den Hjelte-Fjord nach dem Sogne-Fjord. 14,00 Uhr drehten das Schiff vor Gudvangen und fuhren nach dem großen Hardanger-Fjord. 16,30 Uhr passierten Balholmen.

Dienstag, den 14. Juli 1936

9,00 Uhr vor Ulvik. 10,00 Uhr vor Ejdfjord. 13,30 Uhr drehten vor Sundal im Mauranger-Fjord und traten Rückreise an. 18,45 Uhr passierten Haugesund. 19,20 Uhr Kopervik, Lotsen von Bord. 22,00 Uhr passierten das „K. d. F."-Urlauberschiff „Der Deutsche". 22,00 Uhr erreichten die offene See.

Mittwoch, den 15. Juli 1936

Mäßig bewegte See, Wind Süd-West, Windstärke 4. 12,00 Uhr: 56 Grad 07 Min. Nord, 7 Grad 01 Min. Ost. 15,00 Uhr passierten Horns Rev Feuerschiff. 22,30 Uhr passierten Helgoland.

Donnerstag, den 16. Juli 1936

Um 1,00 Uhr passierten Cuxhaven. 7,00 Uhr erfolgte die Ankunft in Hamburg.

Distanzen:

Hamburg-Elbe 1 . . .	77 Sml.	Gudvangen-Ulvik . .	238 Sml.
Elbe 1-Kopervik . . .	340 „	Ulvik-Ejdfjord . . .	10 „
Kopervik-Sogneoksen	118 „	Ejdfjord-Kopervik . .	115 „
Sogneoks.-Gudvangen	92 „	Kopervik--Elbe 1 . .	340 „
		Elbe 1-Hamburg . .	77 „

Gesamtdistanz 1407 Seemeilen = 2606 km

HAMBURG-SÜDAMERIKANISCHE DAMPFSCHIFFFAHRTS-GESELLSCHAFT

⬆ *Monte Sarmiento* cruise summary for passengers on disembarkation.

had a separate sitting room, bedroom and bathroom with toilet, and twelve two-berth staterooms with en suite facilities. In the rest of the accommodation, fifty-one single and fifty-two double cabins had no facilities, but there were thirty-five bathrooms arranged down the centreline so as to be close to the cabins they served. The ship had a dining room that could seat all passengers and senior officers at one sitting, a smoking room, two small writing rooms and a verandah café. It was an all-electric ship and featured forced air heating and ventilation throughout. The ship was very popular and a report of a 1933 cruise noted that they sailed direct from Bergen for the Polar Pack, reaching 80°34'N, before returning to Spitsbergen. In 1930, the *Nottingham Journal* and *Nottinghan Evening News* chartered the ship for one of its Fjord cruises. Prices started at £17 for an inside single, excluding the rail fare to Newcastle, and 8/6 for transfer to the Tyne Commissioners Quay from the railway station, including baggage handling porter fees and quay tax.

In 1930, both vessels cruised to Iceland for the Althing Millennium celebrations. Their annual programme was:

Spring and autumn: Mediterranean and Atlantic Islands
Summer: Fjords, Svalbard, Baltic
Winter: Worldwide cruise out of New York

Bergen Line's *Venus*, although operating mainly on the company service between Bergen and Newcastle, operated cruises to the North Cape in later years. She had accommodation for 182 in first class and fifty-two in second class, all twin-berth cabins.

Perhaps seeing the success of Bergen Line in the cruise business, as opposed to its Hurtigruten coastal passenger and freight operations, Nordenfjledske purchased the laid up 'small' British Royal yacht *Alexandra*[18] in 1925, renamed it *Prins Olaf* and immediately sent it cruising to the North Cape. Over that winter, modifications were made to enable it to carry 100 passengers, although the Royal suite was retained. While Bergen Line's two cruising yachts operated year-round, the *Prins Olaf* generally sailed summers-only on the coast, and was laid up during the winter. Between 1926 and 1930, the yacht operated its Fjord cruises out of Bergen, then in 1930–35 she was based out of Edinburgh. In 1936, the ship was withdrawn from passenger service and converted to passenger/freight configuration for Nordenfjeldske's Hurtigruten service. The Bergen Line continued its regular cruise programmes with both the *Meteor* and the *Stella Polaris* until the outbreak of the Second World War.

During the 1930s the North Atlantic passenger trade was reduced to a fraction of business of that seen during the heady decade of the 1920s. From about a million passengers in 1930, numbers were half that by 1935, with emigration averaging only about 70,000 per year, compared with more than 400,000 per year during the previous decade. Thus lines were forced to look for alternative employment for the ships to maintain some income. Britain was not, at least initially, as affected by the Wall Street crash of 1929 as was America. However, while the devaluation[19] of the pound sterling, when Britain went off the gold standard in August 1931, made it more costly for people to travel overseas, cruises from British ports, which were priced in pounds and guineas, became much more affordable.

British liner companies had a strong presence, and all the major operators put ships into northern cruises. Some emulated Hamburg-Amerika's pre-war itineraries by including the Fjords, Spitsbergen, Jan Mayen and Iceland in their longer cruises. Typically, the northern cruises operated out of places such as Hull, Immingham, Harwich and Newcastle, which saved steaming time, although Lamport and Holt sailed its *Voltaire* and *Vandyck* out of Liverpool, as did Cunard with the *Lancastria*. Leith was also a popular embarkation port and a reduced passage fee was often offered. Southern ports included Tilbury and Southampton.

Canadian Pacific did not abandon its transatlantic service between Britain and St Lawrence, but from 1930 on became heavily involved in almost year-round cruising out of Britain with its cabin-class ships *Montcalm*, *Montclare*, *Montrose* and *Melita*. The Norwegian fjords and North Cape were part of the seasonal rotation of itineraries

⬆ Orient Line's *Viceroy of India* tendering passengers in a Norwegian fjord. (© P&O Heritage Collections, www.poheritage.com)

that also included the Mediterranean, Atlantic Islands and the Baltic. Prices were advertised as being from £1 per day. In 1931, even the *Empress of Australia* undertook two cruises to the Fjords and the North Cape.

As an indication of the extraordinary cruise activity out of Britain in the 1930s, the book *The British Cruise Ship* provides a list of eighty-five cruises departing British ports between 1 May and 17 July 1936, twelve of these were to northern destinations, while the others included short round Britain cruises and those to European ports. On one day in the 1930s seven ships reportedly left Tilbury for cruises.

Royal Mail Line's *Atlantis* and *Avon* cruised regularly from August 1930 to 1939, and were joined by the *Asturias* in 1932. Cruises were offered with lengths from six to twenty-three days, with visits to 'Northern Capitals, Fjords, Spitsbergen and Iceland'. Wilson Line took the *Calypso* and *Eskimo* to the Norwegian Coast as well, and in 1936–39 also employed the *City of Nagpur*, for which Ceres Harper (a popular Hull band leader of the 1920s) wrote a special march. P&O offered cruises on the *Viceroy of India* and its 'electric ships' *Strathnaver* and *Strathaird*. From 1926 its *Ranchi* also offered seasonal cruises around the demands of India service. British India Line took 1,100 children and teachers on the *Neuralia* to the Fjords on school cruises between 1934 and 1935. Also of an educational nature, Orient Lines offered a Scouters and Guiders cruise on the *Orduna* from Liverpool to Iceland, Norway, Denmark and Belgium. A 1928 advertisement stated that a 20,000grt ship left every week during the season for the Fjords. These were probably the thirteen to twenty-four-day first-class-only cruises offered on the *Orion*, *Orford*, *Oronsay*, *Orama* and *Otranto.* The ships combined summer cruises to the Mediterranean with the Fjords, and then reverted to the line's Australian service during the winter. Prices were 20 guineas for thirteen days.

The *Viceroy of India* was an interesting, and quite luxurious, cargo/passenger liner offering northern cruises. Propulsion was an unusual turbo-electric drive, which wasn't used much by the shipping industry until it was widely installed in T2 tankers during the Second World War. For the ship it reportedly gave a remarkably smooth and quiet ride. First class had a smoking room that emulated the great hall of a castle, an eighteenth-century music room, a dining room with marble pillars and an Adam-style reading room. Also unusual for the period, it had a grand inside swimming pool that extended through three decks. In 1934 and 1936, the ship undertook three fourteen-day northern cruises to Trondheim, Murmansk, North Cape, Narvik and Bergen. The fare was 21 guineas round trip from London, or 18 guineas from Leith. The ship cruised regularly to the north from 1930 onwards with trips to Iceland, the Faroes and Spitsbergen. These twenty-three-day cruises were priced from 39 guineas. The ship demonstrated the practice of that period in providing completely separate facilities for first- and second-class passengers, including dining, smoking, reading,

↑ Smoking room on *Viceroy of India*. (© P&O Heritage Collections, www.poheritage.com)

← Second-class single cabin on *Viceroy of India* showing interconnection to a cabin with two beds. (© P&O Heritage Collections, www.poheritage.com)

ladies' and even nursery accommodation. Perhaps because of its main line service between Britain and India, it had a large number of single cabins that could interconnect with twin-berth ones to create a family suite.

Another luxurious ship cruising during this period was Blue Star Line's first-class-only *Arandora Star* with an annual twenty-day itinerary out of Tilbury to the Faroe Islands, Iceland, Jan Mayen, Spitsbergen, Norwegian fjords and Bergen. In 1934 it cost from 30 guineas, but by 1937 the starting price had risen to 34 guineas. The ship had a garden lounge, music lounge, ballroom, smoke room with a dome over, a large dining room with a dome over, ladies' and gentlemen's hairdressers, a dark room, a gymnasium on the observation deck, a games deck, and in later years a swimming pool and a tennis court aft of the funnels. However, like most ships of the period, very few staterooms had en suite facilities. The ship obviously had a family market as a large number of cabins interconnected, as did those on the *Viceroy of India*. It is interesting to note that the quality of even the second-class cabins, although they might lack an en suite bathroom, matched the first class of the ships sailing prior to the First World War.

CGT's *Lafayette* cruised to Svalbard in 1931 and 1937, and its ship *Cuba* also went north in 1931. Although when French ships cruised, they seemed to prefer the Caribbean, some ships did go to Spitsbergen and the North Cape in the 1930s. For example, *Colombie* undertook a twenty-day 'Romantic Cruise to the Norwegian fjords, Spitzbergen, the Arctic Ice barrier Faroe Islands and Iceland' in August 1931 from Leith (£25 tourist, £40 first class), while the *de Grasse* made a twenty-one-day cruise calling at Scotland, Iceland, Spitsbergen, North Cape and the Fjords commencing on 24 July 1939. Prices were Ff6,900 first class, Ff5,200 tourist and Ff2,400 for a special economy fare. Quite how the accommodation worked is not known, as the ship was configured for 399 cabin class and 1,712 tourist.

Even Swedish America Line's flagship *Kungsholm* visited Nordkapp on a Fjords cruise in 1931 and Cie Mar Belge's *Albertville* was chartered by the Norwegian tour operator Bennett in 1935.

American cruising started following Prohibition in 1920. The initial overnight booze cruises segued into longer trips, mainly to Bermuda, but then to the Caribbean and the Mediterranean. Northern cruises seemed to be less popular, but Cunard Line offered forty-five-day North Cape cruises out of New York during the summer period on *Franconia* and *Carmania* from shortly after their mid-1920s delivery until 1939. Then, in September of that year, everything changed and the world was once again at war.

ATLANTIS

During the 1930s there were several ships that had a strong passenger following; P&O's *Viceroy of India* was one, another was Blue Star Line's *Arandora Star*. Looking in depth at Royal Mail Line's *Atlantis*, it is not difficult to see why such ships were popular.

Atlantis started out as the *Andes*,[20] laid down at Harland and Wolff in Belfast in 1912, but delivered to Royal Mail Lines for its Southampton to La Plata line service, and commenced her maiden voyage on 26 September 1913. She survived the First World War, and restarted her pre-war line service on 4 November 1919.

In 1929, Royal Mail decided to move *Andes* into cruising and undertook a comprehensive refit at Liverpool that included conversion to oil firing; the ship also now became *Atlantis*. Reports about the accommodation at the time were that the conversion produced a 450-passenger capacity all-first-class ship; however, this is far from the truth. Examination of a 1930 brochure shows that the ship would be better described as cabin class, and could, if all berths were occupied, carry 557 persons. The 450 figure may be Royal Mail's expectation of a typical passenger complement as the description of the dining room notes that it can 'comfortably accommodate over 400 persons at a single sitting'.

The accommodation offered a substantial number of options, starting with two suites that had separate sitting room, bedroom and private bathroom and toilet. There were also eighteen of what might be called today junior suites that had a bedroom with sitting area and private bathroom. All other cabins, as was the custom of the day, contained a washbasin, but other facilities were elsewhere. There were, however, sixteen single or double cabins with adjoining bathroom that could be configured by the door arrangement to give private facilities.

As an example, berths 226, 227, 228, 229 and 230 were in a three-cabin cluster adjoining a bathroom. Nos 227 and 228 could be offered as a junior suite, 226 could be a single cabin with private bathroom, or the complete bloc could offer a five-berth suite. The cabin with berths 227 and 228 could also have a third Pullman berth at a reduced price per person.

In all, 109 cabins were offered for single occupancy, although some could have a Pullman berth, thus single travellers were an important consideration and not disadvantaged as they are today where the line's focus is to sell a cabin with two persons in it.

The price range was considerable; for a nineteen-day North Cape cruise prices started at 31 guineas for a single cabin (there were only two of these), while a suite cost 255 guineas. Interestingly, prices, like the *Vectis* in 1906, were per berth; only the suites and junior suites were per cabin. In all there were thirty-five price groups, depending on the berth location. Adding a private bathroom cost 16 guineas. This was a time when people bathed and there were only two shower rooms on the ship.

The ship had a remarkable range of facilities, and starting from the upper promenade deck and working down, these were:

F Deck: Upper smoke room, American bar, gentleman's card room, verandah café, deck tennis.
E Deck: Social hall, lower smoke room, verandah café, bar, berths 503–511 in eleven cabins.
D Deck: Swimming pool (not a paddling pool as it extended through three decks), sunbathing deck, photography office, card room, berths 401–477[21] in fifty-five cabins.
C Deck: Shop, gymnasium (including table tennis and Angell golf[22]), tourist bureau, ladies and gents hairdressing salons and public darkroom. Two suites and twenty junior suites, berths 301–380 in fifty-five cabins including eighteen Bibby-type,[23] of which four were convertible to junior suites.
B Deck: Doctor, nurse, consulting room, professional photographer's studio and workroom, berths 100–248 in eighty-five cabins for tourists, of which thirty-six were Bibby cabins, with others assigned to staff, such as the nurse and two lady hairdressers. Ten cabins were convertible with private facilities.
A Deck: Dining room, two private dining rooms and a 'space for dancing', berths 21–61 in twenty-eight cabins, of which twelve were Bibby-style and two convertible.

Between March and October the ship undertook four Mediterranean, one North Africa and Atlantic Islands, two Baltic, one North Cape and one Faroes, Iceland, Spitsbergen and North Cape cruise. The shortest was thirteen days, while the longest was thirty-eight.

Post-War Extravagance

The remarkable flowering of cruise activity that occurred during the 1930s took some time to return after the ravages of the Second World War. It is estimated that 50 per cent of passenger ships afloat prior to the war were no more, or were retained by governments for military service. Those that were released took upwards of a decade to be available to their owners for reconversion and then for them to re-enter service.

Obviously, the focus of reconstruction was on the major routes: transatlantic, transpacific, South America, the Far East and Australasia. Most companies started with smaller ships, many being updated versions of the pre-war cargo-passenger vessel. However, an indication of what was to come was Cunard's *Caronia*, completed in 1949 for the North Atlantic, but mainly intended for cruising.

Also during this period, long-distance air travel began to develop, first using flying boats from the pre-war era because of an initial lack of long civilian runways for landing aircraft. They were rapidly phased out, and BOAC[24] ceased transatlantic flying boat services from Southampton in 1950. In the 1940s, Pan American World Airways ran a DC-4 service across the Atlantic from La Guardia to Hurn, Bournemouth, that took eighteen hours including refuelling stops, so some fortitude was required. Also, at $300–400 one way it was expensive and as a third-class transatlantic passenger liner ticket could be had for as little as $150, with no arguments over excess baggage, there was still an option for people who did not need speed or were on a budget.

⬆ Cunard's 'Green Goddess' SS *Caronia*. (Braun Brothers Collection, Steamship Historical Society Archives, www.sshsa.org)

Air travel developed rapidly during the 1950s, first with pressurised Lockheed Constellations, then the Boeing Stratocruiser[25] was introduced in 1954 and on 5 October 1958, BOAC introduced the first transatlantic jet service[26] with a Comet 4. The trip now took ten hours westbound with a stop at Gander for fuel, but tailwinds gave a non-stop six-hour trip eastbound. The cost at £173 one way was still only for the well-to-do, but the writing was on the wall for passenger ships on the premiere passenger liner route. Just as the US Immigration Act of 1924 had forced the lines into cruising in order to maintain cash flow during the late 1920s and '30s, the availability of air travel hit passenger liners at the top end of their revenue stream, first class, and made cruising essential.

As an indication of how air travel impacted liner shipping, William H. Miller's *Pictorial Encyclopedia of Ocean Liners from 1860–1994* listed more than 400 vessels, and while the book was by no means exhaustive it does give a sense of changing times:

Availability of Passenger Liners 1920–80

Period	New Built	From Pre-War[27]	Total Deployed
1920–29	99	29	129
1930–39	78		207
1940–49	22		22
1950–59	51	52	125
1960–69	31		156
1970–79	19		

As will be seen from the table, the number of ships available in the 1950s was dramatically different from the 1930s. In the 1930s more than 200 ships were available; in the 1950s there were only 125. Most of the post-war ships went into line operations and cruised seasonally, or had to be converted to cruising mode.

The nature of cruising was also changing, dictating more sophisticated accommodation and different destinations, although some ships were still delivered without en suite facilities to every stateroom. As an example, the 1953-built *Kungsholm* was the first transatlantic liner where all cabins had en suite facilities. Such benefits became essential, driven in part by the lines' focus on American passengers who expected such facilities, as well as air conditioning. The Mediterranean was still a popular destination, but the proximity of the Caribbean to the burgeoning American market drew cruising away from destinations such as the Norwegian fjords, Spitsbergen and Iceland that were, or had been, popular with European vacationers. Such cruises were still available, but unlike the 1930s, when Bergen Line offered weekly sailings with two ships, they were now part of an overall itinerary rotation aimed mainly at the American market.

North German Lloyd *Berlin*. (Stephen Barrett Chase Poster Collection, Steamship Historical Society Archives, www.sshsa.org)

These travellers had the funds to take a cruise, while Europe[28] was still recovering from the war and most people could not afford the kind of vacation afloat they might have considered two decades earlier. A market did redevelop in the late 1950s for more affluent British travellers and Royal Mail Lines refitted the 1939-built *Andes* in 1958/59 for full-time cruising, at the same time bringing back Norwegian fjord cruising as part of the ship's itineraries. The company had cruised there regularly in the 1930s. In 1965, the ship called at Iceland, with visits to Akureyri and Reykjavik.

Economic issues during the immediate post-war period applied particularly to the German market, which had been the mainstay of cruising to the Fjords and Spitsbergen pre-First World War. The Potsdam Conference of 1945 called for heavy reparations from Germany and Italy, and there were severe limits on the German merchant marine. The country could not retain more ships than were needed to service its needs, and none could be more than 1,500grt. By 1950, the most stringent restrictions had been lifted and new buildings commenced, although these were relatively small cargo ships. Passenger shipping developed through acquisition, beginning with the 1925-built *Gripsholm* in 1954, purchased by Nordeutscher Lloyd and renamed *Berlin*. The *Berlin* cruised seasonally to the Fjords and Spitsbergen.

In 1957, three ships were purchased: the 1939-built *Pasteur* was renamed *Bremen* and put into service in 1959, and the 1930-built *Empress of Scotland* went to the newly created Hamburg Atlantic Line to re-establish transatlantic service between Hamburg and New York, and the much rebuilt ship entered service in 1958 as the *Hanseatic*. The third ship was the most interesting acquisition as it represented an attempt to recreate the ambience of the *Prinzessin Victoria Luise* from 1900.

The 1951-built Swedish Lloyd cruise/ferry *Patricia* was converted into the small luxury cruise ship *Ariadne*. The ship was extensively remodeled to offer 159 first-class staterooms for 259 passengers, attended by a crew of 159. The ship was mostly air conditioned, had a swimming pool aft and was deployed on Hamburg America's traditional itineraries of the Norwegian coast, Spitsbergen and the Mediterranean.

⬆ *Ariadne* following sale in 1960. (Everett E. Viez Collection, Steamship Historical Society Archives, www.sshsa.org)

⬇ *Ariadne* lounge. (Everett E. Viez Collection, Steamship Historical Society Archives, www.sshsa.org)

The Caribbean was added in 1959, but there simply was not a big enough market for a small luxury cruise ship and she was sold in 1960. However, it is also possible that the design was out of step with the times. The interiors, both cabins and public spaces, harked back to pre-war ships; compare the *Ariadne* lounge photograph with that of the *Viceroy of India*, built in 1925.

A later small cruise ship that continued the yacht approach to design was the *Italia*. Laid down in 1963, it bankrupted the builder before being delivered in 1967. Although not as luxurious as the *Ariadne*, the ship had 213 staterooms on delivery, but these were increased to 251 following a 1973 refit. The ship had a significant number of inside and outside singles. All cabins had en suite facilities and the ship was fully air conditioned and had many features of large ships, including a swimming pool on the lido deck, a large lounge, a casino and two bars on the Riviera deck. The large dining room was one deck down, and there was a cinema on the lowest deck. A 1983 refit, after a sale to Ocean Cruise Lines, added tenders to the foredeck, making the ship suitable for expedition-style cruising. Now trading as the *Ocean Princess*, the tendering capability may have been an attraction to Paquet Lines, which bought the ship in 1990 and took her to the Norwegian fjords and to Antarctica. The company styled the ship as 'A luxury liner with the style of a yacht'. In 1992/93 it offered six eighteen-day cruises. For the 7 January 1993 Antarctic cruise, prices ranged from $7,750pp in a deluxe outside to $4,575pp in a moderate inside double. Other departures were more expensive and air was extra.

⬆ *Italia.* (Michael P. Mudgett Collection, Steamship Historical Society Archives, www.sshsa.org)

Another small ship conversion was Bergen Line's 1952-built steam turbine *Leda*,[29] which was purchased by Dolphin (Hellas) in 1980 and converted for cruising as the *Albatross*, with 202 cabins and a passenger complement of 484. Her first cruises were in 1984, and she started a programme to the North Cape in 1985. Regrettably, despite being a quite well-appointed small ship, she was sold in 1988 and scrapped not long afterwards, no doubt a victim of fuel costs and the inherent inefficiency of turbine machinery.

The Germans continued to grow their passenger fleet through acquisition, buying the 1953-built *Kungsholm* in 1966 and putting it into North Atlantic service as the *Europa*. She offered line service during the summer, then cruised out of New York during the winter. Hamburg Atlantic Line started off with good passenger revenue, but after 1960 air travel began to take a toll. Then, in 1966, the *Hanseatic* was severely damaged by fire and could not be further rebuilt. The company changed its name to German Atlantic Line and after selling shares to its past passengers raised enough capital to order the first German-built passenger liner, the *Hamburg*, which was delivered in 1968. It also purchased the three-year-old *Shalom* in November 1967 and renamed her *Hanseatic*. The ship made a crossing to New York with invited guests and then commenced cruising. In 1968, the company abandoned transatlantic service and focused on cruising. However, it was in serious financial difficulties, paradoxically caused by the strength of the Deutschmark to the US Dollar, and had to sell the *Hanseatic*. The *Hamburg* was renamed, but financial problems persisted, and the ship was also sold, to the Black Sea Shipping Company, and renamed *Maxim Gorkiy*.

The focus of much new building, or in the case of German companies, acquisition and conversion, was on 'Ships of State' that were used by the French, Italians, Dutch and Swedes to promote their national brand. Consequently, they were extravagant vessels, and although some, such as the *Gripsholm*, *Rotterdam* and others, were intended to cruise seasonally to polar waters, most (like the 1961-built *France*) were pure transatlantic liners. However, the *France* did undertake a round-the-world cruise in 1971/72, and called at the Falkland Islands on 24 January 1972. The *Rotterdam*, on a round South America itinerary, called at the Falkland Islands on 7 February 1960. The *Gripsholm*'s visit to the Falkland Islands in 1972 was frustrated by weather although the *Kungsholm* did call, almost on the same day as the *Hanseatic* in November 1969.

The *Gripsholm* probably offered seasonal cruises to the North Cape out of New York from shortly after her delivery, as she was reported there in 1957, and on a forty-seven-day cruise in 1961 that was advertised as offering the 'North Cape, Viking Lands and Northern Europe'. This was similar to the annual offering by the *Caronia* – Cunard's Green Goddess – which sailed out of New York for seventeen years from 1951 on a twenty-eight-day cruise to Reykjavik, Hammerfest, North Cape, Lyngen, Lofoten, Svartisan Glacier, Trondheim, Hellesylt and Merck, Bergen, Oslo, Gothenburg, Queensferry, Oban, Dun Laoghaire, Glengarriff, Le Havre and Southampton. The fare included a return across the Atlantic on either of the two

⬆ *Rotterdam.* (Braun Brothers Collection, Steamship Historical Society Archives, www.sshsa.org)

⬇ *Gripsholm* at Nordkapp, 1957. (© National Maritime Museum, Greenwich, London)

Queens and proved to be a very popular offering. Another British ship that cruised to Spitsbergen, although details as to year and itinerary are missing, was P&O's *Canberra*.

As noted regarding northern cruising during the interwar period, the French did not seem inclined to send their ships into colder regions, however, the second *de Grasse*, ex *Bergensfjord*, was purchased in 1971 as a replacement for the *Antilles*[30] for the run to the Caribbean. She entered service following a six-month refit that gave her 581 first-class berths. However, the expected business was not there and the ship was moved to cruising to European destinations, including the Norwegian fjords. This activity did not work out either and the ship was laid up in 1973.

Although Greek owners tended to keep their cruise ships mainly in the Mediterranean, Chandris offered a regular programme of northern cruises out of Amsterdam in the *Britanis* from 1974. Built back in 1932 as the *Monterey*, Chandris took over the ship in 1970, giving it another major refit and turning it into a single-class cruise ship. She offered three North Cape cruises as part of her annual schedule, and these were sandwiched between an earlier and later cruise to the Faroes, Iceland and the North Cape. This programme continued until 1982. Costa Lines sent its *Enrico C*[31] and *Eugenio C*[32] to the Falkland Islands and the Antarctic during the mid 1970s. The *Enrico C*'s visit to the Antarctic Peninsula in 1973 with 888 passengers was the first large cruise ship to do so. The following season she came back with 803 passengers, and then in 1977 with 989.[33] The *Eugenio C* with 918 passengers also called in January that year.

A number of tourist trips to the Antarctic Peninsula took place, commencing in the 1950s. There were two trips with the Argentine passenger/cargo ship *Les Eclaireus*[34] in 1958, which took a total of 194 tourists, then in 1959 the FANU passenger ship *Yapeyú* took 262 passengers over two cruises, followed by ninety-four passengers in the Chilean transport ship *Navarino*[35] to the same area. Passages were possibly sold to help defray the cost of resupplying national scientific bases. No further activity occurred until Lars-Eric Lindblad's expedition on another Argentine passenger/cargo ship, the *Lapataia*, commencing with the 1965/66 through the 1967/68 seasons. During the next few years there were several visits by Argentine ships including the *Libertad*, *Rio Tunyan* and an Argentine Government charter of Chandris' *Regina Prima* with seven cruises in the 1974/75 season and another six trips the following year. The Spanish passenger/cargo ships[36] *Cabo San Roque* and *Cabo San Vicente* made four and three cruises[37] respectively over the 1972/73, 1973/74 and 1974/75 seasons. These cruises ceased after the 1974/75 season because they became uneconomic due to rising fuel costs.

There was something of a lull during the 1980s and Ushuaia, which had recorded sixty-three calls and 16,824 shipborne tourist visits in the 1970s, only saw thirty-three calls and 3,017 shipborne visits during the next decade. One of the causes was probably the chilling effect of the Falkland Islands conflict in 1982, and the political uncertainties that it brought. The Argentine ship *Bahia Buen Suceso*[38] undertook cruises in 1979/80 on behalf of the Argentine National Directorate of Tourism (DNT), then in 1980/81 Antartur SRL, a private company in Ushuaia, used the ship to take 70 and 139 passengers on two cruises the following season. There was no more Argentine activity until the 1985/86 season, when Antartur started cruises with the *Bahia Paraiso.* In the 1986/87 season, there were two cruises with 155 passengers, and four each in the following two seasons. The ship ran aground on 28 January 1989, and later sank.

Other operators, such as Lindblad and Society Expeditions, were active throughout the 1980s with multiple cruises on the *Lindblad Explorer* and the *World Discoverer.* Some of the initial calls were from Bluff in New Zealand or Cape Town, South Africa, but most originated from Ushuaia. However, both ships were engaged over the 1981/82 and 1982/83 seasons with fly/cruises via King George Island. Activity began to build at the end of the decade as Travel Dynamics brought in the *Illiria*, and Lindblad Expeditions chartered the *Antonina Nezhanova*, probably the very first Soviet ship to be used in the region.

The 1990s saw the entry of multiple Russian research ships, and Antarctic cruise activity took off. In the 1999/2000 season, two of the twenty ships that called, *Aegean I* and the *Ocean Explorer I*, were on round-the-world trips. Also, in January 2000 Holland America's new *Rotterdam* called with 936 passengers and 656 crew.

Cruising in the Canadian Arctic did not return after the Second World War until the *Lindblad Explorer* made its first visit in 1973. The Hudson's Bay Company resupply vessel *Nascopie* had sunk in 1947, and its replacement ships offered limited passenger accommodation. Mackenzie River traffic moved from stern wheel passenger cargo boats that had offered cruises during the 1930s and into the '40s to tugs and cargo-only barges.

The Lindblad Model

Lars-Eric Lindblad decided that travel was to be the focus of his life following a summer job with the Stockholm office of Thomas Cook (the British travel company). He moved to the US in 1951, and eventually set up his own company in 1958. The aim with all his tours was to combine adventure, pleasure and learning, while offering first-class lecturers and great food.

In 1964, he was in Outer Mongolia shepherding a group of adventurous tourists on a sixty-four-day tour into what was then a largely unknown region. One night, somewhat under the influence of koumiss,[39] and challenged about his next trip, he pulled out a Pan American World Airways map to see where they did not go. He noticed that Antarctica wasn't even marked and announced to the party that the next tour into the unknown would be to a place that wasn't on the map – Antarctica.

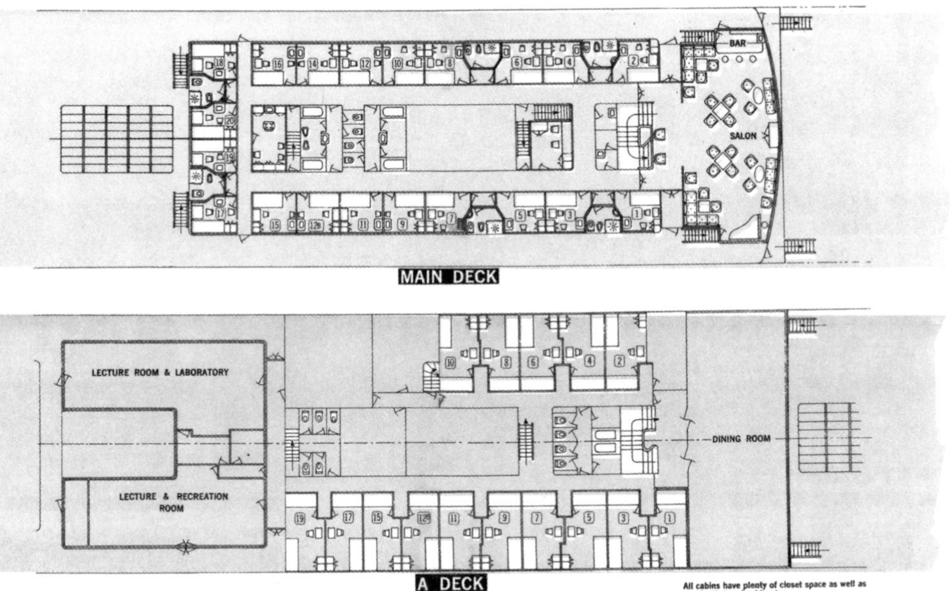

⬆ Deck plan of *Lapataia*. (Courtesy Explorer's Club)

It took some time to make the necessary arrangements, but he was able to charter the Argentine supply ship *Lapataia* for the 1965/66 season, to be accompanied by the naval tug *Irigoyen*.

The trip was to start from New York on 11 January 1966, returning from Buenos Aires on 11 February; prices per person in twin-berth cabins ranged from US$2,800 to $3,000 depending on whether the cabins had immediate access to toilet facilities, or whether these were across the hall. Round trip economy-class air on Avianca was included, with a remarkable (by comparison with today's air pricing) US$250 premium for first class.

The ship had a spacious dining room, as well as a lounge and bar, and could carry fifty-six passengers in reasonable comfort. The trip had a strong scientific focus, which was to be a hallmark of Lindblad cruises, and called at Half Moon Island, Esperanza, Deception Island, Bay of Whales, Le Maire Strait and Anvers Island. The locations included Argentinean, American and British stations, but the ice was too heavy to get to the American base on Anvers Island.

The trip was a resounding success, and the following season, after a tense meeting with Chilean authorities, Lindblad was able to offer three cruises, two on the *Lapataia*, and one on the Chilean *Aquiles*. The 1967/68 season was not so successful

⬆ Stern quarter of *Lindblad Explorer*. (Courtesy Professor Bruce Peter)

in that the twenty-five-passenger *Magga Dan*, which had been chartered for two trips from New Zealand to McMurdo Sound on the Ross Sea, was a dreadful sea boat and was late getting to its destination, where it promptly went aground off the dock. Although it was eventually freed, engine problems delayed the departure and the ship barely got back to Bluff, New Zealand, in time to pick up the second group of passengers. Meanwhile, on the other side of the continent, the Chilean *Navarino*[40] had serious rudder problems and its planned second cruise had to be cancelled. In 1968/69 Lindblad had only one cruise on the Chilean *Aquiles*, while the Argentines took the *Libertad* to the white continent for four cruises.

Lindblad's cruises were popular, despite the cost (the *Magga Dan* trip cost $7,000pp), and the problems with charter tonnage made Lindblad realise that if he was going to continue to offer Antarctic voyages, he needed his own ship. He had a strong idea of the features that it should have, and the Danish Naval architects Knud E. Hansen translated these into the design of the *Lindblad Explorer.*

Lindblad Explorer

Bridge Deck	Small hospital with full medical capabilities, including X-ray, sauna
Boat Deck	Ten staterooms with full en suite facilities
	Penguin Room for lectures and study of marine biology
Main Deck	Explorer Lounge and bar forward with a small library
	Dining room that also had a large buffet table for informal meals
A Deck	Twenty-four twin-berth cabins with en suite facilities
B Deck	Sixteen twin-berth cabins with en suite facilities

Hull	Double skin, built to Baltic 1A ice class, ice knife for the rudder and protected four-blade variable pitch propeller. Bow thruster forward and anti-roll tanks
Equipment	Six Zodiac inflatable boats
Technical	2,398grt, Length 73m, Beam 14m, Draft 4.5m, 2 × 1,800bhp diesels
Capacity	104 passengers, 54 crew

A contract was signed in October 1968 with Nystad Varvet in Finland for $2.5 million[41] and the ship was ready for delivery just over a year later. The shakedown cruise was to Southampton, where the first paying passengers would embark for a transatlantic voyage via the Atlantic Islands to Buenos Aires.[42] On the transatlantic trip, an unattended deep fryer in the kitchen caused a fire that created serious problems to wiring behind the deck head. Drydocking in Buenos Aires for repairs resulted in the first two Antarctic cruises having to be cancelled. The first two cruises had been planned to call at the Falkland Islands, before going to the Antarctic Peninsula, and then turning around in Ushuaia. The third trip was to head to South Georgia, Gough Island, Tristan da Cunha and terminating in Cape Town.

The third planned cruise became the first visit by the *Lindblad Explorer* to the Antarctic. From Buenos Aires the ship called at West Point Island, Carcass Island and Stanley in the Falkland Islands before going on to South Georgia and the Antarctic Peninsula and then on the original itinerary to Cape Town. During a celebratory dinner on board for passengers together with guests from the islands, Lars-Eric Lindblad introduced His Excellency Sir Cosmo Haskard as Governor of the Galapagos Islands and Dr and Mrs Ashmore (Head of Medical Services) as also being from the islands. Rather than correct him, Sir Cosmo, in his role as governor of the Aleutian Islands,[43] thanked Mr Thomas Cook for his hospitality.

The next two seasons went well, although there was a grounding in 1971, but on 10 February 1972 the ship was forced ashore in Admiralty Bay while trying to ride out a storm. The outer hull of the ship was breached in several places and the propeller damaged, but the inner hull held. Eventually, the German salvage tug *Arktis* pulled the ship off and took it to Buenos Aires for temporary repairs. The ship was then towed to Norway where permanent repairs were undertaken, including rebuilding the main engines. Eventually, in August 1972, the ship picked up the interrupted cruise programme with a trip to Spitsbergen, where it managed to get to 82°N, a record at the time for a cruise ship. In a déjà vu moment, the generators failed in a Norwegian fjord earlier in the cruise, but were up and running again twenty-four hours later.

As part of the Spitsbergen itinerary, the opportunity was taken for a barbecue on an ice floe. This attracted a polar bear and the passengers were forced to retreat to the ship. After feeding the bear steaks and a bucket of Coca-Cola, it left. Following Spitsbergen, the ship headed to Greenland with a call at Scoresby Sound on the east coast.

The ship visited the Canadian Arctic in 1973, possibly on an itinerary similar to the one undertaken in 1983. In 1984, the ship made its historic passage of the Northwest Passage.

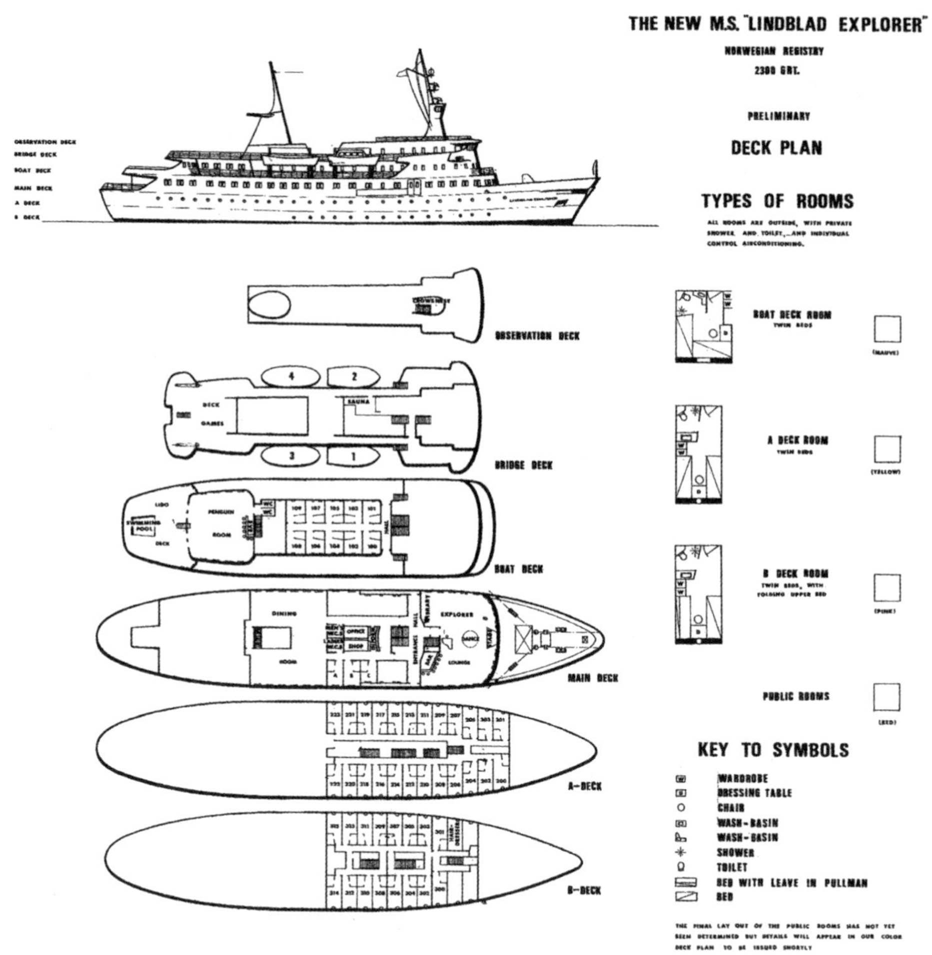

⬆ Deck plan of *Lindblad Explorer*. (Courtesy Knud E. Hansen)

1983 Canadian Arctic Cruise of the *Lindblad Explorer*[44]

Eighty passengers embarked at Reykjavik in Iceland.

Location	Dates	Notes
Gothaab	30 July	
Akpotok Island	2 August	
Shaftesbury Inlet	3 August	
Cape Dorset	4 August	
Mill Island	4 August	
Holsteinborg	8 August	
Sarsanguak	8 August	
Jakobshavn	9 August	
Sondreupernavik	10 August	
Carey Island	12 August	via Melville Bight
Harstein Bay	12/13 August	
78° 18'N	13 August	
Kane Basin	14 August	Stopped by multi-year ice
Cobourg Island	14 August	
Craig Harbour	14 August	
Cape Sparbo	15 August	
Grise Fjord	15/16 August	
Dundas Harbour	17 August	
Navy Board Inlet	18 August	
Eclipse Sound	18/19 August	
Pond Inlet	19 August	
Cape Graham Moore	19/20 August	
Frobisher	24 August	Passengers disembarked

Following repairs to the *Lindblad Explorer* in 1972, ownership changed to Swedish America Line through their Panamanian subsidiary United Cruising Co. Then between 1982 and 1983, ownership switched to Salen Reederi A/B, who transferred ownership to Ferry Services Curacao NV. In October 1985, the German company Discovery Reederei acquired the ship for Society Expeditions and changed the name to *Society Explorer*. In 1992, Liberian company Explorer Shipping became the owner and the name became simply *Explorer*.

There is some confusion about the Lindblad name and expedition cruising. After ownership changed to Salen Reederi A/B in 1982, a new company, under the leadership of Lars Wikander,[45] and called Salen Lindblad Cruising, took control of the ship.

This company was the operator for the 1984 Northwest Passage by the *Lindblad Explorer*. Pricing for that first Northwest Passage ranged from $16,900 to $23,000.

Lindblad Cruises had the market for expeditions on a small specialist vessel to themselves until the *World Discoverer*[46] was taken over by Discovery Cruises in October 1975. The ship was a somewhat larger version of the *Lindblad Explorer* accommodating 137 passengers in seventy-six cabins, versus 104 passengers in fifty cabins. Deployment of the *World Discoverer* followed the Lindblad pattern of cruises to Antarctica and Falkland Islands during November through March; during June through August it cruised in the northern polar regions; then for the balance of the year it headed to remote Pacific and Indian Ocean islands.

The *Lindblad Explorer* (after October 1984[47] *Society Explorer*) was joined by the *World Discoverer* for the 1977/78 season, and these were then the only expedition cruise ships in North Polar waters and Antarctica, until the *Illiria* joined them following the 1987/88 season. From 1989 onwards, more ships arrived every year. Although Argentine ships also had a presence, the only other expedition ship at the time was Peter Deilmann's forty-passenger *Nordbrise*, which offered expeditions to Greenland during the late 1970s; the ship was reported in Antarctica for the 1989/90 season chartered by Mountain Travel Sobek.

Lindblad Travel, Lars-Eric's company, continued with its other tour activities, and in 1987/88 organised tours in Cambodia and Vietnam in contravention of the US Trading with the Enemy Act. The $75,000 fines and associated legal costs forced the company into liquidation in 1989. Following the loss of his eponymous company, Lars-Eric established Creative Travel, and consulted for cruise companies, including Ocean Cruise Line (*Ocean Princess*) and Orient Lines (*Marco Polo*). Both ships cruised to Antarctica; *Ocean Princess* 1990/91–1992/93, and *Marco Polo* from 1993/94 onwards. Lars-Eric Lindblad died in 1994, but his son Sven-Olof continues the family tradition.

The Russians are Coming!

Although the Soviet Union had salvaged a couple of bombed out wartime German hulks[48] and resurrected them as passenger ships, they really did not get involved in building ships that could have a cruise role until the *Ivan Franko* class in the 1960s. Although there was the *Mikhail Kalinin* class of nineteen small passenger/cargo ships that could accommodate 333 passengers,[49] built at Matthias Werft in the 1950s, except for the lead vessel these little ships were mainly used internally. The *Mikhail Kalinin*, though, was removed from its Leningrad to London service and refitted as a small cruise ship at Rijeka in 1973/74. On completion the ship had four suites and 90 two-, three- and four-berth cabins, all with en suite facilities. The ship was now stabilised, fully air conditioned and had two restaurants, two bars, a lounge/bar, hairdresser and a shop. She operated quite successfully as a small cruise ship, mainly on charter to CTC Lines. The ship cruised mainly in the south, but did venture into Norwegian fjord country on a seasonal basis.

CTC Lines (Charter Travel Company) was formed in the mid 1960s to offer budget cruises in the UK market. It used Soviet ships, and had a major interest in the UK–Australia passenger ship trade. It ran the *Mikhail Lermontov*[50] from Tilbury to Lerwick, Reykjavik, Spitsbergen, Hammerfest, Honningsvåg, Tromsø, Trondheim, Bergen and Rotterdam, and *Maria Yermalova* from Hull to Florø, Harstad, Honningsvåg, Murmansk, Kirkenes, Hammerfest, Trondheim and Bergen, alternating with the Baltic and the Canaries. Revenue was a major source of hard currency for the Soviet government. The company eventually closed in 1996.

One pre-war ship that survived, and obviously had somewhat better accommodation as it served until the late 1980s, was the *Baltika*.[51] This was one of two 437-passenger cargo/passenger ships built in Holland for operation between Leningrad and London. She was frequently used as a 'Ship of State', and took Nikita Khrushchev to New York for his belligerent appearance at the United Nations in 1960. In later years, as cargo needs declined, the ship was used for cruising in the Black Sea and the Far East, and later offered Norwegian fjord cruises among the usual suite of Mediterranean and Atlantic Islands itineraries. However, the accommodation was a throwback to an earlier era, with first, second, third and tourist. Accommodation and catering was described as uninviting, which was not helped by each block of cabins being overseen by a formidable lady of mature years.

The *Ivan Franko* class was a series of five 20,000grt ships, all of which were used for cruise purposes at different times, no doubt as a means of earning hard currency. The ships were described as somewhat austere, but offered good value for money and the bar tariffs were considered excellent. Most have now been scrapped but the *Alexandr Pushkin* became the 22,080grt *Marco Polo*[52] in 1991, and had a long history of polar cruising for Orient Line commencing in the 1993/94 Antarctic season. The ship is now owned by Cruise and Maritime Voyages (CMV), which was founded in 1996 by the principals of CTC Lines, hence the presence of the *Marco Polo* and *Astor* in the CMV fleet.

The 1970s saw a major expansion in activity with a series of five ro-ro/passenger vessels (the Azerbaydzhan class) intended for Black Sea service. All were involved in a certain amount of cruising and were fully converted to cruise mode in the late 1980s. Another four ships were acquired during the early 1970s, and one of these, the *Maxim Gorkiy* (ex *Hamburg*), cruised regularly to Spitsbergen, nearly sinking in 1989. Another, the *Odessa*, cruised out of the USA until President Reagan imposed sanctions on Soviet ships in 1982. All have now been scrapped.

Also during the 1970s a series of eight small ice class passenger ships was built for the Soviets in Yugoslavia; this was the Maria Yermalova class. Three are still operating within Russia, and only the *Alla Tarasova*, now the *Ocean Adventurer*, remains of the four ships in the series that were involved in polar cruising. The others were the *Lyubov Orlova*, which sank off Ireland in 2013, the *Maria Yermalova* (employed by Marine Expeditions in the 2000/01 Antarctic season) and the *Antonina Nedzanhova* (chartered by Lindblad for the 1988/89 season), which sank in Japan in 2004 during a storm. Another ship, which has since been scrapped, operated for Lindblad for the 1997 season in the Antarctic. This was the *Olga Sadoskaya* and was renamed *Ocean Star* for the single season charter.

Around the same time as the Azerbaydzhan class of ro-pax ferries were being converted, a fifth offshore acquisition was made, the 1987-built, 20,704grt *Astor*. Purchased in 1988 by Black Sea Shipping, she operated for some years as the *Fedor Dostoevsky*. In 1995 she reverted to *Astor* and has continued to cruise regularly in polar regions, from 2013 on behalf of Cruise and Maritime Voyages.

During the 1980s, the Soviets commissioned a series of seven ro-pax ships from Poland. The Dmitri Shostakovich class was delivered in 1980–86 and several operated as cruise ships. Two, the *Konstantin Chernenko* and the *Konstantin Simonov*, were sold and converted to full cruise configuration as the *Ocean Atlantic* and the *Ocean Endeavour*. Both of these ships have operated on expedition voyages in polar regions. Apart from two ships of the series that are still operating within Russia, the other three in the class have been scrapped.

⬆ *Akademik Ioffe.* (Daisy Gilardini, courtesy OneOcean Expeditions)

Not as obvious as the entry of the Soviet Union into the international cruise business through the vehicles of the Black Sea and Baltic Shipping companies was the remarkable build-up of research and oceanographic ships, also during the 1980s. While all had at least nominal ice strengthening, some were true icebreakers. Almost all of the ships were built in Finland and had facilities for 50–100 scientists with varying degrees of comfort.

The growth in Soviet passenger and research shipping in the 1980s overlapped with the crumbling of the Soviet Union after Mikhail Gorbachev opened Pandora's box in 1985 with his policy of Glasnost. The Berlin Wall fell on 9 November 1989, and the accelerating deterioration of the Soviet Bloc was effectively complete by 26 December 1991.

After the collapse of the Bloc, the research ships became available, primarily for charter, but later for outright sale in some cases. The research ships, and the small ice class passenger ships, formed the backbone of the nascent polar expedition fleet. They came with competent crews that understood navigating in ice, had acceptable, if basic, accommodation, and charter rates were very reasonable. A list of expedition-type ships of Russian origin is given in the Appendices.

The importance of these Russian ships in the development of expedition cruising can be appreciated from the fact that prior to their availability from about 1991

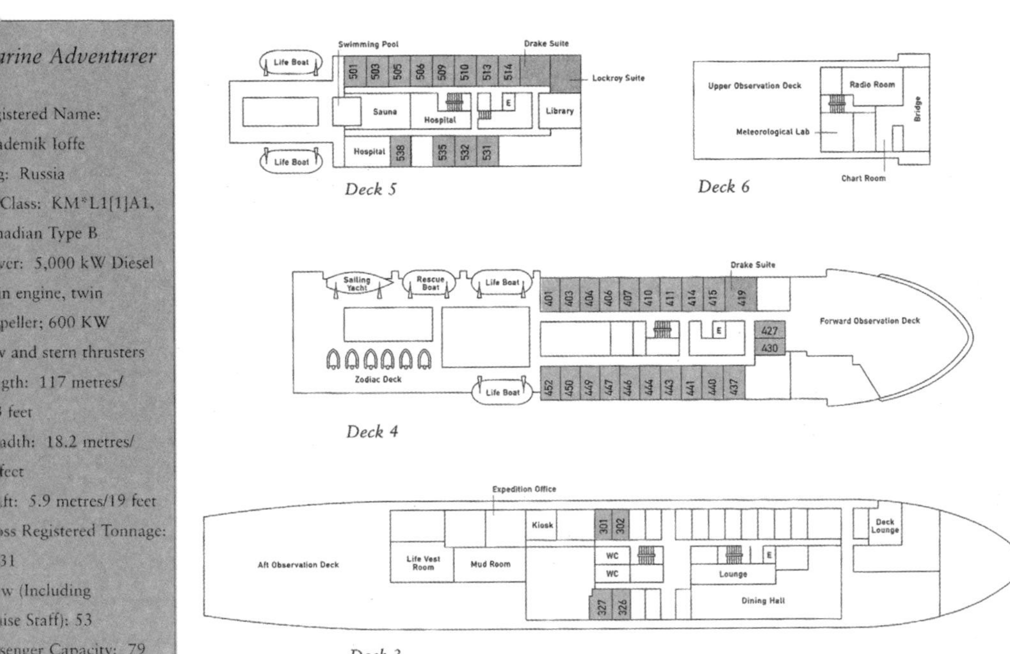

⬆ *Akademik Ioffe* deck plan.

← Lounge on the *Akademik Sergey Vavilov.* (Courtesy OneOcean Expeditions)

onwards, there were only three small ships cruising in polar regions; the *Illiria*, built in 1962; *Lindblad Explorer*, built in 1969; and *World Discoverer*, built 1975. In 1989, the *Delphin Clipper* came on the scene (now the *Silver Explorer*), in 1990 the *Frontier Spirit* (now the *Bremen*) was delivered. Then, in 1991, the *Society Adventurer* was completed, but never sailed under this name due to the insolvency of the owning company. It became the *Hanseatic* (now RCGS *Resolute)*.

Two companies, Quark and Marine Expeditions, were early adopters of the Russian research ships for polar cruising. Marine Expeditions, with Sam Blyth as President, was based in Toronto and incorporated in 1993. Earlier charters were undertaken as Blyth and Company.

Quark Expeditions, led by Lars Wikander, was incorporated in 1991 and was based in Seattle. In addition to taking some research ships on charter, the company also pioneered North Pole cruises with Russian icebreakers.

Today's Fleet

When does history become the present? For the purpose of this chapter we have taken as a starting point the formation of the International Association of Antarctic Tour Operators (IAATO) in 1991, and provided brief profiles of the seven companies that participated in its creation. At the time, these were the primary polar operators. Argentina and Chile had been active through the 1970s and '80s, both with their own ships as well as some charters; the last Argentine season with passengers was 1988/89 and Marinsular of Chile took the *Pomaire*[53] to the Antarctic in the 1990/91 season. However, companies based in both Chile (Punta Arenas) and Argentina (Ushuaia) continue to have a strong presence in Antarctic tourism.

The focus from the 1990s onwards has been on companies with specific polar cruise programmes, rather than cruise companies that incorporated northern destinations or the occasional Antarctic programme, although Holland America has sent its ships to the South Shetlands for many years, with *Zaandam* going there seven times during the 2017/18 season. Companies such as Fred Olsen Line might have been expected to be involved in Norwegian cruising from an early date, but it did not participate until the conversion of the *Black Watch* in 1986/87, and then to the Atlantic Islands where it had, and continues to have, other commercial interests. The line's first northern cruise was not until *Black Prince* in 1993.

The Magnificent Seven

ANI International

ANI is based in the UK, but registered in Canada, and like Mountain Travel, primarily an air/land operator. ANI demonstrated the possibility of safely landing an aircraft on a bare ice runway, eventually setting up a base camp for air-supported visits from Punta Arenas to Antarctica at Patriot Hills. It participated in the charter of the Chilean ship *Pomaire* (ex *Aquiles*) in 1990/91, and was also noted as the charterer of the *Grigory Mikheev* in the 2000/01 Antarctic season, in addition to operating air-supported, land-based tours that season. ANI last operated in 2002 and was dissolved in 2003, although continuing in operation as Antarctic Logistics and Expeditions (ALE).

Mountain Travel Sobek

This company is essentially a land-based adventure tour operator. However, Mountain Travel was noted as the operator for two cruises by the Argentine supply ship *Bahia Paraiso* in 1987/88, and in 1989/90 with the *Nordbrise*. Sobek Expeditions was the operator for two cruises of the Chilean yacht *Rio Baker* in 1987/88, in conjunction with ANI. Both companies are still operating.

Ocean Cruise Lines

Paquet acquired Ocean Cruise Lines, and its principal asset the *Ocean Princess*, in 1990, perhaps with the intent of offering expedition-style voyages because it had been outfitted with tenders during the 1984 refit. Lars-Eric Lindblad acted as a consultant to the company, and may well have travelled with the ship on one or more of its Antarctic voyages. It is likely that Lindblad persuaded Pacquet to limit the number of passengers to facilitate landing, and that the upper limit of 500 passengers for ships offering landings was introduced by IAATO to accommodate the *Ocean Princess*.

← *Ocean Princess.*

↓ *Bremen.* (Courtesy Hapag-Lloyd Cru

The ship successfully made cruises to the Antarctic for three seasons, even though it had no ice class. It sank in the Amazon in 1993 after hitting an unknown obstacle; considered a constructive total loss by the insurers, it was sold. Ocean Cruise Lines folded after the loss of the ship and Paquet did not return to the Antarctic.

Salen Lindblad Cruising

The company was created by Lars Wikander[54] in 1982 when Salen AB purchased the *Lindblad Explorer*. Despite its name, Salen Lindblad was not related to Lindblad Travel, which was managed by Lars-Eric Lindblad. The ship continued to be operated by Salen under its original name until purchased by Discovery Reederei GmbH in October 1985 for Society Expeditions. It is not known what ships it used for expedition cruises after 1985, but press reports stated that in 1989 Salen Lindblad had been appointed operator and sales agent for the *Caledonian Star*, which was operated in the

Baltic, Mediterranean and Indian Ocean. Salen Lindblad was closely associated with Noble Caledonia, which was owned by Christer Salen. Salen Lindblad did not appear as a ship operator in the Antarctic until into the 1990s.

In 1992, a new expedition company was formed – Seaquest Cruises – that was owned by three Japanese companies, together with Caledonia Shipping and Hapag-Lloyd. Seaquest acquired Salen Lindblad and the *Caledonian Star* intending to operate the ship in tandem with Frontier Cruises' new expedition cruise ship *Frontier Spirit*, built at the Mitsubishi yard in Japan. *Frontier Spirit* was delivered to Frontier Cruises at the end of 1990, and first appears in the Antarctic, under Salen Lindblad management, for three cruises in early 1991. This arrangement obviously did not work out as Seaquest went out of business following the 18 August 1992 sailing of the *Frontier Spirit*. She was given an overhaul in 1993 and then went on charter to Hapag-Lloyd as the *Bremen*. Hapag purchased the ship two years later. There is no mention of the fate of the *Caledonian Star*, but she was sold in 1997, becoming the *Endeavour*, and now operates as *National Geographic Endeavour* in the Galapagos Islands. Noble Caledonia has a very limited direct involvement in polar cruises.

Society Expedition Cruises

The company was created in 1976 as Society Expeditions and chartered the *World Discoverer*[55] from Adventure Cruises. In 1987 the company was purchased by Discovery Reederei GmbH (owned by Heiko Klein), who had acquired the *Lindblad Explorer* in 1985, and was renamed Society Expedition Cruises. The *Lindblad Explorer* also changed name, to *Society Explorer*.

A further expansion was planned by Heiko Klein with the order for a third vessel and an option for a fourth from the Rauma Shipyard in Finland. Delivery of *Society Adventurer*[56] was refused a week before its maiden voyage in July 1991. Rauma was to bareboat charter the ship to Klein, but this was contingent on Abercrombie and Kent International (North American sales agent for Society Expedition Cruises) having a minimum of $9 million in advance sales. Technical and contractual issues were cited as the reason for refusal, but it would seem that sales were soft and the company filed for Chapter 11 bankruptcy in the United States (reorganisation under bankruptcy protection) on 28 January 1992. The company did manage to recover, but by taking space on other ships, Klein chartered the *World Discoverer* to Clipper Cruise Line and sold the *Society Explorer* to Abercrombie and Kent. The *Society Adventurer* was chartered to a new German company, Hanseatic Cruises, and sailed as the *Hanseatic*.

The *World Discoverer* hit an uncharted reef in the Solomon Islands in 2000 and was wrecked. The company filed for Chapter 7 bankruptcy in 2004 and is no longer in operation. The *Society Explorer*, under the name *Explorer*, sank in the Antarctic in 2007.

Polar Circle. (Courtesy Ulstein Group)

Travel Dynamics

Originally formed in 1969 as Classical Cruises, the company was a pioneer in small ship educational cruising with some owned, but most chartered, ships. It chartered the *Illiria* for the Arctic and Antarctic, operating to the Antarctic from the 1988/89 through 1992/93 seasons. For the 1990/91 season it brought in the icebreaker *Polar Circle* for its Antarctic programmes. The *Polar Circle*[57] was a new polar resupply and passenger ship built by GC Rieber Shipping, the German specialist in ice support vessels. The *Illiria* was also used in Greenland and the Canadian Arctic in 1991 and 1992. Travel Dynamics variously chartered the *Orion*, *Corinthian II* and *Clelia II* for its programmes in the Antarctic from 2003/04 through the 2013/14 season. The *Clelia II* was also used in the Great Lakes, Greenland and the Canadian Arctic.

In 2014 its owned ships *Arethusa*, *Artemis* and *Corinthian* were acquired by Grand Circle Cruises, which has continued Travel Dynamic's itineraries. The balance of assets was reportedly purchased by Ponant.

Zegrahm Expeditions

The company was founded in 1990 by a group of seven, one of whom was the ex-VP of Planning and Operations at Society Expeditions. It had reportedly planned to commence Antarctic operations during the 1990/91 season but did not. Zegrahm does not own ships and typically operates between one and three charters in the Antarctic. It specialises in small ship cruises to unique destinations, as well as land tours and safaris.

Other Companies

After the 1991/92 season, a number of new operators came into the Antarctic taking advantage of the availability of Russian research ships. As noted, Marine Expeditions was one, and another was Quark Expeditions. However, most were small and did not operate over many seasons. For example, Elegant Cruises brought the *Andrea* to the Antarctic between the 2003/04 and 2008/09 seasons; the German tour operator Plantours offered cruises intermittently with different ships; and Clipper Cruise Lines initially had a strong presence with the *Clipper Adventurer* before fading to a single cruise in the 2007/08 Antarctic season, and it was gone thereafter. The *Clipper Adventurer* was also chartered to Adventure Canada for cruises in the Canadian Arctic. One company that has survived, and flourished, is Lindblad Expeditions, which grew out of a parallel company established by Lars-Eric's son Sven-Olof in 1979 and which was not affected by the bankruptcy of Lindblad Travel in 1989.

Marine Expeditions came on the scene in 1993 and was active between 1992/93 and 2000/01. Quark, now a major presence in expedition cruising, also commenced service in the Antarctic in the early 1990s, as did Abercrombie and Kent.

The following are brief details of selected companies. Some of these came and went, while others have started to make their presence known. Also included are a few cruise companies that took their ships to the white continent. There are other companies that offer a polar cruise experience that do not, or did not, get involved with Antarctic travel; these are also covered.

Abercrombie and Kent

Reportedly founded in 1962 in East Africa, A&K was an important travel company by 1990 given its role with Society Expeditions, for whom it acted as general sales agent. The company has gone through a number of ownership changes in recent years, from Fortress Investment Group to Zhonghong Holdings, a Chinese real estate company, and now to the Heritage Group, the Monaco-based holding company of Manfredini Lefebvre d'Oividio, who sold part of his holdings in Silversea Cruises to finance the deal. Heritage holds 85 per cent of the company, while Geoffrey Kent holds the balance.

In recent years A&K has regularly offered between four to six cruises in Antarctica. However, in a three-season period commencing with the 2004/05 season it offered ten and eleven cruises each season using the *Minerva*. The ship operated as *Explorer II* until March each year and then switched to operate as the *Alexander von Humboldt*. The complicated arrangement came from the charter agreement where A&K had the *Minerva* for about six months either side of the New Year (operating as *Explorer II*), then Phoenix Seereisen took the ship from March onwards as *Alexander von Humboldt*. A&K sometimes had one and two cruises with the ship in March after the charter arrangements, and name, changed during this period. After Phoenix terminated its arrangement with the owners, A&K continued chartering the ship under its original name until it was sold in 2010. It then took full ship charters from Compagnie du Ponant, and this relationship continues today, although with a reduced number of Antarctic cruises.

Adventure Canada

Adventure Canada is a family-owned and operated company based in Mississauga, Canada. It started in 1987 with land-based adventure travel into remote Canadian destinations, and became involved in ship chartering in 1994 after being asked to manage a visit by a large group to Cape Dorset, the Inuit printmaking capital of Nunavut. The ship used was the *Alla Tarasova*; from 1998, *Clipper Adventurer.* Since then seaborne expeditions to the Canadian Arctic, Labrador and other maritime destinations have become a major part of the business. Today, the *Ocean Endeavour* is the main vessel, but other smaller ships are used for unique locations such as Haida Gwai on the Pacific coast. The company partners with the Explorer's Club and also groups associated with Canada's Arctic; in 2011 it acquired Cruise North Expeditions q.v.

Antarpply

Antarpply is based in Ushuaia Argentina and operates a single ship, the eponymous *Ushuaia*, on Antarctic cruises. Originally built for the United States National Oceanic and Atmospheric Administration (NOAA) as the *Malcolm Baldridge* in 1970, the ship was acquired by the Ushuaia Adventure Corporation in 1990. The first reported appearance in Antarctic waters was on a single cruise for Mission Antarctica in the 2002/03 season. Antarpply is noted as the operator thereafter, with an increasing number of cruises each season, currently in the fifteen to seventeen range. The ship is typically laid up during the austral winter season, although in 2005 it was chartered by the newly created Cruise North Expeditions for six cruises in the Canadian Arctic. Cruise North subsequently chartered the *Lyubov Orlova.*

Antarctic Shipping

The company started in 2002 with the acquisition of the ex-Chilean Navy research vessel *Piloto Pardo.* The ship was completely rebuilt over 2003 at the Chilean shipyard ASEANAV into the small (2,180grt) luxury expedition ship *Antarctic Dream.* The ship then offered cruises from Punta Arenas for up to eighty guests to the Antarctic Peninsula, commencing with the 2004/05 season. A complementary programme was offered in northern polar regions from 2008, but the company was unable to continue

⬆ *Ushuaia*. (Weishing Lin, courtesy Antarpply)

profitably beyond the 2011/12 season. The reason given was the economics of operating such a small cruise ship. However, examination of IAATO statistics suggests that the issue may have been an inability to maintain a reasonable occupancy rate. While Quark had occupancy rates well over 90 per cent, Antarctic Shipping rarely achieved 80 per cent and in some seasons this was a lot less. The ship is still operating today in the Arab Gulf, but under the Mongolian flag.

Antarctica 21 SA

Originally operating as Antarctica XI (the company changed its name in 2019), they started in a small way with thirty-seven guests on the *Grigory Mikheev* during the 2003/04 Antarctic season. It has subsequently built up to a remarkable nineteen cruises on the *Ocean Nova* during the 2017/18 season, although it has chartered the *Hebridean Sky* in other seasons as well. The company's unique offering, hence the large number of cruises, is a fly/cruise model using a BAe 146 STOL aircraft configured for seventy passengers flying from Punta Arenas to and from the airfield at the Chilean base of Eduardo Frei on King George Island. This approach converts the often stormy two-day transit of the Drake Passage into a two- to two-and-a-half-hour flight. However, there are hazards as weather can frustrate flight plans. The company will offer a dedicated ship from the 2019/20 season with a long-term bareboat charter of the *Magellan Explorer* currently being fitted out by the ASEANAV yard in Chile. The ship is a 100-passenger expedition ship with a PC6 ice class that fully meets the requirements of the Polar Code (see Chapter 6). It will operate in Antarctic waters with seventy-three guests.

Aurora Expeditions

Aurora is Australia-based and has had a long-term presence in the Antarctic with ten to twelve cruises each season on its dedicated ship *Polar Pioneer* (ex *Akademik Shuleykin*). The company also offers northern polar cruises to Iceland, Svalbard, East Greenland and Franz Josef Land. Aurora has another small ship that operates in Australian waters, and has taken a long-term charter on two of Sunstone's Chinese new-builds. The *Greg Mortimer* will become its flagship from 2020, replacing the *Polar Pioneer*. A sister vessel will go on charter in the third quarter of 2021.

Bark Europa

The ship is the company. The *Europa* is a three-masted barque (two forward masts square rigged, third mast fore and aft rigged). The ship was originally built in Germany in 1911 and was rebuilt and re-rigged in the Netherlands over an extended period in the 1980s. As a sail training vessel the *Europa* offers up to forty-eight trainees the opportunity to 'learn the ropes' with a largely Atlantic-based sailing programme that includes four to five Antarctic cruises each season. The Falkland Islands is included as part of itineraries and booking notes interestingly state that passage fees exclude Falkland Islands landing fees, which will be added to the passenger's bar bill at the end of the voyage.

The ship first appeared in Antarctic trip reports in 2000/01 under Smit Tall Ships BV, but then from 2002/03 with Bark Europa. The company website notes that the ship suffered an incident prior to 2010 that damaged its figurehead. In that year a new one was fitted in Ushuaia.

Compagnie des Iles de Ponant and Ponant

Ponant was the brainchild of Jean-Emmanuel Sauvée, who gathered a group of retired French naval officers to create a new small ship cruise company that started in 1988. Its first ship was the three-masted barque *Le Ponant*,[58] delivered in 1991. Financing was arranged through a special French programme for ships that would be registered in French overseas territories. The company's second ship, *Le Levant*, was an elegant mega yacht for ninety-four passengers.

After a successful intervention by the author with the design of the ship, whereby the original sweeping bridge wings were trimmed flush to the hull and the lifeboats moved 30cm inboard, it went on to a well-received series of seasonal cruises in the Great Lakes that commenced in 1999. *Le Levant* undertook a number of northern polar cruises, including the Canadian Arctic, but never went to the Antarctic. After being operated for a time by Paul Gauguin Cruises, the ship is now owned by Grand Circle as *Clio*. Since *Le Levant*'s deployment into the Canadian Arctic in 2000, Ponant has offered regular northern cruises, although its first Northwest Passage was not until 2013 with *Le Soleal*. In 2018, heavy ice prevented any cruise ship passages, and the planned transits by *Le Boreal* and *Le Soleal* were frustrated.

Ponant's first foray into the Antarctic was with the ex *Song of Flower*, refitted as *Le Diament*[59] in 2003. The ship operated successfully in northern and southern polar regions, but was sold to a group of investors in 2011, who chartered it to Quark as *Ocean Diamond*.

In 2006, the company was purchased by the French container line CMA/CGM and its headquarters moved from Nantes to Marseilles, where the new owner had its head office. Access to better funding enabled the company to commence a significant expansion and in 2010 the first of a series of four sister ships,[60] *Le Boreal*, *L'Austral*, *Le Soleal* and *Le Lyrial*, was delivered. These ships have nominal 1D ice strengthening, but have been deployed

⬆ *Le Laperouse*. (Philip Plisson, courtesy Ponant)

extensively into the Arctic and Antarctic, including Northwest Passages. Ownership changes brought changes in name; originally Compagnie des Iles de Ponant, the company became Compagnie du Ponant in 2004, and from 2014 simply Ponant.

In 2016, Ponant entered a further expansion phase with an order for another four small luxury ships called the Explorer Class.[61] These have a slightly better 1C ice class, together with a unique 'Blue Eye' underwater lounge that enables guests to observe and hear, via integrated hydrophones, the underwater world. In 2017, the company ordered what will become the world's only ice-breaking cruise ship, the 270-passenger, 30,000grt *Le Commandant Charcot*, which will be capable of independent North Pole cruises. Then, in 2018, a further two ships in the Explorer class were ordered.

Expansion has no doubt been facilitated by ownership changes since the CMA/CGM acquisition. Ponant first moved to Bridgeport Capital in 2012, then the Artemis Group[62] in 2015. By 2022, the company will have the world's largest luxury expedition fleet, including its original sail-assisted cruise ship, ten ice-classed ships and an icebreaker. As a measure of its polar activities, its first Antarctic season in 2004/05 offered two cruises in one ship; by the 2017/18 season it was up to twenty-seven cruises in three ships.

Cruise North Expeditions

Cruise North was a Canadian expedition cruise company[63] established by Dugald Wells (previously President of Marine Expeditions) and supported by the Makivik Corporation and the Province of Quebec. Makivik is an Inuit-owned investment corporation and the legal representative of Quebec's Inuit; it was established in 1978 under the terms of the James Bay and Northern Quebec Agreement. The intent of Cruise North was to develop tourism activities focused on Nunavik, the northern part of Quebec. Some cruises were run out of Kuujjuaq, but others turned around in Churchill, Iqaluit and other northern locations. The company's first ship was the *Ushuaia* in 2005; from 2006 until 2010 it chartered the *Lyubov Orlova*. Operations ceased after the 2010 season. In 2007 it ran eight cruises on five itineraries, plus an inbound positioning cruise featuring the Torngat Mountains on the Labrador coast. The eight-night positioning cruise sailed from St John's, Newfoundland, on 20 June and was priced from $3,295; the Arctic cruises were from $3,855.

G.A.P. and G Adventures

Based in Toronto, Ontario, the company has a worldwide presence in nine distinct tour formats, and was founded as G.A.P. Adventures in 1990 by Bruce Poon Tip. The company had to change its name to G Adventures in 2011 after the GAP clothing line successfully challenged its name over brand confusion. The company also has a

↑ *Expedition* in Svalbard Islands. (Courtesy G Adventures)

non-profit partner – Planeterra – that undertakes some fifty social projects in countries where the company sends tours. These range from a refugee-run hotel in Vienna to a women's cooperative in Belize. In 2017, the company acquired the Page and Moy brands Travelsphere and Just You from the liquidators of the All Leisure Group.

The different tour formats are offered with strategic partnerships, and polar voyages on the dedicated ship *Expedition*[64] (ex ferry *Alandsfarjan*) is just one of the areas covered. The ship underwent a $13 million conversion in 2008 and was then chartered for the 2009 northern polar season for Spitsbergen cruises. The ship headed south, but further work was needed in Las Palmas over the 2009/10 winter, including the main engines. These continued to be a problem and were replaced in Italy in 2015. The ship offers a combination of suites, single, double and triple cabins, and G Adventures typically offers ten to twelve cruises each season in the Antarctic with a full programme of north polar cruises including the Norwegian fjords, Nordkapp, Spitsbergen, East Greenland and Iceland. Prior to bringing in the *Expedition*, the company operated the *Explorer* from the Antarctic 2004/05 season until its sinking in 2007.

Hapag-Lloyd

Through its predecessor companies, Hamburg-Amerika Line (HAL) and Nordeutscher Lloyd (NDL), Hapag-Lloyd (Hapag) can claim a longer association with polar cruising than any other company. The HAL *Columbia* sailed to Spitsbergen in 1893, followed by NDL's *Stettin* the following year. The companies re-established a presence during the interwar years and again after the Second World War. However, until Hapag took over the *Frontier Spirit* in 1993 and renamed it *Bremen* it did not have a dedicated small cruise ship in the model of the *Prinzessin Victoria Luise*. The *Bremen* has since cruised steadily in polar waters for part of each year. Although the *Hanseatic* has cruised in polar regions from 1993, this was on behalf of Hanseatic Tours. After Hapag-Lloyd purchased the company in 1997 she joined the *Bremen* as part of its expedition fleet.

Both ships have undertaken Northwest Passages and the *Hanseatic* transited the Northern Sea route in 2014. On this voyage advantage was taken of an unusual ice-free zone for the ship to sail to 85° 40'N, or about 250 nautical miles from the North Pole.

Hapag never took its small four-star *cColumbus* to southern polar waters, even though last-minute requirements by the St Lawrence Seaway Management Corporation prior to its maiden Great Lakes programme gave it bow reinforcement that would have protected against ice impacts. Plantours, who took over the ship after Hapag declined to renew its bareboat charter from Conti Reederei, had no such qualms, and the *Hamburg* has undertaken regular polar voyages, including to Antarctica. The ship has two excellent high-speed catamaran tenders, as well as zodiacs, that make it eminently suitable for expedition-style cruises.

Hapag took its then new luxury ship *Europa*[65] on traditional northern trips to the Fjords following delivery in 1981, and also to the Antarctic over three seasons, 1990/91, 1992/93 and 1994/95. These would have been sightseeing as the ship was not set up for landings.

The company came to an agreement with OneOcean Expeditions for a long-term charter of the *Hanseatic* to it, and she returned to the Antarctic in the 2018/19 season as RCGS *Resolute*. The *Bremen* is also leaving Hapag, and has recently been sold to the Swiss river cruise operator Scylla, which will take delivery in 2021. Scylla, like Scenic and Viking, is looking at moving into ocean expedition cruising. The *Bremen* will be taken on a five-year seasonal charter by Polar Latitudes and renamed *Seascape* for operation in the Antarctic over the 2021/22 season. A summer charterer is yet to be announced.

Hapag will deliver three new luxury expedition ships under the Hanseatic brand, commencing in late 2019.

Heritage Expeditions

Heritage is a New Zealand-based company that operates its own expedition ship, the *Spirit of Enderby*[66] (ex *Professor Khromov*). It has a relatively small but unique long-term presence in the Antarctic, offering two to three cruises each season. Cruises started in 1993/94 season with the *Akademik Shokalskiy*, the sister ship to the *Khromov*. These cruises are to the 'Other Antarctic', the Ross Sea and New Zealand sub Antarctic Islands, not the Antarctic Peninsula. However, the company's main area of speciality is the Russian Far East, with cruises to Kamchatka, Kuril Islands, Wrangel Island and the Sea of Okhotsk.

Hurtigruten

Hurtigruten is the generic name for the year-round Norwegian Coastal Express service established in the late nineteenth century to link communities along the country's deeply indented and mountainous coastline. Eventually, the service extended from Bergen to Kirkenes in the far north.

In the 1980s the role of shipping in this service began to change as other modes of travel became available to the communities. Tourism, rather than basic ferry service, became of more importance to the shipping companies. Two of these, Ovotens og Vesteraalens D/S (OVDS) and Trans Fylkes D/S (TFDS), merged in 2006 under the Hurtigruten banner. The company went private in 2015 after being acquired by TDR Capital, a UK investment company with a diverse portfolio.

OVDS started cruising in the Antarctic with eight cruises on the *Nordnoge*[67] in 2002/03. Although occupancy for the first programme was only 40 per cent, it had significantly improved to more than 70 per cent two seasons later. In 2007/08, Hurtigruten undertook a remarkable twenty-three cruises with the *Fram*[68] and *Nordnoge*.

More recently, the ship used has been the *Midnatsol*,[69] part of the expedition fleet that includes *Fram*, the classic 1956-built *Nordstjenen*,[70] and *Spitsbergen*.[71] The ships cruise regularly in the Svalbard Islands, Faroe Islands, Greenland and occasionally into the Canadian Arctic; *Fram* was in the Canadian Arctic in 2018. The company is building two, possibly three, advanced expedition cruise ships: *Roald Amundsen*[72] and *Fridjof Nansen* were delivered in 2019.

⬆ *Fram* in the Svalbard Islands. (Courtesy Hurtigruten)

Lindblad Travel, Lindblad Expeditions[73]

While Lindblad Travel had lost access to the *Lindblad Explorer* in 1982, it returned to the Antarctic in 1986/87 with cruises on what was now the *Society Explorer*. The following year Lindblad used the *Illiria*, and in 1988/89 ran seven cruises with the *Antonina Nezhanova*. For the 1997 Antarctic season it took the *Olga Sadoskaya* and renamed her *Ocean Star* for the single-season charter.

Lindblad Expeditions Inc. was founded in 1979 by Sven-Olof Lindblad, Lars-Eric's son. The goal of the company was to offer innovative and educational expeditions to the world's noteworthy destinations. The company expanded into areas other than polar regions, particularly those that demanded marine access. In 2004, the company came to a strategic relationship with the National Geographic Society and since then its ships have all had that name in their title. Lindblad Expedition Holdings was incorporated in 2010 and stock commenced trading on NASDAQ on 9 July 2015. In 2013, Lindblad acquired Orion Expedition Cruises, together with the *Orion*, which became *National Geographic Orion*. As of 2016, the company reported it had six owned vessels and five on seasonal charter. Of the owned ships, *National Geographic Explorer* and *National Geographic Orion* currently offer polar cruises, while the others are dedicated to specialist areas, such as the Galapagos Islands. The peak year for Antarctic trips was 2008/09 with sixteen cruises on the *National Geographic Endeavour* and *Explorer*.

Marine Expeditions

Marine Expeditions was incorporated in 1992 and based in Toronto, Canada. In the early days, it had the following Soviet research and cruise ships[74] on charter, but others were used at different times:

Marine Adventurer	*Akademik Ioffe*
Marine Voyager	*Akademik Sergey Vavilov*
Marine Discoverer	*Alla Tarasova*
Marine Explorer	*Professor Multanovsky*
Marine Spirit	*Akademik Shuleykin*
Marine Challenger	*Livonia*

Marine Expeditions' main polar business was the Antarctic, but it did offer some cruises in the Canadian Arctic with the *Akademik Ioffe* and *Kapitan Khlebnikov*. In 1992, the company also chartered a small ice-classed resupply boat that served the Labrador coastal communities. The *Northern Ranger* was somewhat basic, and not a good sea boat. The positioning voyages were difficult, but it did deliver a season of cruises in the Antarctic.

➡ *Northern Ranger* on the Labrador coast.

Bauer reported that the company had more than 30 per cent of the business in Antarctica during the 1996/97 season with 2,362 passengers, and carried 3,751 passengers in the 1999/00 season in conjunction with a related operation – the World Cruise Company (WCC). However, the 1999/00 numbers may not be accurate. The numbers relate to two ships:[75] the *Aegean I*, and the *Ocean Explorer I* with a reported 889 on board. The *Aegean I* carried two passenger loads,[76] but the *Ocean Explorer I* number is probably the all-berths capacity of the ship. She is thought to have had about 500 passengers on board, which is reasonable given that Holland America's *Rotterdam*, also in the Antarctic that season, was operating at the equivalent of 60 per cent occupancy. These two cruises appear to have been completed successfully; however, the second round-the-world cruise using the *Riviera I* was abandoned in Tahiti on 25 May 2000.

Marine Expeditions barely survived this incident, although only for the 2000/01 season when it was down to two vessels, the *Maria Yermalova* and the *Luybov Orlova*, with a total of eighteen cruises and 2,132 passengers. By the following year the company was no more, no doubt a victim of its, and WCC's, unwise excursion into low-cost round-the-world cruises. Additionally, the *Ocean Explorer I*, while a stately and beautifully outfitted passenger ship, was woefully fuel uneconomic.[77]

Oceanwide Expeditions

The Dutch company was established in Vlissingen in 1993 and specialises in North and South polar cruises with a range of owned ships. The company's origin goes back to 1983 with the formation of the Plancius Foundation (based at the University of Groningen Arctic Centre) that undertook research into Dutch whaling at Smeerenburg in the north of Spitsbergen Island. The foundation purchased and converted a small vessel as the *Plancius* in 1979 to support its work, but due to financial

⬆ *Plancius*. (Sandra Petrowitz, courtesy Oceanwide Expeditions)

problems had to sell it a few years later. Oceanwide continued the tradition of cruises to the Svalbard Islands.

The company has four ships, with a fifth, the *Hondius*,[78] being delivered in 2019, and a sixth, *Janssonius*, in 2021. *Rembrand van Rijn* is a tall ship with a focus on the northern hemisphere, *Noorderlicht* is also a sailing vessel and is usually frozen in not far from Longyearbyen to act as a base camp for winter land expeditions in Spitsbergen. During the northern summer it offers cruises within the Svalbard Islands. The mainstay of the company's Antarctic programme are its ships *Plancius*[79] (ex Dutch Navy *Tydeman*) and *Ortelius*[80] (ex *Marina Svetaeva*).

Oceanwide commenced its Antarctic programme with charters of the *Grigory Mikheev* through the 2008/09 season. The *Plancius* then offered cruises the following season, with the *Ortelius* joining her in 2011/12. In 2017/18 both ships were active with a total of twenty-one cruises.

OneOcean[81]

Andrew Prossin, a native of Cape Breton, Nova Scotia, established the company in Squamish, British Columbia, in 2007, following his sale of Peregrine Adventures in 2006 to the UK's First Choice Holidays. Peregrine was an Australian expedition operator that he had established with a successful Antarctic business. Prossin had started in

⬆ RCGS *Resolute*. (Jason Ransom, courtesy OneOcean Expeditions)

strategic analysis with Canadian Pacific Railways, but a stint with Marine Expeditions in Toronto got him hooked on the polar region.

The company steadily expanded from two Antarctic cruises on the *Professor Multanovskiy* in 2008/09 to twenty-five cruises in the 2017/18 season on the *Akademik Ioffe* and the *Akademik Sergiy Vavilov,* which were their primary ships from the 2012/13 season. Commencing with the 2019/20 season, these ships were joined by the RCGS *Resolute* (ex *Hanseatic*). However, the Shirshov Institute in Kalingrad, which owns the *Akademik Ioffe* and the *Akademik Sergey Vavilov*, unexpectedly, and in contravention of its agreements with OneOcean, withdrew both ships in May 2019. The company has a strategic alliance with the Royal Canadian Geographic Society and was one of the main operators of cruises in the Canadian Arctic. Andrew Prossin is attempting to restructure the company, but there was no news as of December 2019. The RCGS *Resolute* was laid up in Buenos Aires on 27 October 2019.

Orient Lines

The company was created by Gerry Herrod, who had acquired the Soviet cruise ship *Alexandr Pushkin* in 1991; he then spent two and a half years totally rebuilding the ship into the *Marco Polo*. Lars-Eric Lindblad consulted with Orient Lines regarding polar cruising and the ship first went to the Antarctic for the 1993/94 season. The ship operated under the Orient Lines banner until the 2007/08 season, then the next season Transocean Tours took her for four cruises. The ship has not visited the

Antarctic since, but it has cruised to Greenland and the Norwegian fjords. Since 2010 it has been operated by the UK-based Cruise and Maritime Voyages.

Orient Lines was sold to Norwegian Cruise Lines in 1998, which was then taken over by Star Cruises in 2000. An attempt was made to relaunch Orient Lines as an independent entity using the ex-Russian ship *Maxim Gorkiy*. Regrettably, the 2008/09 recession put paid to this idea.

Peregrine Adventures

Even though Peregrine has a continuing presence in Antarctic and northern polar waters, it was only listed in IAATO travel data up to 2008. As noted under the OneOcean profile, the company was sold in 2006 to First Choice Holidays, which also bought Quark. Its cruises are now integrated with Quark, with whom it is closely associated in the Australian market. The company is also part of the broad-based Australian travel company the Intrepid Group, and offers a wide-ranging programme of specialist cruises in the northern hemisphere, including Iceland, Svalbard Islands, Jan Mayen and North Pole cruises. The company is also active in temperate destinations such as Southeast Asia. The ships offered for polar cruises are *Ocean Adventurer* (also used by Quark), and *Ocean Nova* (used by Antarctica 21). The *Ocean Nova* is the ship proposed for a unique fly-cruise opportunity out of Reykjavik into East Greenland.

Polar Star Expeditions

This was a single-ship company established by Martin Karlsen, a Halifax, Nova Scotia-based shipowner who ran the long-established Karlsen Shipping Company. The *Polar Star*[82] was the ex *Njord*, a Swedish icebreaker, and it operated successfully in polar regions and in Antarctica from the 2001/02 season. Although there were engine problems in 2010, the end of the road came in 2011 following a grounding that caused the company to lose the balance of the season and sail the ship to Las Palmas in the Canary Islands for repair. The ship never got out of dry dock before the Spanish government put a lien on it for $1.4 million, and then the bank holding the mortgage took fright and called it in, even though the company had a solid book of future cruise business.[83] The company was forced into liquidation in May 2011, and as of 2017 the ship was still at Las Palmas. There is now no trace of it and it may have been scrapped.

Polar Star worked with Cheesman's Ecology Safaris and Students on Ice for some of its cruises. From 2005 the ship offered one or two cruises in the Canadian Arctic and also cruised in Svalbard, Iceland and Greenland.

Poseidon Expeditions

Since 2010, Poseidon has been an alternative charterer to Quark of the Russian icebreaker *50 let Pobedy* for North Pole cruises. The company is based in Cyprus and was reportedly founded in 1999. However, it only started to offer a cruise to the Antarctic in the 2015/16 season with the *Sea Spirit*. It does offer a wide range of north polar programmes, including the little-visited Franz Josef Land in the Russian Arctic. Like some other companies, it has itineraries, also with the *Sea Spirit*, that include East Greenland as an integral component of a cruise from Spitsbergen to Reykjavik.

Quark Expeditions

Prior to incorporating Quark in 1991, Lars Wikander and Mike McDowell undertook a (successful) trial charter of an Atomflot icebreaker *Rossiya* for a 1990 North Pole cruise. Regular North Pole tourist voyages began in 1991 in the last days of the Soviet Union with *Sovetskiy Soyuz*. From 1992, two or three charters each year were undertaken, mainly with the *Yamal*. It had the North Pole market pretty much to itself until 2010, when Poseidon came on the scene. From 2011, the primary icebreaker was *50 let Pobedy* (*50 Years of Victory*), and Quark and Poseidon shared the business, with each having two or three charters per season. Other tour operators book groups onto these cruises through the principals.

Quark started its Antarctic operations with a couple of chartered Russian research ships in the 1991/92 season, and early Russian research ships that the company chartered were the *Professor Molchanov* and *Professor Khromov*, as well as the *Kapitan Khlebnikov*. For the 1994/95 Antarctic season it had the *Alla Tarasova* and *Professor Khromov* on charter. In the 1996/97 season it took 1,028 guests to the Antarctic using four ships, and 1,153 in the 1999/2000 season. These numbers remained fairly stable until the demise of Marine Expeditions, after which Quark's Antarctic cruise numbers and passengers increased steadily through the 1990s and into the 2000s. Their peak year for Antarctic activity was 2006/07, when the company offered fifty-nine cruises with six ships and carried 3,908 guests. In the 2017/18 Antarctic season, Quark deployed four ships on forty-five cruises with close to 7,000 passengers. In 2011/12, the company took the *Kapitan Dranitsyn*, a close sister to the *Kapitan Khlebnikov*, for two cruises to Franz Josef Land and Novaya Zemlya in the Russian Arctic.

In 2007, the company was acquired by the UK travel company First Choice, which was then acquired by TUI Travel Plc. In 2016, ownership changed again to Travelopia.

Seabourn Cruise Line

The *Seabourn Quest* is designated as Seabourn's expedition vessel and was outfitted in 2013 with Zodiacs, cranes for handling them and an adapted marina area to facilitate boarding. The ship then started regular Antarctic cruises in the 2013/14 austral season and also visited Greenland and Iceland in 2014.

The ship is scheduled for four Antarctic cruises each season, which is the longest it stays in any one destination. Cruises are offered that take in northern destinations such as Greenland, Iceland and the North Cape and the Baltic, but the ship spends most of the year in temperate regions. The *Seabourn Quest* does not have an ice class, and Seabourn may offer more cruises with a polar orientation following the delivery of its two new ships in 2021 and 2022. These have a PC6 class, so will be quite capable of cruising into ice-infested waters.

Silverseas Cruises

The *Silver Explorer*[84] was acquired by Silverseas in 2007 and undertook a major refit in 2008, starting visits to Antarctica in the 2008/09 season as the *Prince Albert II*. There were eight cruises in the first season, of which one was taken by Abercrombie and Kent. Canadian Arctic visits commenced in 2013 with a turnaround in Churchill for two cruises that originated and ended in Greenland. The ship, which has an Ice 1A class, regularly cruises to Spitsbergen, Iceland and Greenland as well other northern destinations. Its *Silver Cloud*[85] was ice-strengthened during a refit in 2013 and then deployed to the Antarctic in the 2017/18 season. The *Silver Wind* will receive a similar refit in 2020, which will presumably give it an Ice 1C Class similar to its sister ship, as well as Zodiacs. Silverseas plans to deploy the ship to the Arctic and Antarctic following the refit.

Yachts and Tall Ships

The start of polar cruising can reasonably be ascribed to Lord Dufferin and the account of his 1856 Arctic voyage in his schooner yacht *Foam*. Several private yacht owners took confidence from his light-hearted story and sailed to the Arctic, mainly Svalbard, in subsequent years. Steam yachts, such as HAL's *Meteor* and the Bergen Line's *Stella Polaris*, then set the tone for polar cruising, and yachts (both commercial and private) have remained an important part of regional and seasonal cruising.

In the Canadian Arctic, many 'adventurers' have challenged the Northwest Passage, encouraged by media stories of retreating ice, only to find the reality is somewhat different. Numbers increased dramatically from 2011, reaching twenty-eight in some seasons, although not all attempted a transit between the two oceans. Another class of yacht that calls in the region are mega yachts. These are private craft over 30m in

⬆ Schooner *Noorderlicht* frozen in at Spitsbergen. (Courtesy Oceanwide Expeditions)

length[86] and sometimes carry passengers as a small cruise ship. The late Paul Allen's ice-classed mega yacht *Octopus* frequently used the Northwest Passage for its original purpose, a shortcut between the Atlantic and Pacific. The boat has also visited the Antarctic on a number of occasions.

The Antarctic and islands in the Southern Ocean sees a large number of yachts every season. Many of these are operated for small group expeditions and accommodate twelve passengers or fewer. Larger ones have been categorised as small cruise ships, although primarily sail-propelled. Some mega yachts have also appeared, and EYOS has brought in one such, the twenty-six-passenger *Legend*, in recent years in addition to smaller craft. During the 2017/18 Antarctic season, there were twenty motor and sail yachts registered with IAATO that visited. The number of private yachts is not known. In Greenland for the 2018 season, NORDREG reported sixteen larger vessels, including the *Legend*, and nineteen adventurers.

The tall ship *Europa* has been classified as a small cruise ship due to its capacity of forty-two trainees, but *Hanse Explorer*, offered for group charters, is classified as a yacht because its capacity is only twelve persons. Oceanwide operates both a schooner and tall ship to Svalbard, while there are several Icelandic operators of small yachts that offer cruises to East Greenland. One such is North Sailing, which has several classic schooner rigged sailing vessels in its fleet.

The Future

At the time of writing this book, and excluding large cruise ships, there are some thirty-eight expedition-style cruise ships either currently operating, or having recently operated, specific Arctic and Antarctic polar voyages. By 2023, and dependent on any retirements from the existing fleet, there will be close to eighty ships that target expedition-style polar cruises. The current numbers include some small cruise ships that are designated by their owners as expedition ships, an example being *Seabourn Quest*. Other ships, such as Cruise and Maritime Voyages' classic small cruise ships *Marco Polo* and *Astor*, have recently operated on polar itineraries, but are not currently scheduled. Silverseas does not have any new buildings, but will have both its *Silver Cloud* and *Silver Wind* as ice-reinforced expedition ships by 2023 to complement its small but high-ice-class *Silver Explorer*. Included in the count are some yachts and sail training vessels that undertake polar cruises.

Other cruise companies schedule the occasional cruise ship to Antarctica for sightseeing. Holland America has been a fairly regular caller since the *Rotterdam* in 1960, and the *Prinsendam* and *Zaandam* were there during the 2018/19 season. Many other companies include Stanley, the North Cape, Longyearbyen, Tórshavn, Reykjavik, Akureyri and the Greenland coast on their itineraries. Visitor arrivals at these destinations are dominated by large ship activities.

Such a plethora of ships looking to develop original polar itineraries to take advantage of the capabilities of their ships will put considerable pressure on destinations. For example, there were thirty-one ships in the Antarctic for the 2018/19 season that offered 304 cruises, mainly to the Antarctic Peninsula. Could the region safely accommodate a doubling of this level of activity without materially impacting the environment and guest experiences?

Another aspect resulting from the extraordinary number of new ships arriving in the marketplace may be the appearance of a two- or even three-tier price structure. Almost without exception, the new ships are targeted at a luxury market with a claimed five- and six-star level of accommodation and service. The existing ships will have to differentiate their offerings based on price, as the new ships may exceed the capabilities of the old fleet relative to access.

A number of vessels are quite old, and a justification for the extraordinary number of vessels on order is that these will need to be replaced. However, there do not seem to be any specific regulatory requirements coming up that would require costly structural work that the older ships would need to meet. The Polar Code may cause some to be retired due to survival requirements, although the International Maritime Organisation (IMO) requirement for safe return to port for ships that exceed 120m in length came into force in 2010. As a consequence their continuing presence in the market will be governed by the willingness of the owners to undertake some initial investment followed by periodic refits and upgrades. However, contractual issues may take some ships out of the market, as has been the case with two Russian ships operated by OneOcean. All cruise ships are refreshed from time to time, and such activity runs the gamut from a simple redecoration and replacement of carpets to a major overhaul that may include replacement of main engines. It is interesting to compare the actual hull age of the ship with the perceived age, based on the year of the last refit.

Active Polar Fleet by Decade

	<1969	1970–79	1980–89	1990–99	2000–09	2010–19
By Year Built	3	4	8	10	7	16
By Year of Refit[87]	0	0	0	5	9	23

Eleven ships were delivered in 2019, and most of the future fleet is being built for companies that have had a presence in polar waters, and are either upgrading their fleet or developing new ships that may replace, or supplement, ones that have been chartered. Some are newcomers to the market.

As part of a suite of announcements about polar waters in October 2019, Russian sources stated that the country is considering building an unspecified number of 350-passenger ships for the expedition market, at a cost of about $300m per ship.

The following are snapshots of company new-building activity.

Antarctica 21

The *Magellan Explorer* was scheduled to undertake an inaugural cruise from Punta Arenas on 28 November 2019. It then commenced fly-cruise operations based at Eduardo Frei on King George Island. The ship has a sixty-day operational capability.

Magellan Explorer: 73/100 passengers, 60 crew,[88] 4,900grt, PC6 Ice Class.

Aurora Expeditions

The company will replace their small ex-Russian research ship *Polar Pioneer* with a charter from Sunstone for the *Greg Mortimer*, commencing with the 2019/20 Antarctic season and a second Sunstone newbuild in 2021. The *Polar Pioneer* appears to be moving to New Zealand coastal cruises for the 2019/20 winter season.

Greg Mortimer: 120 passengers, 74 crew, 20 staff, 7,400grt, PC6 Ice Class.

Crystal Yacht Expeditions

Crystal Cruise Line is probably best known for its Northwest Passage transits in the *Crystal Serenity* in 2016 and 2017. However, this ship had no ice class and was accompanied by the *Ernest Shackleton* as a backup in case of a serious incident. Their three new ships, of which the *Crystal Endeavour* is first of class, are called mega yachts by the company and will not require such support. They have many unique features, including dynamic positioning, two helicopters, two small submarines and a remote-operated vehicle. The first deployment is reported to be the Kamchatka Peninsula in August 2020, with a visit to the Ross Sea area of the Antarctic in January 2021.

Crystal Endeavour: 200 passengers, 200 crew, 25,000grt, PC6 Ice Class.

(Representation Courtesy Crystal Yacht Expeditions)

Hapag-Lloyd

The company has been associated with polar cruising for 125 years, and its three new ships will continue its tradition of luxury cruises into ice-infested waters. The first vessel, although delivered late by Vard at the cost of the first two 2019 cruises, will be *HANSEATIC Nature*, to be followed later in the year by *HANSEATIC Inspiration*. The third vessel, *HANSEATIC Spirit*, will be delivered in 2020. The *Inspiration* will be fitted for Great Lakes cruises and is designated their international ship, with programmes in both German and English. The *Nature* and *Spirit* will be German only.

HANSEATIC Nature: 230 passengers (199 for Antarctic expeditions and circumnavigation of Spitsbergen), 175 crew, 15,650grt, PC6 Ice Class.

(Courtesy Hapag-Lloyd Cruises)

Hurtigruten

Hurtigruten is materially upgrading its fleet as well as introducing two new large expedition vessels.[89] Three ships will have cabins and suites upgraded, be fitted with battery packs, and have engine upgrades to Tier III[90] over 2020 and 2021 in a $100m programme. The *Trollfjord* will be renamed *Maud*, *Finnmarken* will become *Otto Sverdrup* and *Midnatsol Eirik Raude*. The *Fram* is also to undergo a total makeover in 2020. It is not clear what the passenger capacity will be for these two ships after their refits.

The first new polar ship is the *Roald Amundsen*, to be delivered in 2019, after which it will undertake a Norwegian coast and Svalbard cruise, continue to Greenland and then undertake a Northwest Passage en route to the Antarctic. The second vessel, *Fridjof Nansen*, was delivered early in November 2019; the third ship for 2021 delivery is yet to be named. The new builds have hybrid propulsion systems using battery packs, and will also use biofuels.

Roald Amundsen: 530 passengers, 151 crew, 20,889grt, PC6 Ice Class.

(Courtesy Hurtigruten)

Lindblad

The new buildings for Lindblad for delivery in 2020 and 2021 will use Ulstein's unique X-Bow design. The first one will be named *National Geographic Endurance*, the second will carry the name *National Geographic Resolution*. The ships will carry a remote-operated vehicle, be fitted with hydrophones and underwater video cameras and carry a helicopter landing pad.

The itinerary for the maiden voyage will include a Svalbard cruise, a Northeast Passage and a cruise on the eastern coast of Greenland.

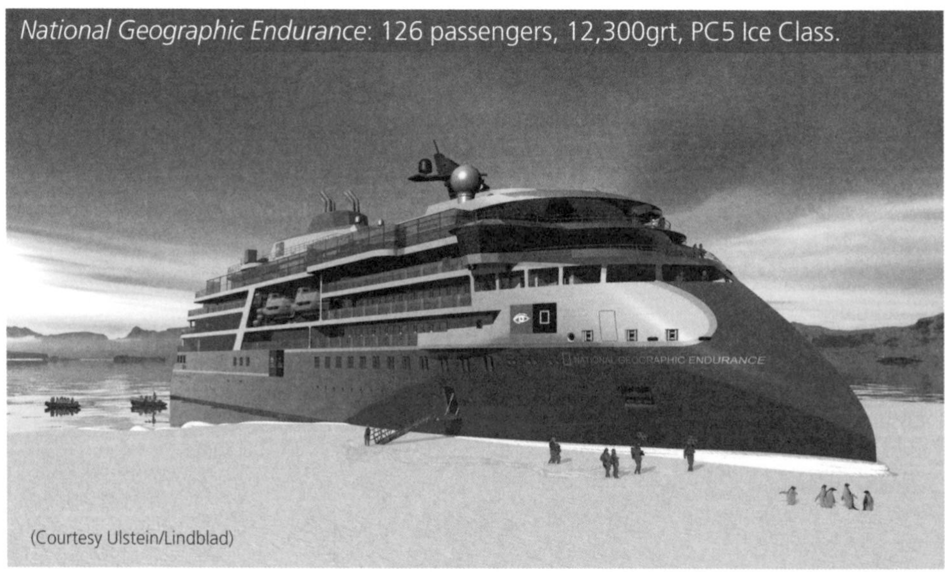

National Geographic Endurance: 126 passengers, 12,300grt, PC5 Ice Class.

(Courtesy Ulstein/Lindblad)

Mystic Cruises

The company is a brand of Mystic Invest, which has two subsidiaries heavily involved in river cruising. DourAzul operates on the River Douro in Portugal, while Nicko Cruises runs riverboats in central Europe. The parent is a family owned financial holding company with multiple brands in travel and tourism.

The *World Explorer* is the first of three expedition ships being built at the Portuguese shipyard West Sea and was delivered in 2019. Nicko Cruises has marketed the ship in Germany with Norwegian fjord, Baltic and Arctic cruises. Quark will charter the ship for the 2019/20 Antarctic season. The second ship, *World Voyager*, is scheduled for delivery in 2020, with the *World Navigator* the following year. Mystic have stated that up to ten expedition ships will be built, with four assigned to a new brand – Atlas Ocean Voyages in the USA.

World Explorer: 228 passengers, 9,200grt, 1B Ice Class.

(Courtesy Mystic Cruises)

Norwegian Yacht Voyages

The company proposes to build a series of four mega yachts with deliveries commencing in 2022. The first of class will be *MY Caroline* in the summer of 2022, with subsequent yachts arriving at eighteen-month intervals. The design is by Deltamarin, with construction proposed at Metalships in Vigo, but there is very little detail available about design features.

MY Caroline: 222 passengers, 127 crew, 16,500grt.

Oceanwide

Hondius was delivered during 2019 with a flexible power management system designed to reduce fuel consumption and thus CO_2 emissions. Interestingly, the ship reverts to a traditional form of heating, steam, rather than electricity, again as a means of reducing power consumption. The ship uses LED lighting throughout, and is fitted with bow and stern thrusters for better manoeuvrability. Oceanwide has committed to a sister ship – *Janssonius* – for delivery in October 2021. The company has upgraded *Plancius* and *Ortelius* and installed more user-friendly gangways on the *Hondius*.

Janssonius: 176 passengers, 72 staff and crew, 5,590grt, PC6 Ice Class.

Hondius: 176 passengers, 72 staff and crew, 5,590grt. PC6 Ice Class.

(Courtesy Oceanwide Expeditions)

Ponant

By mid 2022, Ponant will have the world's largest fleet of polar expedition vessels. Adding to its existing fleet of four Boreal class Ice 1D ships and two Explorer class with Ice 1C designation will be four more Explorer class and finally its icebreaker in 2021. *Le Commandant Charcot* will have a hybrid electric drive with high-capacity batteries as well as a dual fuel capability with on-board Liquified Natural Gas (LNG) storage. The ship will also have two helicopters housed in an on-board hangar.

Northern Polar itineraries focus on the Svalbard Islands and Iceland with cruises to Greenland, the Aleutians and Alaska. The company schedules one or two transits of the Northwest Passage each season, but was frustrated in 2018 by ice conditions.

Explorer Class: 184 passengers, 110 crew, 9,900grt, 1C Ice Class.

Le Commandant Charcot: 270 passengers, 30,000grt, PC2 Ice Class.

(Courtesy Ponant)

Quark Expeditions

In addition to its other season charters, Quark will take Mystic's *World Explorer* on a seasonal basis. Quark is also building a dedicated vessel at Brodosplit in Croatia for delivery in time for the 2020/21 Antarctic season. The ship will be capable of up to forty days of independent operation and fully compliant with safe return to port requirements. It will have dynamic positioning, up to twenty Zodiacs and two helicopters.

Ultramarine: 200 passengers, 116 crew, 13,500grt, PC6 Ice Class.

REV Ocean

An unusual new vessel is being built for REV Ocean as an expedition yacht. The company is a not-for-profit created by Norwegian billionaire Kjell Inge Røkke. The PC6 ice class ship will have a crew of thirty-six and a mix of passengers and scientists making up the ninety-person complement. At a proposed 16,000grt, she will be the world's largest yacht when delivered in 2021 and be available for full ship charters.

Scenic Luxury Cruises and Tours

Scenic Eclipse, the company's first ocean-going vessel, was seriously delayed in its delivery due to financial problems at the Croatian shipyard Uljanik. The Scenic Group, which includes Emerald Tours, is a worldwide inland waterways operator and was forced to bring in independent subcontractors to complete the ship's outfitting. At the time of writing, the issues that have plagued Uljanik may not have been resolved.

A separate joint venture that includes the Italian yard Fincantieri was proposed to work with the shipyard and focus on delivery of *Scenic Eclipse II*, due in 2020, as well as the next generation of Scenic's discovery yachts. However, it would appear that the Croatian government was not in favour due to its cost, and it has approached the Chinese for assistance. It is understood that construction of the second ship is continuing. The ships will have two helicopters and a six-seat submarine capable of dives of 300m as part of its outfit.

Scenic Eclipse: 228 passengers (200 for Arctic and Antarctic cruises), 17,085grt, PC6 Ice Class.

Seabourn Cruise Lines

Seabourn Venture is scheduled to debut in the second quarter of 2021, with its sister a year later. Both ships will offer all-veranda suites and carry two custom submarines as well as kayaks and twenty-four motorised Zodiacs for guest exploration.

Seabourn Venture: 264 passengers, 23,000grt, PC6 Ice Class.

Seadream Yacht Club

Founded in 2002 with the purchase of two mega yachts from Cunard that had been built in 1984 as *Sea Goddess I & II*, the company operates with the slogan 'Yachting not Cruising'. *Seadream I & II,* with 112 passengers and 95 crew, have typically operated in temperate waters. The new ship was to be able to use shore power, where available, and have battery packs to give up to four hours of silent cruising. It was to have been built at Damen's Romania yard and delivered in the third quarter of 2021. In December 2019, Seadream and Damen announced the ship's cancellation, but the company hopes to announce new projects in 2020.

Seadream Innovation: 220 passengers, crew 190–210, 15,300grt, PC6 Ice Class.

(Courtesy Seadream Yacht Club)

Sunstone Ships

Sunstone is a successor to International Shipping Partners under the presidency of Nils-Eric Lund. Its innovative Infinity Class expedition ships are being built in China, with plans for an eventual series of ten. Sunstone has so far committed to the construction of seven, with the first of class being delivered in 2019. The Infinity vessels can be configured to between 160 and 200 passengers with 75–100 crew and fifteen to twenty-five staff. They all utilise Ulstein's unique X-Bow for better sea keeping and come with dynamic positioning, zero speed stabilisation, a safe return to port machinery installation with Tier III engines, and PC6 Ice Class. All are about 7,400grt. The seven ships are:

Name	Delivery	Passengers	Charterer
Greg Mortimer	August 2019	120	Aurora Expeditions
Ocean Victory	October 2020	200	Victory Cruise Lines[91]
Ocean Explorer	January 2021	160	Vantage Cruise Lines[92]
Sylvia Earle	September 2021	120	Aurora Expeditions
Ocean Odyssey	May 2022	160	Vantage Cruise Lines
Ocean Discoverer	September 2022	160	To be announced
Ocean Albatros	October 2022	186	Albatros Expeditions

Viking Cruises

Viking Cruises has both river (Viking Longships) and ocean cruise brands. Its Polaris expedition ships will be a new venture, but little information was available when completing this book, although they will be Great Lakes fitted. *Viking Polaris* and *Viking Octantis* are scheduled for delivery in 2022, and there are options for another two. Viking is expanding aggressively, and has an order book with Fincantieri for up to ten additional ocean ships through 2027.

The ships are rumoured to be dual fuel, with the ability to use LNG where available. They will carry submarines and have an expedition staff of twenty.

Polaris Class: 378 passenger capacity, 30,150 grt, PC6 ice class. No data on crew numbers.

Vodohod

Vodohod is a Russian river cruise operator that recently announced their entry into ocean cruising with two new builds at the Helsinki Shipyard for 2021 and 2022. The shipyard is owned by Algador Holdings, which also owns Vodohod. Each will reportedly cost $115m and carry 148 passengers. No other details are currently available.

2

POLAR CRUISING DESTINATIONS

Alaska

Capital: Juneau, 58° 18′N 134° 25′W
Population: 739,795

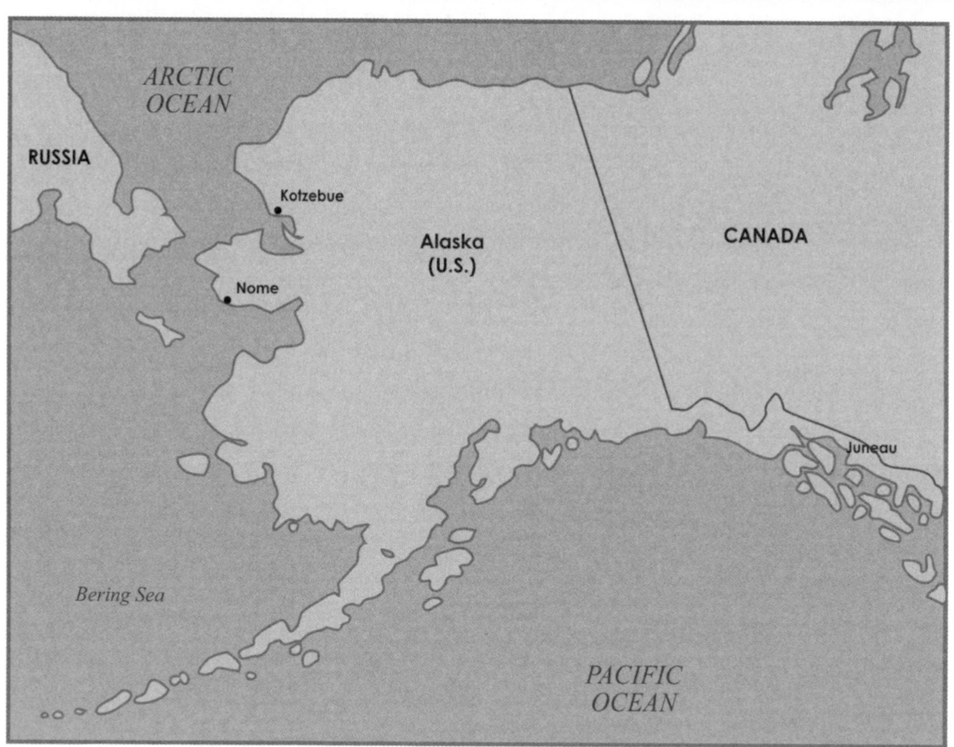

⬆ Map of Alaska.

Today, although Alaska is a well-established cruise destination, all activity is focused on south-east Alaska, which is well south of the Arctic. The accessibility of the Le Conte Glacier in Glacier Bay offers cruise passengers a sense of the Arctic, without going far north. Some cruise companies offer Nome as part of an Alaskan itinerary; but these cruises usually complete in Japan. Other ships may call at Nome as part of a Northwest Passage itinerary. However, both Nome and Kotzebue used to be offered as regular cruise calls.

A service from mainland US to Alaska began following the purchase of Alaska from Russia for $7.2 million on 30 March 1867, but serious attention by shipping companies did not occur until after the discovery of gold in the Yukon and the start of the Klondike gold rush in 1896. After this date almost anything that could float was pressed into service, first to Skagway, and then to Nome, after discovery of gold there in 1898. Shipping companies sailed mainly to Nome, but the nearby community of St Michael was close to the mouth of the Yukon River and prospectors could readily take riverboats up to the Klondike.

One company that had a major role in trade, both through the inside passage and to Nome, was the Alaska Steamship Company, which was formed in 1895 and immediately offered serious competition to the incumbent operator, the Pacific Coast Steamship Company. Established fares from Seattle to Juneau were $50 per person, and $11/ton freight; Alaska Steam offered travel at $12pp and $5/ton. These fares produced a rush of people to try the route and Pacific Coast[1] was forced to reduce its rates. The two companies competed for traffic in the Pacific Northwest for many years, but Alaska Steam proved to have greater staying power.

Fares in 1900 were reported as $100 first class, and $75 second class between Seattle and Nome. Many companies were established to take advantage of the trade but either fell by the wayside or were absorbed by the Alaska Steamship Company, which ultimately had a near monopoly on freight and passenger service to northern communities.

One of Alaska Steam's major assets was the SS *Victoria*, built originally for Cunard as the first *Parthia*[2] in 1870. The ship was brought to the West Coast as one of three ships to operate Canadian Pacific's Transpacific service in 1887 and was then operated by the Northern Pacific SS Co. from 1892, before that company merged with Alaska Steam in 1908. The following year it challenged Pacific Coast *Senator* to a race from Nome back to Seattle. Despite the *Senator* leaving twenty-five hours earlier, the *Victoria* arrived in Seattle a day ahead. She underwent many upgrades, but a major one in 1924 materially upgraded the accommodation and in 1934 the ship inaugurated an Alaska Steam cruise programme to Nome and Kotzebue. Her 1in iron plating and powerful engines meant she could easily manage northern ice conditions and was often first in and last out at Nome. In 1950, the bell was returned to Cunard for installation in their second *Parthia* – a cargo/passenger liner.

⬆ SS *Victoria* after the 1924 refit. (Henry W. Uhle Collection, Steamship Historical Society Archives, www.sshsa.org)

⬇ *Corwin* at edge of ice, Nome, 1907. (Courtesy University of Washington Special Collections, Nowell 5384)

Another ship that also claimed the first in, last out title was the SS *Corwin*. Originally built as a revenue cutter in 1877, she was adapted for Arctic work in 1880 with 1in oak planking, going from 2 feet above to 6 feet below the waterline, and a removable ice prow of ⅜in iron plate.

Sold in 1900 to a group from Boston for use in mining support, she was sometimes used as an icebreaker and in 1908 cut channels to let three steamers get into Nome. This was after shipyard work in 1901 and 1904 when her passenger accommodation

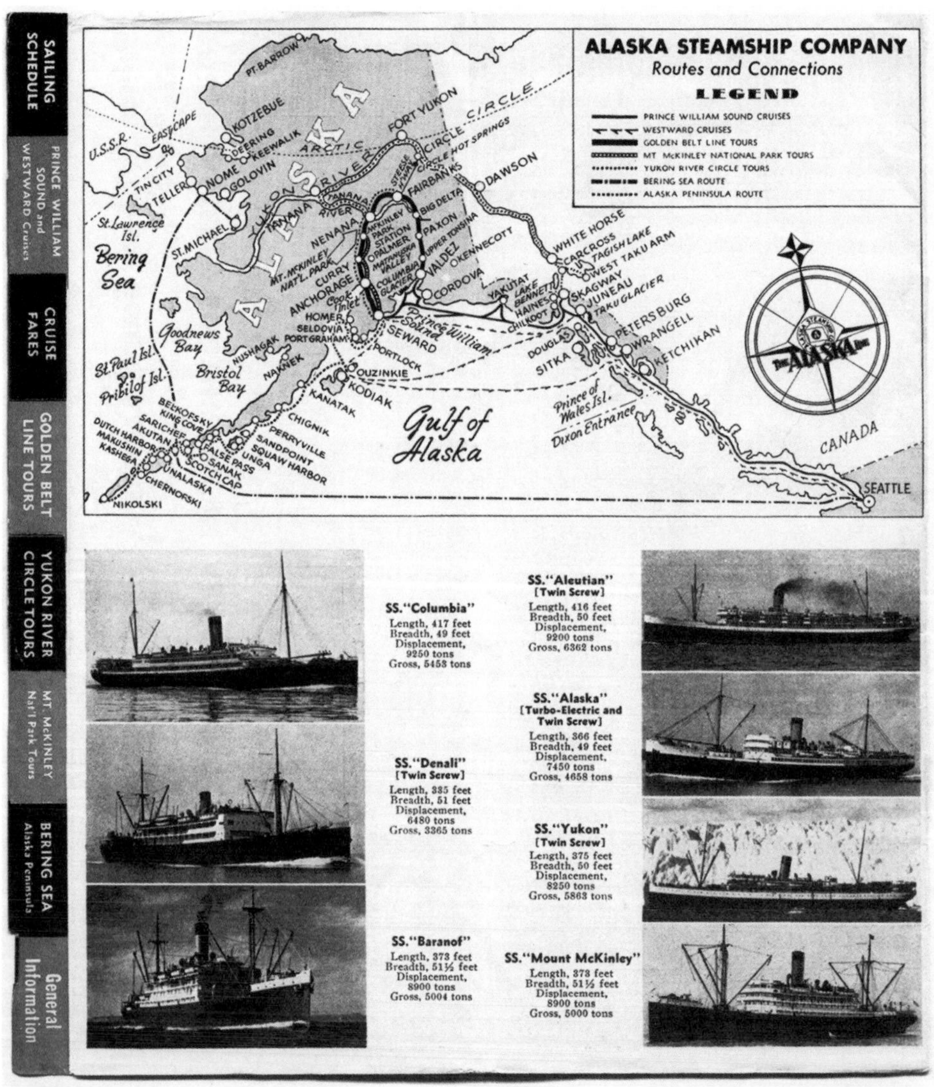

↑ Alaska Line routes and ships, 1941. (Courtesy Explorenorth)

was increased from thirty-five to forty-one first class and fifty to sixty steerage. She was reportedly the first ship into Nome 1902–09, 1913 and 1914. In 1914 it was arranged that she would lead the fleet into Nome. Most of the crew were Inupiat as they were considered less likely to desert and go prospecting.

In 1931, Richard Bonnycastle, Hudson's Bay Company District Manager for the Western Arctic, caught the last sailing by the *Victoria*, from Nome to Seattle en route home to Winnipeg after the company steamer *Baychimo* was caught in the ice and had to be abandoned for the winter. In making arrangements for his and the crew's repatriation, he noted in his diary that first-class fares were $115 and steerage $50 (although for $10 more you could dine with everyone else). There were no second-class cabins available. The scheduled departure of 22 October was delayed a day to enable passengers flying in from Deering, Alaska, and some of the *Baychimo*'s crew flying from the north, to make the sailing.

By the start of the Second World War, Alaska Steamship had sixteen vessels operating out of Seattle, providing service as far as Nome. The company advertised its itineraries to potential tourists, and while the 1941 brochure focused on south-east Alaska and circular tours by plane and rail, two ships (out of their seven-ship passenger fleet) offered sailings to the Bering Sea. The SS *Columbia* and SS *Mt McKinley* offered two sailings each, commencing on 30 May at $100–120pp depending on the deck: round-trip fares were double one-way fares. Steerage was available at $60pp, but noted as for men only. However, after the war the company focused on the panhandle, offering vacation travel to essentially the same communities as today. Passenger service was abandoned in 1954 due to air competition, and the company pulled out all together in 1971.

Antarctic and South Shetlands

Capital (Notional): Presidente Eduardo Frei Montalva Base, 62°12'0'S 58°57'51'W
Population: 1,100–4,000 depending on season

The Antarctic continent was discovered by Fabian von Bellinghausen in 1820 during a Russian circumnavigation of the globe intended to discover whether there was land close to the South Pole. The first to land was probably the American sealer John Davis in 1821, but the first territorial claims were not until 1908, when Britain made various claims encompassing the Falklands and other islands, as well as at least parts of the continent itself. Over the next fifty years seven countries claimed different sections of Antarctica; some of these areas overlapped, while other areas had no claims at all. Although sovereignty is not resolved, all differences have been essentially put on hold by the Antarctic Treaty of 1961. Fortunately, there was never an indigenous population, and the penguins did not have a say in writing the treaty.

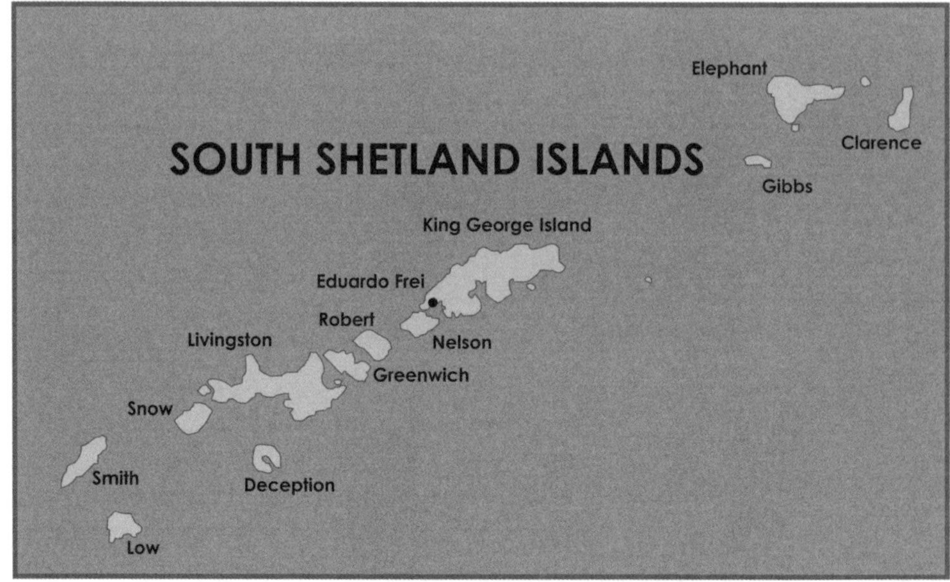

Map of South Shetland Islands.

The Antarctic Peninsula, including the South Shetland Islands, is claimed by Argentina, Chile and the United Kingdom. King George Island in the South Shetlands is where ten countries have bases, with the Chilean base being the most established and notional regional capital with an airport that is used seasonally by fly-cruise operators. The largest population, though, is at the American McMurdo base on Ross Island with some 1,000 scientists and support staff in residence. Other national bases have small resident research populations.

Early Polar Cruising

If a Thomas Cook tour, which was advertised in 1909, had been successful, the first expedition cruise to Antarctica would have taken place to McMurdo Sound from New Zealand in 1910. Another unsuccessful promotion was by Ernest Shackleton's captains J.R. Stenhouse and Frank Worsley, who proposed to leave New York on a Holland America Line ship in 15 December 1931, returning on 18–19 April 1932. If it had not been for the prevalent economic conditions, the cruise might have taken place, as might the one promoted by the shipping line for the following season.

The earliest cruise tourists may have arrived at Deception Island in the South Shetlands on board the mail ship *Fleurus* in the late 1920s. The ship was the Tonsberg Whaling Company supply ship and was chartered, by Britain, for four trips[3] each year between Stanley and South Georgia to provide a mail connection to Grytviken.

⬆ *Libertad* at Paradise Harbour. (Courtesy Histarmar)

In the years when whaling was active at Deception Bay, the ship called there as well. The ship is reported to have been in Stanley in 1924, and most commentators agree that the charter started then and continued for nine years. Most trips by the ship are reported as carrying passengers. Apparently a 'saloon' to South Georgia and Port Foster on Deception Island cost £10 return; while a cabin was half the price. A tourist round trip was advertised for some of the sailings, however there is no direct evidence that tourists took advantage of the ship's itinerary.

The *Fleurus* departed for England on 2 July 1933, so the last visits may have been earlier that year. The ship's duties were assumed by the *Lafonia* in 1934. Also in 1933, members of the University Club of Buenos Aires, together with an Argentine journalist and his family, visited Laurie Island, South Orkney Islands, on the Argentine merchant vessel[4] *Pampa*; another visit with tourists was made by the same ship in 1937. It is not known whether any tourist shipping activity then took place until 1958 when the Argentine transport ship *Les Eclaireus* took ninety-eight passengers on a cruise from Ushuaia to South Shetland on 16 January and another ninety-six passengers on a second cruise on 31 January. These were demonstration visits and the Argentine Navy filmed the cruises and used the footage for promotional purposes. The following year the FANU passenger ship *Yapeyú* undertook two cruises with a total of 262 passengers to the same area, while in the same season the Chilean transport ship *Navarino* took ninety-four passengers[5] to South Shetland. It is presumed that activity did not continue into the 1960s because of the limited local market for such a trip. The trip on the *Yapeyú* was advertised at 13,800 pesos. In January 1959 the exchange rate[6] to the US$ was 65.40, implying a fare of about US$211.

There was then no further activity, of which we are aware, until Lars-Eric Lindblad chartered the Argentinean naval transport *Lapataia* in 1966 and 1967, offering Antarctic cruises to the American market. For the 1967/68 season he chartered the Chilean passenger ships *Aquiles* and *Navarino* for two similar cruises, together with the twenty-five-passenger capacity Danish ship *Magga Dan* for two trips from New Zealand to McMurdo Sound. In 1969 he again chartered the Chilean transport ship *Aquiles* for cruises to the Peninsula. Lindblad's Antarctic Peninsula cruises were typically eight to twelve days in length and he made a point of beach landings with a very disciplined approach. The Argentine National Directorate of Tourism (DNT) chartered the *Libertad* for four cruises for the 1968/69 season, reportedly mainly with Argentineans on board, but also some Europeans living in the country.

The *Lindblad Explorer* commenced regular cruises to the region in 1970 and was in Antarctica over the 1972/73 season as the ship met up with the *Cabo San Roque* on 31 January at the Argentine Admiral Brown Station in Paradise Harbour. Also in the 1970/71 season, *Rio Tunyan* made two cruises, then DNT chartered the *Regina Prima* for seven trips in the 1974/75 season and six cruises in the 1975/76 season. The Spanish passenger/cargo ships[7] *Cabo San Roque* and *Cabo San Vicente* made four and three cruises respectively over the 1972/73, 1973/74 and 1974/75 seasons.

⬆ Antarctic cruising. (Ben Haggar, courtesy OneOcean Expeditions)

There was a peak of eleven voyages over the 1974/75 season with possibly 4,000 passengers. During the 1970s the first big ship visit took place when the *Enrico C*[8] cruised the South Shetlands in 1973 with 888 passengers. In 1974 there were two cruises with more than 1,700 passengers, one cruise in the following season, and finally in the 1976/77 season 989 passengers were carried.

In the early 1980s, DNT chartered the *Bahia Buen Suceso* and sailed with seventy passengers in the 1980/81 season. It undertook two trips in the 1981/82 season, with 139 passengers on the second cruise. Commencing with the 1985/86 season, the Argentine resupply/tourist ship *Bahia Paraiso* started taking tourist groups to the Antarctic. There was one trip in 1985/86, two the following season with 155 passengers, four cruises in 1987/88 with 327 passengers, then in the 1988/89 season there were three trips before the ship was wrecked after visiting Palmer Station on the fourth visit.

During the 1980s the *Lindblad Explorer* (after its sale in 1985, *Society Explorer*) and *World Discoverer* visited each season with multiple cruises. From two ships each season during the early 1980s, activity began to increase after the 1987/88 season, when they were joined by the *Illiria*, then more ships thereafter. Lindblad Expeditions chartered the *Antonina Nedzhanova* for seven trips in 1988/89; Ocean Cruise Lines brought its *Ocean Princess* in commencing with the 1990/91 season until the 1992/93 season, possibly with passenger numbers limited to 480. Orient Lines *Marco Polo* then commenced seasonal cruises in the 1993/94 season.

A typical *Marco Polo* cruise from Ushuaia had the following elements:

Day 1 Ushuaia
Day 2 Drake Passage
Day 3 Hope Bay
Day 4 Half Moon Island, Deception Island
Day 5 Paradise Harbour, Neumayer Channel, Port Lockroy
Day 6 Port Lockroy, Lemaire Channel
Day 7 Drake Passage
Day 8 Cape Horn, Ushuaia

If the cruise had commenced in Buenos Aires, it would have been twelve days with a call at Stanley, Falkland Islands, on Day 4, and then following the itinerary from Day 2 above. In 1995/96 the ship undertook four cruises with a total of 1,687 passengers, then another four cruises in 1997/98 with 2,012 passengers. The ship was a regular visitor until the 2008/09 season.

Some comparison of pricing is possible between the *Ocean Princess* in 1993, Blyth and Company with the *Northern Ranger* in 1993, Marine Expeditions with the *Akademik Ioffe* (sailing as the *Marine Adventurer*) in 1995 and the *Antonina Nedzhanova* in 1989.

In 1993, Ocean Lines offered three itineraries with six departures, all eighteen to nineteen days in length. Their least costly departure was that on 7 January and ranged from US$7,750 to US$4,575pp double occupancy for an inside twin with upper and lower berths; an outside single was available at US$8,895. Air was not included (air add-ons were offered and the round-trip fare from New York was US$845), also port taxes of US$135 were extra. Also in 1993, Blyth and Company offered a fourteen-day cruise on the *Northern Ranger*, at US$3,995 to US$2,850pp in a quad; a single cabin was offered at US$4,395. Again port taxes were extra at US$225, but air was included.

A couple of years later, related company Marine Expedition's pricing for the *Akademik Ioffe* was US$6,495 to US$3,595pp double occupancy, plus port fees and taxes of US$495, air included. Lindblad Travel fares for the comparatively luxurious *Antonina Nedzhanova* in the 1988/89 season ranged from $5,300 to $3,950pp double occupancy for the fifteen-day itinerary and $700pp more for the seventeen-day itinerary. Discounts were offered for the company Intrepids Club members, however air was extra (the indicative round trip air from New York to Buenos Aires was US$975).

Wildlife

Because of the lack of any significant vegetation, wildlife in the Antarctic is almost exclusively marine dependent. The dominant species are, of course, different penguins, while seals and whales are found offshore and nesting birds where there are cliffs. On the mainland the chief penguin species are chinstrap and Adélie, with smaller numbers of gentoo and macaroni. The photogenic emperor penguins are only found here, again in relatively small numbers. One of the largest colonies is at Snow Hill Island.

There are four types of seal to be found in the immediate Antarctic region: leopard, crabeater, fur and Weddell. The leopard, recognisable from its spotted fur, is a ferocious hunter of penguins and smaller seals. It can be found near penguin colonies. Weddell seals will be found on fast ice, while crabeaters live among the pack ice and consume mainly krill. Elephant seals are found mainly on South Georgia and the Falkland Islands. Fur and elephant seals were heavily hunted from the late eighteenth century, but have made a remarkable comeback.

Sperm, blue, humpback and killer whales are found in waters around the Antarctic continent. As in the Arctic, whales were hunted virtually to the point of extinction, and during the primary whaling period of 1904–79, 1,474,578 whales were taken, 50,436 in 1960/61, which was the largest seasonal catch. Although different whale species were protected in different years from 1935 onwards, this was largely ignored by factory whalers operating in the region. A global pause was instituted in 1982, and there has been some recovery of stocks. However, minke whales are still taken annually by the Japanese and their catch hit 856 animals in the 2005/06 season. The take is much lower now[9] partly due to the actions of Greenpeace and the Sea Shepherd Society. The Japanese also lost a court case in July 2013 regarding the legality of their claim to taking whales for 'scientific' purposes and have now abandoned southern, in favour of domestic, whaling.

Penguins in the Antarctic Region[10]

Species	Height cm	Breeding Pairs	Main Locations (Those with more than 100,000 breeding pairs)
Adélie	70	2,500,000	Antarctic Peninsula, South Orkney Islands
Chinstrap	70–75	7,500,000	Antarctic Peninsula, South Sandwich & South Orkney Islands
Emperor	120	220,000	Antarctic Continent & Peninsula
Gentoo[11]	75–90	300,000	Falkland, South Georgia Islands
King	90	1,800,000	South Georgia, Prince Edward, Crozet, Kerguelen & Macquarie Islands
Macaroni	70	9,200,000	South Georgia, Prince Edward, Crozet, Kerguelen, Heard & MacDonald Islands
Magellanic[12]	70	130,000	Falkland Islands
Southern Rock Hopper[13]	45–55	300,000	Falkland Islands
Eastern Rock Hopper	45–55	600,000	Prince Edward, Crozet, Macquarie Islands
Royal	70	850,000	Macquarie Islands

Among the many bird species in the Antarctic, terns, cormorants, Cape petrels, kelp gulls and blue-eyed shags use cliffs as nesting sites. Other birds are found in the neighbouring sub-Antarctic islands.

Other Antarctic Islands

There are twenty-two major islands and groups as well as 800 individual islands and island groups in the Southern Ocean surrounding Antarctica. For example, the Falkland Islands archipelago has two main and 776 smaller islands, and is one of two of the major destinations, from a cruise perspective, that have been described separately. The South Shetland Islands are an essential component of cruises to the Antarctic Peninsula. Other islands, or groups, tend to be visited depending on turnaround port, or ports.

Most islands had a history of sealing for fur and elephant seals, some supported exploitation of penguins for oil and skins. Whaling operations were based at some islands and many have associated shipwrecks. Science stations are also supported on some of the islands. Today, the wildlife, other than whales, has recovered and there are large penguin colonies on South Orkney, South Sandwich, Crozet, Prince Edward Island, Heard and MacDonald, Kerguelen and Macquarie Islands.

As noted earlier, South Orkney[14] was visited in 1933 and 1937 by the Argentine Flag *Pampa*, mainly to relieve the base personnel, but also carrying tourists. The Orcadas base on Laurie Island is the longest continuously operated base in Antarctica, having been established in 1903 by a Scottish expedition and handed over to the Argentineans a year later. There is little information about subsequent visits until the 1980s when the *Lindblad Explorer* and *World Discoverer* are reported to have visited. Polar cruise vessel visits picked up with the rise in general Antarctic activity during the 1990s.

The French territory of Kerguelen is perhaps the most visited of the islands as the resupply ship from Réunion – *Marion Dufresne* – calls four times each year and has accommodation for fifteen tourists. The round trip takes twenty-eight days and usually calls at Crozet Island, Kerguelen (La Grande Terre) and Île Amsterdam. The cost is reported to be €9,000. A couple of expedition cruise companies have included Kerguelen in an Antarctic itinerary.

The Australian-administered Macquarie Island is a UNESCO World Heritage Site. There is a small scientific station and cruise ships are limited to four per year with no more than 600 passengers in total. The island is often visited by yachts, and there is some conflict over numbers permitted to land.

The Antarctic is losing six times the amount of ice each year than it did forty years ago. During the period 1979–90 it is estimated the continent lost 40 gigatons of ice each year, and this loss has risen to 252 gigatons a year during 2009–17. It was found that, over the past three years, a cavity almost the size of Manhattan Island and up to 300m deep had formed under Thwaites Glacier. A major multinational expedition was investigating this glacier in 2019.

South Georgia and the South Sandwich Islands

Administrative Centre: King Edward Point, 54°17'00'S 36°30'00'W
Population: 20–40 depending on season

South Georgia, together with the South Sandwich Islands, is a British Overseas Territory about 750 nautical miles south-east of the Falkland Islands. Although sighted in the seventeenth century, South Georgia was not claimed for England until James Cook landed in 1775. Based on his reports of extensive seal and whale populations in the vicinity, sealing started in 1786, but the island only became a base for

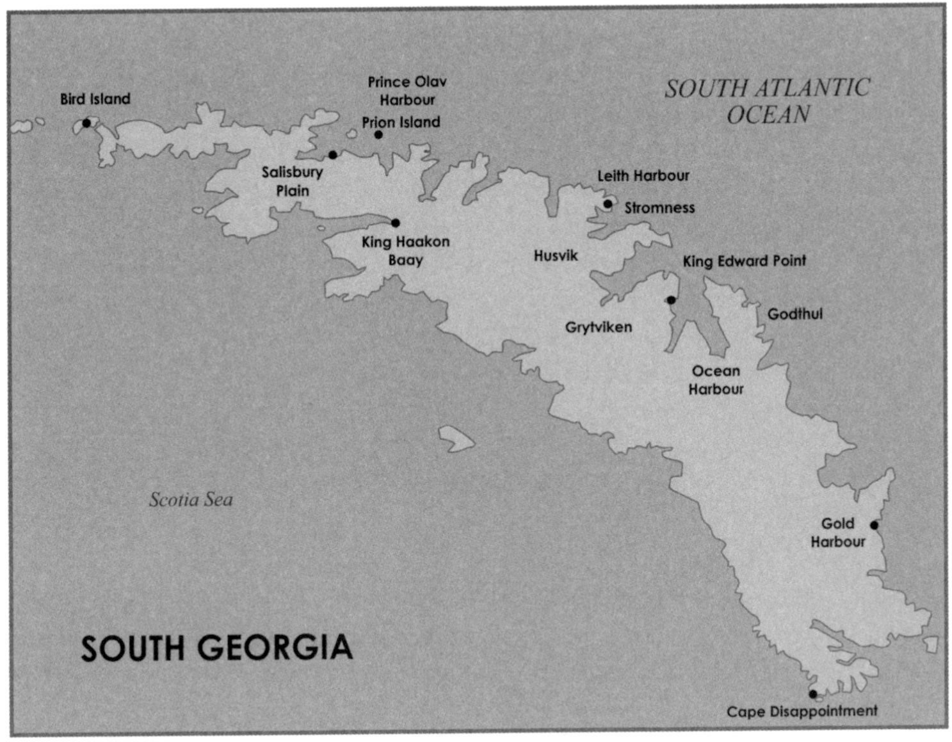

⬆ Map of South Georgia.

whaling in 1904 when a station was established at Grytviken, which operated until 1965. Seven whaling stations were eventually operated under lease from the Falkland Islands governor, mainly on the north coast that offers a number of sheltered harbours. Christian Salveson, the main operator of factory and shore whaling in later years, did not formally give up its leases until 1992.

During the whaling period, a female blue whale was landed at Grytviken that measured 33.58m in length. This is the largest animal ever recorded.

The only preserved buildings that remain in Grytviken from the whaling era are the church and the South Georgia Museum in the old manager's house; the contents can be viewed online at www.ehive.com/collections/3408/south-georgia-museum. Another attraction in Grytviken is Shackleton's grave. The research station at King Edward Point is operated by the British Antarctic Survey and manned year-round. Several derelict whale catchers were scuttled in Stromness Bay.

The islands mostly rise steeply from the ocean, with the peaks being covered by snow and ice year-round; South Georgia also has a number of glaciers. The South Sandwich Islands are of volcanic origin and the Protector Shoal is a submarine volcano. In 2008 there was a series of strong earthquakes centred on Bristol Island.

The islands have no airports and no regular marine links, although visiting cruise ships offer the occasional vessel of opportunity for a connection with Stanley in the Falkland Islands. Commencing in 1924, there was a regular service between Grytviken and Stanley using the SS *Fleurus* under a charter arrangement with Britain. This was primarily a mail contract that occasionally extended to Deception Bay in the South Shetland Islands, and operated until 1933.

Cruise Ship Activity

After the departure of the *Fleurus* in 1933, it is not known whether other commercial ships called carrying passengers, although military vessels continue to visit annually. The sole indication of later calls was the *Lindblad Explorer* and the Argentine *Rio Tunyan* in early 1970; two calls by the *Lindblad Explorer* in 1972, and again in the 1974/75 and 1975/76 seasons. This ship and the *World Discoverer*, after its first reported call in the 1979/80 season, have called most years. Other ships that have been reported as calling include the *Columbus Caravelle* in 1992. The islands have since become a popular itinerary call for expedition vessels, rising from eleven ship visits in the 1991/92 season to seventy-three in 2018/19. Typically passenger numbers average 100–130 per call.

↑ *World Discoverer.* (Courtesy Knud Hansen)

Wildlife

There are no native terrestrial mammals, and the reindeer that were introduced onto South Georgia have been culled because of damage to the local ecosystem. Rats, which were an involuntary introduction from visiting ships, have also been eradicated because of damage to the local ecosystem.

The waters surrounding the islands have a high level of biodiversity and a Marine Protected Area was established in 2012, covering more than 1 million sq km. A major source of revenue for the islands is licenses for fishing Patagonian toothfish (Chilean sea bass), and other cold-water fish.

The islands are considered important bird areas and support a vast bird population including subspecies of shag, pipit and pintail that are unique to the region. There are large colonies of king, gentoo and macaroni penguins. Seals, including a large colony of elephant seals, and 95 per cent of Antarctic fur seals, as well as whales, are common in the surrounding waters.

Falkland Islands

Capital: Stanley, 51° 42'S 57° 51'W
Population: 3,398 (2016)

The Falkland Islands (Islas Malvinas) is an archipelago that shares a cool temperate climate with other outlying island groups that surround Antarctica. There are two main islands – West and East, separated by Falkland Sound – and more than 700 smaller islands, most of which are privately owned sheep ranches. Although well outside the 60°S boundary considered as the limit for polar cruising, the islands have been included because of their importance as a component of Antarctic cruise itineraries.

Given their position off the tip of South America, the islands have had a long maritime history linked to ships heading to or from Europe and North America around Cape Horn. Calls were made for water, provisions, repairs and as steam supplanted sail, coal as well. The islands were a centre for sealing, and New Island had a major whaling operation from 1908–16. During the mid-nineteenth century this island also supported a guano[15] mining activity.

As examples of the type of ships calling, the English barque *Tynemouth* stopped in July 1862 with 350 passengers from London en route to Vancouver (BC). The ship's stay of a week was probably welcomed by the emigrants heading to British Columbia. Another call was made in December 1853 by the steamship *Great Britain*[16] en route from Melbourne, Australia, to London with 199 passengers and 164,824oz of gold dust.

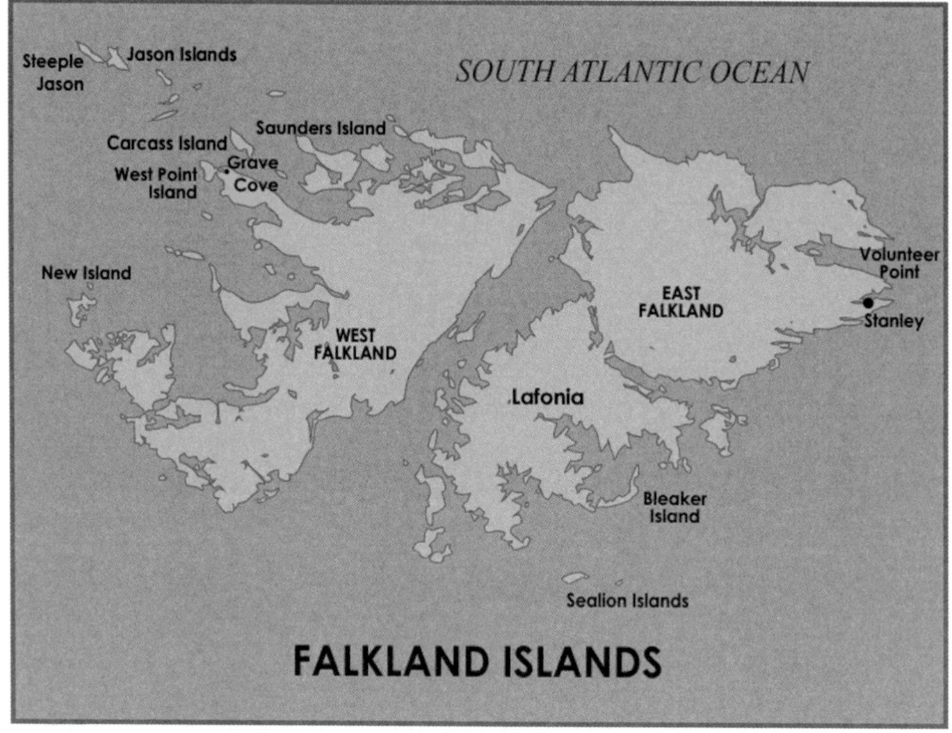

Map of the Falkland Islands.

The location of the islands that at one time made them a convenient stop for ships rounding Cape Horn now makes it perfect for incorporation in round-the-world itineraries, South America circumnavigations and particularly for ships heading to or from the South Shetlands and Antarctica. In addition to the attraction of a call at Stanley for large ships, the extensive and unique wildlife opportunities offered by the many islands has led to an increasing number of calls by smaller polar cruise vessels on Antarctic cruises.

Early Cruise Activity

The American schooner *Tekoa* with nine passengers was reported to be on a cruise in October 1854, and may have been the first cruising yacht to arrive. Thomas Cook advertised annual round-the-world cruises, and the one for 1888 proposed the steam yacht *Victoria* 'fitted up with all the latest improvements and electric light throughout' at £600 for one person in a cabin; couples or two friends sharing at £500 each. The cruise was scheduled to leave Gravesend on 1 November, and return on about 24 July, calling at the Falkland Islands[17] on its homeward leg. There is no evidence in Falkland

⬆ *Hanseatic*. (Braun Brothers Collection, Steamship Historical Society Archives, www.sshsa.org)

⬇ Falkland Islands. (Courtesy Falkland Islands Tourism)

Islands shipping records of the ship calling in 1889. A later cruise by the same company was advertised on the *Orcoma* in 1908.[18] This cruise took advantage of the Pacific Steam Navigation Company's regular voyages from Liverpool to South America's Pacific coast. Departing Liverpool on 3 December 1908, it was due to call at Stanley on 13 January. In the brochure Stanley is described as 'resembling a small town in the Scottish highlands'. While the *Orcoma* did not call on 13 January 1909, the *Oriana* did. The inclusive fare London to London was £300, or Ffs 7,600 Paris to Paris.

The *Fleurus*, which supplied links with the mainland and South Georgia from 1924 onwards, was described as 'an uninspiring and far from glamorous steamer'. The ship took Sir Arnold Weinholt Hodson, then Governor of the Falkland Islands, on a South Georgia inspection trip on 6–13 August 1927. It was replaced in 1934 by the *Lafonia*, and different ships provided an essential marine link for the islands until the *Darwin* was retired in 1971.

There are no reports of cruise calls until the *Rotterdam* visited in February 1960, while on a round South America cruise. A decade later, the Swedish America Lines *Kungsholm* and the German Atlantic Line *Hanseatic* called within days of each other in November 1969. The next decade saw considerable activity, commencing with the *Lindblad Explorer* in February 1970 on its first Antarctic cruise; she was a regular visitor thereafter. The *Kungsholm* was due to call again in November 1970 on a round-the-world cruise, but the visit was cancelled due to bad weather; however, the *Gripsholm* did call in February 1971. The Argentinean liner *Libertad* called in January 1972 before heading to Antarctica, then the *France* called on 24 January 1972 on its first round-the-world cruise, apparently with a high proportion of widows in the passenger complement. The Spanish Ybarra cargo/liner *Cabo San Roque* called in February 1973 on its return to Buenos Aires from an Antarctic cruise. This was the first of several calls and the ship visited in January 1974 with 800 tourists, and then in February 1975 there were 700 passengers aboard. Costa Lines *Enrico C* commenced a regular programme of calls in 1973, returning twice the following year, in January with 803 passengers and then with 896 passengers in February. The ship came back with 912 tourists in January 1975. This was a busy year as the *Regina Prima*[19] called three times and the *Lindblad Explorer* was also in Stanley in January, and February as part of Antarctic cruises, then again in December at West Point en route to South Georgia,[20] where it called a few days later. Both the *Enrico C* and the *Eugenio C* visited in 1977, while the *Franca C* had been scheduled for a call in February, but cancelled.

Through the 1980s and into the '90s the *Lindblad Explorer* (later *Society Explorer*), *World Discoverer* and *Frontier Spirit* all visited regularly. After Hapag-Lloyd acquired suitable tonnage for polar voyages, the *Hanseatic* and *Bremen* have also called most seasons.

Wildlife

The Falklands is home to about 500,000 breeding pairs of five penguin species, and also to 70–80 per cent of the breeding pairs of the black-browed albatross. Many islands host colonies of the albatross as well as gentoo, southern rockhopper, king and Magellanic penguins. The locations identified on the Falkland Islands map are frequently visited by expedition cruise ships for bird, penguin or seal watching.

The ubiquitous orca, or killer whale, is fairly common around the islands, as are several types of dolphin. Long-finned pilot whales can also be found. Although technically a large oceanic dolphin, at up to 7m in length and 2,300kg they are quite large and can be found in pods. Sealion Island is home to most of the Falkland Islands' elephant seal population, while fur seals are limited to the northern islands. Leopard seals, which breed in Antarctica, visit the Falkland Islands. There are many bird species to be found; some, such as the upland goose and steamer duck, are unique to the islands. A large percentage of all striated caracara, or johnny rooks, are found in the islands.

Canadian Arctic

Nunavut
Capital: Iqaluit, 63° 75'N 68° 52'W
Population: 35,944
Nunavik
Capital: Kuujjuaq, 58° 11'N 68° 42'W
Population: 13,204

The Canadian Arctic Archipelago covers a vast region, and includes more than 30,000 islands. It stretches from Cape Columbia on Ellesmere Island at 83° 06'41"N and Cape Dyer on Baffin Island at 61° 22'0"W to Cape Prince Alfred on Banks Island at 124° 77'07"W. The islands, together with parts of the mainland to the south, form the Territory of Nunavut.

The Inuit homeland was carved out of the Northwest Territories, which still retains some islands in the west, but is mainly around the Mackenzie River, Great Bear Lake and Great Slave Lake. Nunavut has three administrative regions: Qikiqtaaluk (mainly Baffin Island) in the east; the Kivalliq west of Hudson Bay; and Kitikmeot in the west. Nunavut's capital is Iqaluit at the head of Frobisher Bay, but administration is decentralised to Rankin Inlet in the Kivalliq and Cambridge Bay in the Kitikmeot as well as some other communities.

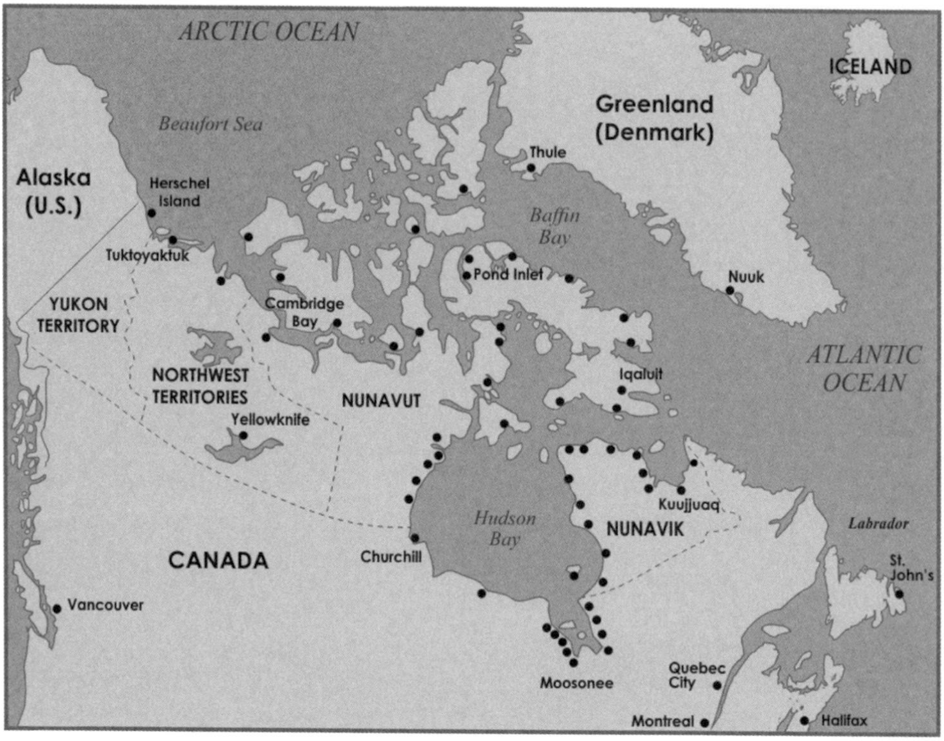

⬆ Map of the Canadian Arctic; each dot represents a community.

Northern Quebec is also predominantly Inuit, and is often referred to as Nunavik. Technically, this is the Kativik Region of Quebec encompassing the province north of the 55th Parallel. The administrative centre is Kuujjuaq.

Early Cruise Activity

For Canada, Arctic cruising really started as river cruising on the Mackenzie River after the completion of the Alberta and Great Waterways Railway between Edmonton and Waterways on the Clearwater River in 1922.[21] The Clearwater led, via the Athabasca and the Slave Rivers, and Lakes Athabasca and Great Slave, to the Mackenzie.

Alberta and Arctic Transportation Company Passage Rates, 1923 season

Location	Miles	Downstream From Waterways $	Upstream From Aklavik $
Waterways	0	-	150.00
Fort MacMurray	6	1.00	148.00
Fort MacKay	40	5.00	142.00
Point Bruce	153	9.50	133.25
Lake Athabasca	176	13.50	131.50
Fort Chipewyan	192	15.00	130.00
Mouth of Peace River	222	18.00	127.00
Fort Fitzgerald	292	22.00	120.00
Fort Smith	308	27.00	115.00
King's Sawmill	352	31.50	110.00
Fort Resolution	512	37.00	100.00
Hay River	587	42.00	92.00
Wrigley Harbour	621	45.00	89.50
Fort Providence	665	47.00	85.00
Fort Simpson	821	57.00	70.00
Wrigley	973	67.00	55.00
Fort Norman	1,125	77.00	40.00
Norman Oil Well Discovery	1,175	82.00	32.00
Fort Good Hope	1,298	87.00	25.00
Arctic Red River	1,512	97.00	10.00
Fort MacPherson	1,566	102.00	5.00
Aklavik	1,666	107.00	-

Meals: Breakfast $0.75, dinner and supper $1. Berths lower $1.50, upper $1. Children 5–12 half fare.

In 1922, the Alberta and Arctic Transportation Company (AATC) offered its new steamer service with a special round trip fare of $240[22] excluding berth and meals between Waterways and Aklavik. The round trip took about one month; the full tariff is given in the preceding table.

The AATC brochure extolled opportunities for fishing as well as big and feathered game. The trip 'combining splendid state rooms and meals make this one of the most unique and interesting tourist trips to be found anywhere'. The AATC had the *Slave River* on the upper route with the *Distributor* on the lower route, while Northland Trading had the *Northland Echo* and *Northland Trader*, and the Hudson's Bay Company (HBC) offered its sternwheelers *Athabasca River* and *Mackenzie River*.

The upper and lower portions of the route were separated by the rapids between Fort Fitzgerald and Fort Smith. Here the AATC offered passenger transportation in a Winton Six touring car over the 16-mile portage.

In 1923, there were three carriers, but due to the collapse of the fur market on which the companies depended for most of their revenue, by 1924 there was just the Hudson's Bay Company.

In the June 1925 issue of *The Beaver*, the HBC published a promotional piece about the river trip, saying, 'in commodious and up to date steamers we may travel in absolute comfort to the very rim of the world, the home of the Eskimo and the land of the Midnight Sun'. Business on the river obviously improved, and by 1927 the HBC was offering a thirty-five-day round trip to Aklavik at $325 including meals and was unable to keep up with the passenger demand.[23] At this time, it was running the *Athabasca River* and *Northland Echo* on the upper route, and the *Distributor* and *Mackenzie River* on the lower route.

Hudson's Bay Company Passenger Boats 1930s

Route	Boat	Built	Dimensions L × B × d	Berths
Upper	*Athabasca River*	1922	147ft 5in × 35ft 6in × 4ft 6in	58
	Northland Echo	1923	137ft 6in × 24ft 3in x 4ft 5in	40
Lower	*Distributor*	1920	151ft 4in × 35ft 3in × 4ft 6in	60
	Mackenzie River	1911[24]	126ft × 26ft × ?	30

Not all boats operated every season. L = Length, B = Breadth, d = Draft

Passenger travel on the Mackenzie effectively ended in 1949 when the HBC stopped being a common carrier.

In 1971, a small expedition-style cruise ship, the *Norweta*,[25] entered service running cruises from Hay River to Inuvik (eight days downstream, ten days upstream). Reportedly, the eighteen-passenger boat was run for four years, and was then purchased as a standby vessel for Beaufort Sea exploration. In 1991, a local family purchased her, refurbished the boat and again ran it as a small cruise ship, but the *Norweta* was laid up in 2009 and is for sale.

Cruising in the eastern Arctic might have commenced in 1923, when the Hudson Bay Tourist Syndicate of Winnipeg proposed to charter the Canadian Pacific liner *Montreal*[26] for a cruise to Hudson Bay, Port Nelson and Fort Churchill. However, bookings were less than half the necessary number (the company had expected to book 300 passengers) and deposits were refunded.

⬆ The abandoned Hudson's Bay Company post at Fort Ross. (David Mceown, courtesy OneOcean Expeditions)

Tourist trips to the eastern Arctic commenced a decade later with HBC's venerable SS *Nascopie*. Built in 1912 in partnership with Newfoundland's Job Brothers, the ship was the mainstay of HBC seasonal resupply. In 1932, control of the *Nascopie* was transferred from London to the Canadian Committee in Winnipeg, and from 1933 onwards Arctic resupply trips started in Montreal, not Britain. At this time, the HBC consolidated its position with the Dominion Government's Eastern Arctic Patrol[27] (EAP), agreeing a lucrative space charter commitment from 1933 onwards. According to an advertisement in *The Beaver*, accommodation was expanded to include additional berths for possible cruise passengers. The advertisement asks that prospective passengers write to the Fur Trade Commissioner for pricing and accommodation. In fact, Ralph Parsons, the Commissioner at the time, personally vetted all requests and 'chose the passengers carefully in order to maintain the "right" atmosphere aboard ship'.

After embarking passengers in Montreal, the *Nascopie* typically dropped them off at different posts, also picking up way passengers (i.e. between posts) as well as post employees heading to Churchill to take the train south. There was a major turnover when the ship reached Churchill; from here, the *Nascopie* served northern Arctic posts on its return voyage, so in addition to cargo being loaded, passengers joined the ship for northern posts, or the trip to Halifax.[28] In 1933, the *Nascopie* embarked three American tourists in Montreal, then when it left Churchill, passengers included Dr Colin Ross and family, noted as a German newspaper correspondent; Harold E. O'Neil, Sunday editor of the *Daily Home News*, New Brunswick (NJ); and Owen Russell from the *New York Times* publicity department.

Tourist Numbers on the Nascopie[29]

Embarking	1933	1934	1935	1936	1937	1938	1939	1940	1941
Montreal	5	0	6	8	5	8	12	4	5
Churchill	4	4	0	3	8	6	7	7	5

Apparently a decision was made in 1941 to get out of the tourist business on the rationale that tourists were bad for Inuit health. This is unlikely to have been an HBC decision, and was probably driven by the Dominion Government, which was taking a greater interest in Inuit welfare. More than likely there were also security considerations as the ship disembarked tourists at Port Alfred in Quebec in 1940, carrying those that embarked at Churchill via Ivigtut in Greenland, a key Allied source of cryolite for aluminium smelting.

For the 1939 season, the tourist fare from Montreal to Churchill was $300; Churchill to Halifax was $350 and a Montreal round trip was $650.

As far as we can find, there was then a hiatus in cruise activity in the Canadian Arctic until Lindblad brought the small expedition ship the *Lindblad Explorer* north in 1973, when the ship sailed to 82° 12'N, although it is not stated where this occurred. However, the 1983 cruise itinerary suggests that it might have been in the Kane Basin. *Lindblad Explorer* cruises are known to have taken place in 1973, 1982 and 1983, and then the first Northwest Passage by a cruise ship in 1984.

Although some cruises start at places such as St John's, Newfoundland, Greenland[30] is the preferred origin/destination in many cases, due partly to Canadian cabotage rules, but also the unwieldy permitting process. By utilising Greenland ports, long sea passages can be avoided, allowing for more days of scenic Arctic activities. Also, air uplift capabilities are better, and most communities can offer a dock for passenger and baggage transfer, rather than using Zodiacs over a beach. Churchill was frequently used as a turnaround port in Canada, probably because the two-day and two-night train trip to/from Winnipeg offered a unique experiential addition to the cruise experience. Due to storm activity in 2016, the Hudson Bay Rail line was washed out and VIA Rail[31] later recovered its engine and coaches, stranded in Churchill, and shipped them back to Montreal. In 2018, the federal government approved transfer of ownership to a Canadian consortium, together with a promise of operating subsidies. The line has now been repaired and VIA Rail has recommenced service.

Calls by selected ships and years on eastern Arctic itineraries

MV *World Discoverer*	MV *Ocean Endeavour*
31 July–14 August 1989	16–26 July 2017
Upernavik (Greenland)	St John's (NL)
Dexterity Fjord	Cruising Labrador Coast
Eclipse Sound	George River
Pond Inlet	Akpotok Island
Admiralty Inlet	Douglas Harbour
Resolute Bay	Digges Island
Strathcona Sound	Cape Dorset
Nunavik	Kimmirut (Lake Harbour)
Sermilik Glacier (Greenland)	Lower Savage Islands
Pond Inlet	George River
Holsteinborg (Sisimut, Greenland)	Akpotok Island
	Douglas Harbour
	Nuuk, Greenland

Wildlife

⬆ Muskox on Devon Island. (Stimpson, Courtesy OneOcean Expeditions)

Canada's Arctic wildlife[32] is extensive and is partially protected by five National Wildlife Areas, six National Parks, fifteen Migratory Bird Sanctuaries, three Marine Protected Areas, fourteen Territorial Parks in Nunavut and two Nature Wildlife Areas in Quebec. The Lancaster Sound Marine Protected Area, which has probably the most diverse marine and bird population in the Canadian Arctic, is to become a National Marine Conservation Area.

Birds protected in these areas include geese, Arctic sea ducks, eiders, loons, northern fulmar, thick-billed murre, red knots and red phalaropes.

Sea mammals include bowhead and beluga whales, and ringed and harp seals are common sights. The region is also home to 90 per cent of the world population of narwhals; the HBC used to sell their tusks as unicorn horns. Land mammals include polar bears, muskox, Peary caribou and the ubiquitous Arctic fox.[33]

Greenland

Capital: Nuuk, 64° 10'N 51° 44'W
Population: 56,144

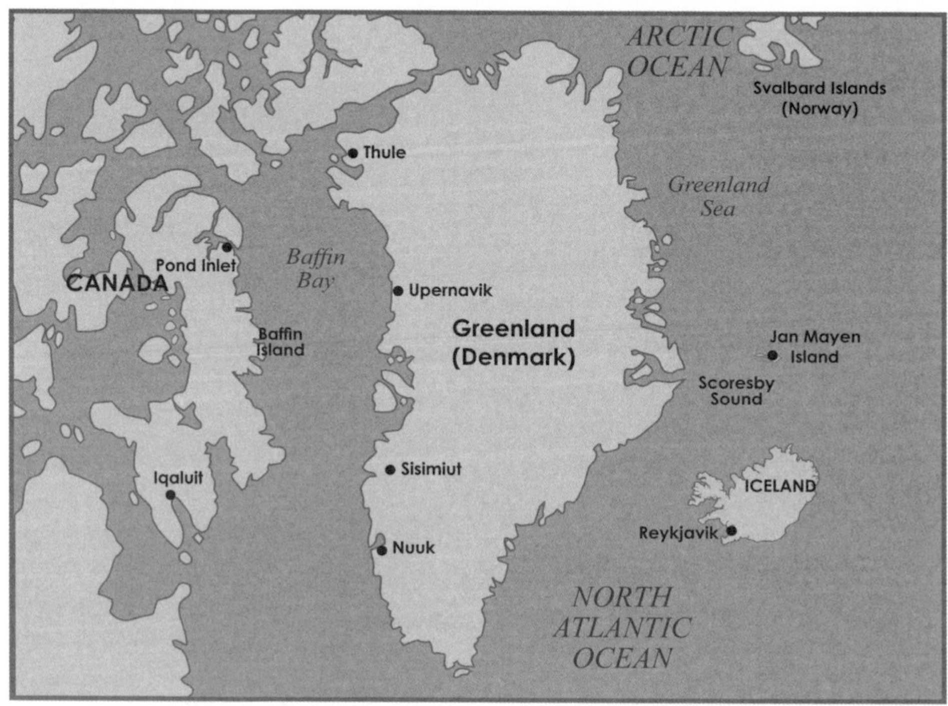

⬆ Map of Greenland.

At more than 2 million sq km, Greenland is the largest island in the world, and also has the second largest ice sheet after Antarctica. Habitation is only feasible on coastal strips, mainly on the west coast. While it has long been home to the Inuit, it is perhaps best known for its settlement by Viking adventurers from Iceland in AD 985 during the Medieval Warm Period.

Despite changes in sovereign rule from Scandinavia, the island was virtually forgotten until 1721 when Hans Egede, a Christian minister, together with missionaries, sailed from Copenhagen to determine if the inhabitants were following Christian precepts. The descendants of the Norse were not found, but the Inuit had settled the southern part of the island and Egede decided to stay on as an administrator.

There is some question over the demise of the Norse, but it seems that they did not survive the Little Ice Age, which probably began in the 1300s and was at its coldest in the 1600s. The last written record about the Norse was of a marriage in 1408 at Hvalsey Church, one of the best-preserved buildings from the period, which was visited, and photographed, by William Bradford during his 1869 art cruise.

In 1776, Denmark established the Royal Denmark Trading Company, which became the model for a paternalistic support of the colony providing education and health care. Inuit home rule was granted in 1979, although Denmark continues to support Greenland.

Early Cruise Activity

Greenland has always benefited from a relatively ice-free west coast and communities could be serviced over an extended season by ice-strengthened vessels. The lack of ice relatively far north attracted William Bradford with his cruise in the *Panther* in 1869. Thomas Cook's *Excursionist* of March 1881 noted that through special arrangements with the 'Arctic Committee', it could book passengers to accompany an expedition to Disko Island at $500 first class and $300 second class, leaving in June from London. However, no such expedition appears to have taken place.

In the nineteenth century, the west coast passenger service was by a variety of cargo/passenger ships catering to day passengers only. The first ships with cabin accommodation were the Ice 1A *Kununguak*[34] delivered in 1964 (219 berthed passengers) and the Ice 1A *Disko*[35] (200 berthed passengers) delivered in 1968. The two ships provided a service similar to the Hurtigruten on the Norwegian coast and tourists reportedly flew from Copenhagen to explore the attractions of the coast.[36] They operated until three new small passenger ships[37] were introduced in 1992. These were *Sarpik Ittuk* (sold 2006 and now *Ocean Nova*), *Sarfaq Ittuk* and *Saqqit Ittuk* (sold 2007 and now *Sea Endurance*). The first two were lengthened in 2002 and 2000 respectively.

⬆ *Costa Deliziosa* at Ilulissat, 2011. (Gert Bjerre, courtesy Bjarne Rasmussen)

If the ship's 1983 itinerary was followed, the *Lindblad Explorer* probably called in 1973, en route from Reykjavik to the Canadian Arctic. There is, however, little record of cruise ship calls prior to the 1990s, although Peter Dielmann's *Nordbrise* offered expedition-style cruises to the east coast in the 1970s. Other expedition-style ships no doubt visited communities and many Canadian Arctic cruises, such as the *Society Explorer* in 1990, and Northwest Passages commenced or terminated in Greenland. In terms of large ships, Hapag-Lloyd's *Europa* (now *Saga Sapphire*) cruised[38] the Greenland coast in 1985. The next reported call was by the *Royal Odyssey* (now *Albatros*) in 1993. The present *Europa* called in 1996 and then the *Royal Princess* (now *Artania*) in 1998. The *Lyubov Orlova* undertook at least two cruises in 2000 prior to a series of Canadian cruises. These may not be the only cruise ship calls, but they are the only ones for which we have any information. Many ships reported in Greenland waters are actually passing through scenic Prins Christian Sound as part of a Europe/North America voyage.

An analysis of the 2018 cruise schedule shows that out of forty-two ships calling at Greenland, twenty-one were large, with one being of 2,500-passenger capacity. Although a significant number of smaller ships do call, cruise activity is dominated, as in the Faroes and Spitsbergen, by large ships.

Wildlife

Most Arctic wildlife can be found in Greenland, although what may be seen depends on the region and the time of year. Polar bears are found mainly in the north and east, while the rare Arctic wolf is found only in the north. Herds of muskox can be found around Kangerlussuaq, with pockets of reindeer on the east coast, and barren-ground caribou on the west coast. Marine mammals are common, and most species of whales can be found in coastal waters in late summer and early autumn. It is estimated that there may be 2 million seals of different kinds in Greenland. The most common types are harp, ringed and hooded seals. Walrus are generally found in the north and east. There are many nesting bird species, from the magnificent white-tailed sea eagle in the south-west to the tiny northern wheatear, which nests in all coastal areas.

The West Greenland Current that today keeps ice clear from Greenland's west coast for much of the year as far as Disko Island was also a boon to English and Scottish whalers from the late eighteenth century to the start of the First World War. It enabled them to hunt the Greenland right whale almost to extinction. After 1817, when a way through the North Water was found to the Canadian side of Davis Strait, the whales were pursued to Lancaster Sound and Pond Inlet. While seals and walrus were also taken in vast numbers, these stocks have recovered. The whales have not and remain an endangered species.

Iceland

Capital : Reykjavik, 64° 08'N 21° 56'W
Population: 338,349

Iceland is a relatively new island from a geological perspective and straddles the Mid-Atlantic Ridge. As a result it is volcanically active, with some 200 volcanoes in a south-west to north-east zone across the island. A neighbouring island, Surtsey, was created by volcanic activity in 1963, and in 1973 the town of Vestmannaeyjar was devastated by the eruption of the Eldfjell volcano. The townsfolk pumped vast quantities of sea water onto the lava flows and were able to protect their harbour. The town was reoccupied in 1974.

The country has three national parks, and as a result of geothermal activity has several hot springs, of which the Blue Lagoon is the best known.

Because of its isolation, the island never had an indigenous population and the first recorded settlers were from Scandinavia in the ninth century. It is speculated that Irish missionaries may have visited earlier, but today the primary legacy is Norse with some Gaelic influences believed to be from the serfs who came with the early settlers.

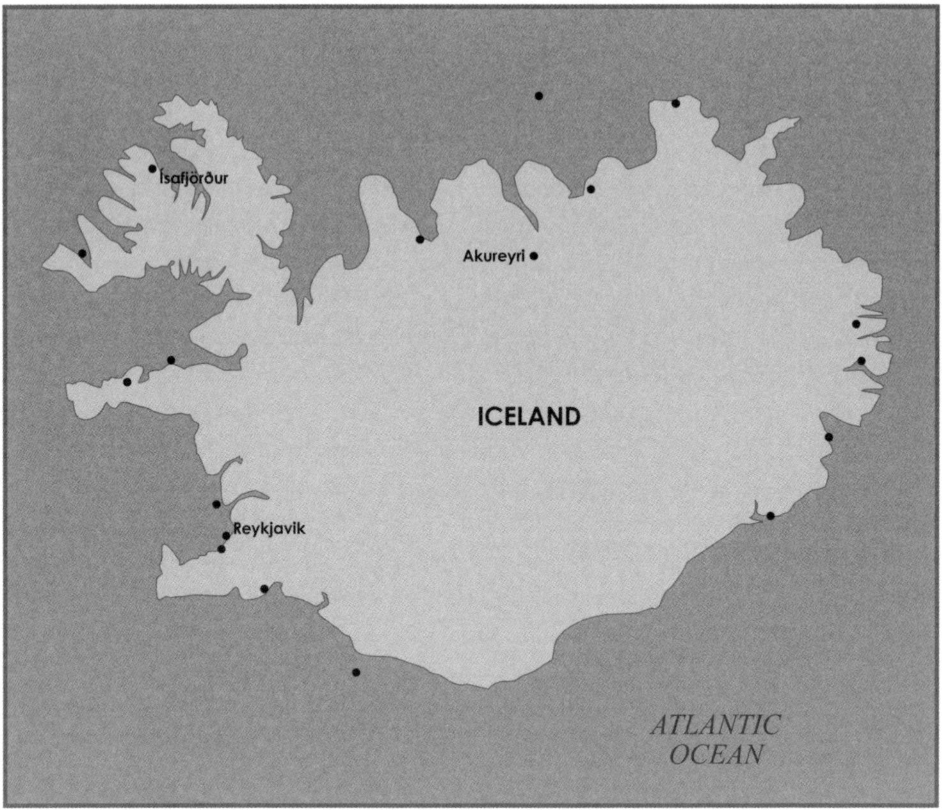

⬆ Map of Iceland; each dot represents a community.

Early Cruise Travel

The first cruise to Iceland might have been in 1874 when Isaac Hayes (who participated in the William Bradford cruise to Greenland in 1869) travelled with four others on the *Albion*, chartered from the Edinburgh and London Shipping Company. Apparently the party could not find a suitable ship in America, so went to Scotland. The *Albion* was not a passenger ship and the five members of the party had to sign on as ordinary seamen. They sailed from Aberdeen on 21 July, visited St Magnus Cathedral and the ancient burial site at Maeshowe in Kirkwall, Orkney, then to Lerwick in Shetland to visit the ruins of the seventeenth-century castle at Scalloway, and arrived at Tórshavn, Faroe Islands, on 26 July. They did not seem overly impressed and continued to Iceland to join twenty or more vessels from around the world that were present for the island's millennium celebrations.

Thomas Cook was advertising trips to Iceland in 1879 and popular cruises in 1883. Its 1890 catalogue included United Steam Ship Company sailings from Copenhagen and Granton (Scotland) commencing on 18 April until November at about three-week intervals. Sailings on the Leith and Iceland Steam Ship Company's SS *Copeland* to Iceland were monthly at a first-class fare of £5, £8 return with provisions at 6*s* 6*d*/day. However, these trips could not really be termed cruises, as Cook, in line with its practice, was using existing services and ships to offer guided excursions.

The 27 May 1899 edition of Thomas Cook's *Excursionist and Tourist Advertiser* offered what may have been one of the first true cruises to Iceland. As a part of its 'Yacht Cruises to the Norwegian Fjords' feature, it offered a twenty-nine-day cruise departing from London on 11 July to the Fjords, Spitsbergen and Iceland on Orient Lines' *Ophir*. The itinerary is one that was popular with many cruise companies and sometimes included the Faroe Islands as well.

Another early cruise that included Iceland was Hamburg-Amerika's cruising yacht *Prinzessin Victoria Luise* in 1905; she visited both Akureyri and Reykjavik. As she was in Spitsbergen that year, it is likely that she could have been on a similar itinerary to the *Oceana* the following year. In 1906, the *Oceana*, with 300 German and American passengers, arrived in Reykjavik from Hamburg via the Shetlands and left for Ísafjörður, Akureyri and then Spitsbergen.

In a 1907 advertisement aimed at the American market, Hamburg-Amerika Line offered several sailings each season from Hamburg to the Norwegian coast, Nordkapp, Spitsbergen, Akureyri and three locations in Iceland as well as Reykjavik, then returning via Tórshavn, Faroe Islands, Kirkwall, Orkney and Leith in Scotland. Prices were from $175 upwards including stateroom and meals. The company's cruise ship *Victoria Luise* undertook two sailings each season from 1912 to 1914, when only one was possible because of the start of the First World War.

⬆ German cruise liner *Victoria Luise* in Reykjavik, 1912. (Courtesy Guojon Fridrikson)

← German cruise liner *General von Steuben* in Reykjavik, 1930s. (Courtesy Guojon Fridrikson)

Iceland continued to be a popular destination for cruise ships during the interwar period, combined with cruises to Spitsbergen and Norway both from America and Europe. Reported sailings included Royal Mail *Atlantis* in July and August 1932, Blue Star Line's *Arandora Star* in July 1936 and 1938; these were probably annual trips as the ship was cruising regularly from 1932 until 1939. Also in 1938, Orient Line's *Orduna* visited in August. Although dates and frequency are uncertain, *General von Steuben* called some time between 1930 and 1938, and may have been a regular visitor as the Nordeutscher Lloyd ship cruised regularly in northern waters, both as *Munchen* and after being rebuilt and renamed in 1930. Hamburg South America Line *Monte Rosa* also called between 1931 and 1934, when it was acquired by the German KdF operation.

The Cunard 'Green Goddess' *Caronia* spent the month of July between 1951 and 1967 sailing from New York to Reykjavik then on to the North Cape and Norwegian fjords before completing the cruise in Southampton.

Reykjavik and Akureyri remain popular cruise destinations, with an increasing number of turnarounds for cruises to West and East Greenland. Akureyri is extending its cruise dock to offer better accommodation for the increasing number of ships.

Wildlife

The only native terrestrial species that existed in Iceland prior to settlement is the Arctic fox; other animals such as the ubiquitous Icelandic horse and reindeer were introduced by, or to serve, the settlers. The horse used to be an essential means of transport and is frequently mentioned by early visitors. The reindeer were introduced in 1775 and are limited to the north-east of the island. There are several breeds of seal that can be seen and whale watching can usually find humpbacks, minke and killer whales. Among bird species, Iceland has one of the world's largest colonies of puffins. More than half of the world population of Atlantic puffins breeds in Iceland, about 3–4 million pairs. The total population of birds in Iceland is estimated to be 8–10 million.

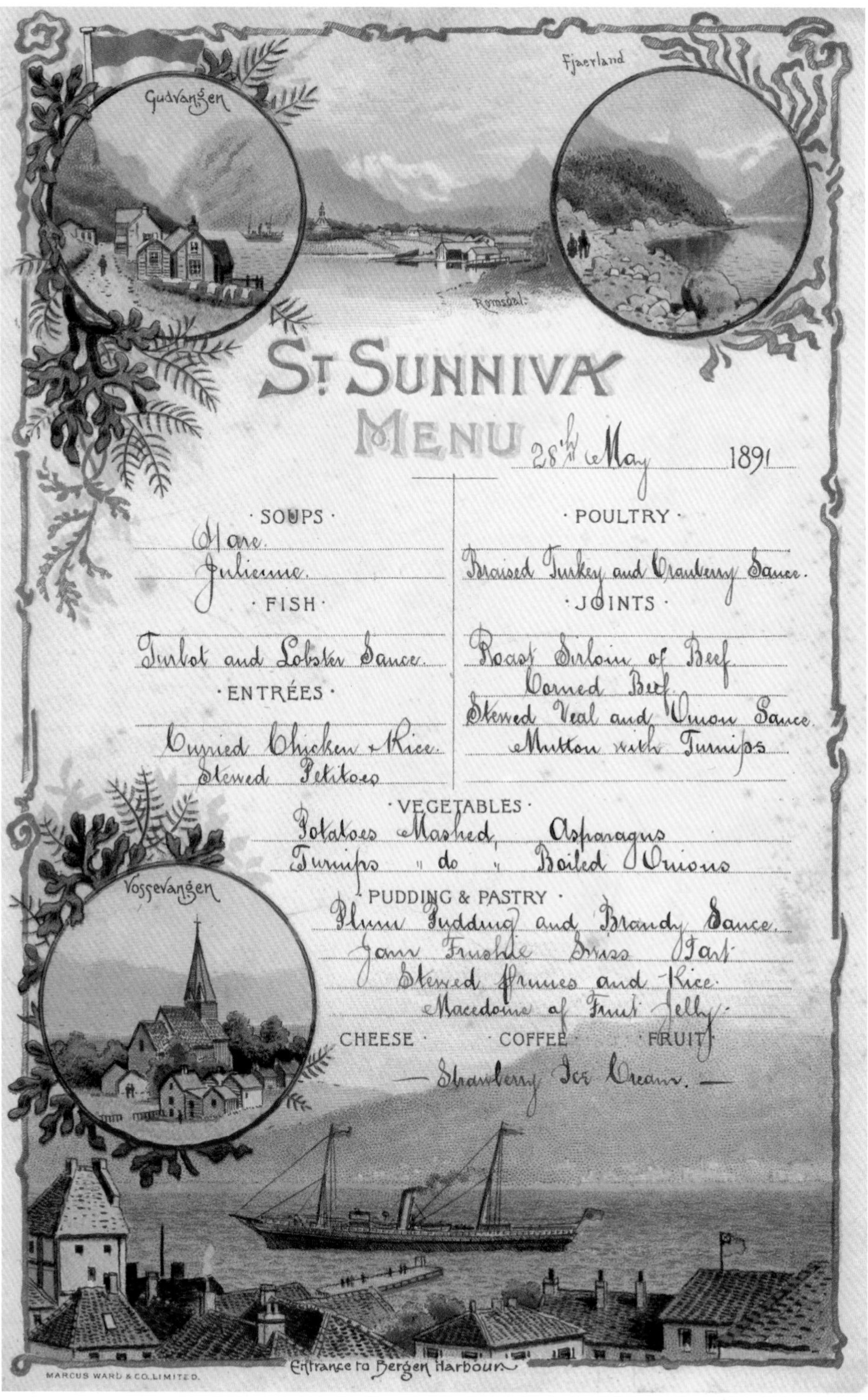

⬆ *St Sunniva* menu. (Courtesy of Shetland Museum and Archives)

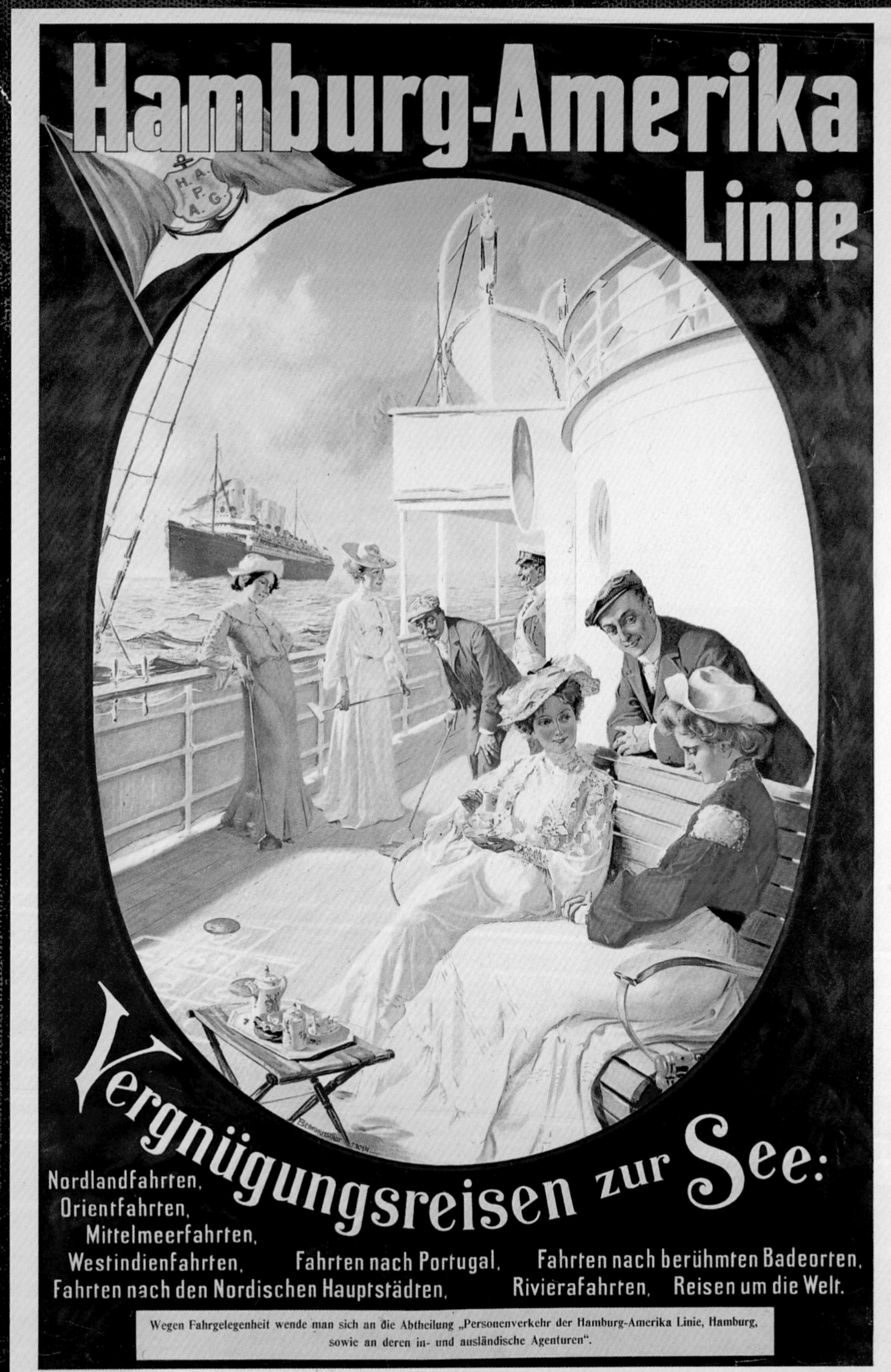

⬆ Early twentieth-century advertisement for Hamburg-Amerika Linie cruises. An identical poster in English with a Paris address was provided for the American market. (Courtesy of Hapag-Lloyd AG Hamburg)

⬆ 1920s Bergen Line poster for the *Meteor.* (Stephen Barrett Chase Poster Collection, Steamship Historical Society Archives, www.sshsa.org)

⬆ 1930s poster for P&O *Ranchi*. (Stephen Barrett Chase Poster Collection, Steamship Historical Society Archives, www.sshsa.org)

⬆ Cunard advertisement for *Caronia*, probably 1950s. (Stephen Barrett Chase Poster Collection, Steamship Historical Society Archives, www.sshsa.org)

⬇ Advertisement for *Lindblad Explorer*. (Courtesy of Lindblad Expeditions)

Our Ship, The M.S. Lindblad Explorer

The new M.S. LINDBLAD EXPLORER is the first ship to be expressly built for rugged exploration service while retaining all the comforts of a modern cruising vessel. The design of this exciting ship has evolved as a result of experience gained during past Lindblad expeditions to the less accessible parts of the world.

By luxury cruise standards she is a small ship, but for adventure cruising the "Lindblad Explorer" is ideal: 240 feet in length, 2,480 tons, a cruising range of 6,000 miles and a speed of better than 15 knots. A bow thruster and variable pitch propeller give her added maneuverability, and an up-to-date stabilizing system ensures greater passenger comfort.

The M.S. LINDBLAD EXPLORER has fifty double rooms, all outside with private shower and toilet. They are compact and comfortable — all except a few have twin-beds, dressing table (a boon to the ladies), individually controlled air-conditioning, and piped music.

One of the many special features of the "Lindblad Explorer" is an Observation Deck, with a Crow's Nest that will give our passengers a panoramic view from the highest point of the ship. For landing through shallow water or directly onto the shore, our ship is equipped with special landingcraft, in addition to two fiber glass launches. In the ship's movie and lecture auditorium, ornithologists and oceanographers will brief passengers in their particular subjects.

The M.S. LINDBLAD EXPLORER also offers all the usual cruise amenities, including Lido deck and swimming pool, lounge for dancing and entertainment, dining room, bar, hairdressing facilities, shop, and laundry. A doctor/surgeon will be in attendance on board.

It will be possible to communicate with the ship by radio.

SAFETY INFORMATION

The M.S. LINDBLAD EXPLORER is of Norwegian registry and meets the international safety standards for new ships developed after 1968 and meets the 1966 fire safety requirements.

The Lindblad Explorer off Praslin Island

⬆⬇ Hamburg-Amerika Line *Prinzessin Victoria Luise*, built 1900. Lounge with light well to dining room; Dining room. (Courtesy of Hapag-Lloyd AG Hamburg)

⬆⬇ *Marco Polo,* built 1965, many refits, operated by Cruise and Maritime Voyages. Waldorf restaurant; Standard twin stateroom. (Courtesy Cruise and Maritime Voyages)

⬆⬇ *Kapitan Khlebnikov*, built 1981, owned by Far East Shipping Company and chartered by Quark Expeditions. Dining room; Standard cabin. (Courtesy Quark Expeditions)

⬆⬇ Ponant Explorer-class ships. First of class *Le Laperouse,* delivered 2018. Blue Eye observation lounge, 8 feet below the water line; Prestige cabin. (Courtesy Ponant)

⬆ Polar bear. (Roger Pimenta, courtesy OneOcean Expeditions)

⬆ Rockhopper penguin. (Adeline Heymann, courtesy OneOcean Expeditions)

⬇ Magellanic penguin. (Courtesy Falkland Islands Tourism)

⬆ Sea lions. (Ben Hagar, courtesy OneOcean Expeditions)

⬇ Arctic fox in summer coat. (Ira Meyer, courtesy OneOcean Expeditions)

⬆ Falkland Islands grass wren. (Courtesy Falkland Islands Tourism)

⬇ Walrus. (David McEown, courtesy OneOcean Expeditions)

⬆ Narwhal. (Nathan Small, courtesy OneOcean Expeditions)

⬇ Atlantic puffin. (Tony Beck, courtesy OneOcean Expeditions)

Striated caracara. (Adeline Heymann, courtesy OneOcean Expeditions)

Humpback whale. (Dave Sanford, courtesy OneOcean Expeditions)

⬆ Emperor penguins at Snow Hill Island. (Courtesy of Robert Headland, Scott Polar Research Institute)

⬇ Elephant seals. (Courtesy Falkland Islands Tourism)

Faroe Islands

➡ Map of the Faroe Islands.

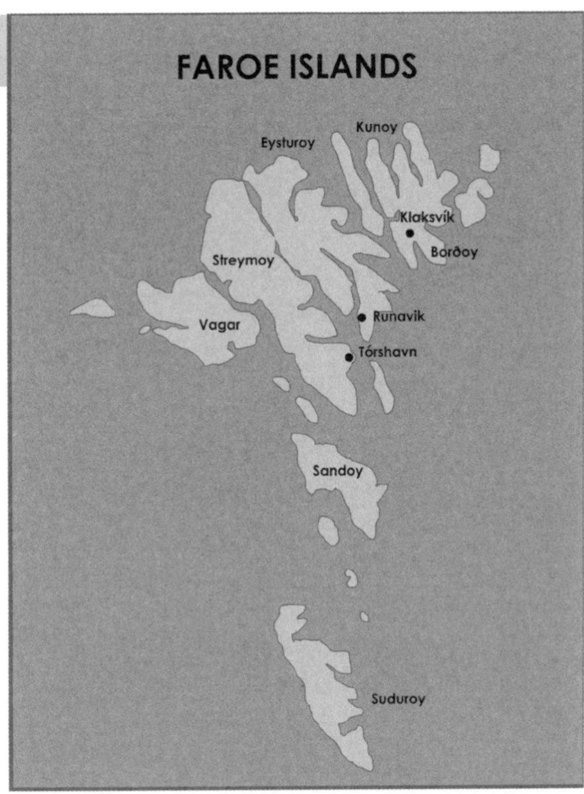

Capital: Tórshavn, 62° 00′42″N 6° 46′03″W
Population: 51,095

Like Iceland, the Faroe Islands have a relatively recent geological history. However, plate tectonics have moved the islands away from the volcanically active zone of the Mid-Atlantic Ridge. Also, like Iceland, the islands were relatively remote, and never had an indigenous population. It is possible that monks from Scotland or Ireland settled in the period AD 400–600, but the most authoritative accounts of settlement come from AD 825. As these mention the presence of sheep, it would seem that these must have been imported in earlier times. In fact, Faroe Islands derives from old Norse, meaning 'Sheep Islands'.

Originally a part of the Denmark/Norway Kingdom, the Treaty of Kiel in 1814 dissolved the sovereign duality and the islands became a part of Denmark. With the occupation of Denmark by Nazi Germany during the Second World War, Britain pre-emptively occupied the islands to deny their possible use as a submarine base. While Britain left the islands in 1945, a lasting affection for British chocolate and candies remained.

Like Svalbard, coal was found, and mining of brown coal was undertaken on the island of Suderoy from the 1770s. While some minor mining continues, commercial coal mining ended after the Second World War.

Early Cruise Calls

The 1874 charter by Isaac Hayes, Cyrus Field and others of the *Albion* to cruise to Iceland called at Tórshavn on 26 July. Isaac Hayes noted that there were no formal wharves, only heaps of stones surrounding a landing area. He considered the islands to be like Greenland with a stench of dead fish everywhere. They were not the first party to call, and two Danish warships carrying King Christian IX had preceded them. This was the first visit by a monarch since Danish rule had been established, and the town's mayor was so overwhelmed by the occasion that he died on completion of his speech.

While it is likely that cruises started earlier, given the location of the islands, the first mention of scheduled cruises was in an advertisement in the American market in 1908. The Hamburg-Amerika Line offered:

> Special summer cruises to Norway, Spitsbergen, North Cape, Iceland, Scotland, Orkney, Faroe Islands by the magnificent twin screw steamships *Oceana, Meteor, Koening Wilhelm II.* Duration from 14–24 days (starting from Hamburg). Rates $62.50 and up including all expenses on board steamer.

⬆ Meinschiff and Samson. (Courtesy Tórshavn Head of Sales and Marketing)

In the early days, the principal port of call would have been Tórshavn, although ships now call at Runavik (first cruise call 2005) and Klaksvík. The focus appears to be on large ships rather than expedition vessels, which represent only a small proportion of cruise calls. Tórshavn advises that the port is being expanded to enable it to accommodate more large ships, with a 300m pier extension in 2019 and another 600m by 2020, all with a minimum depth of 15m.

Wildlife

All land animals were introduced by settlers or visitors, but some, such as the Faroese goose and sheep, are unique to the islands because isolated breeding over 1,000 years has essentially created a subspecies.

The islands are an important breeding area for many seabirds, with the signature species being the puffin. However, the puffin population has collapsed from about 1.5 million to 300,000 in recent years; it is thought that climate change is the primary cause. The islands are home to one of the largest colonies of storm petrels in the world and, in addition, there are significant colonies of northern fulmars, black-legged kittiwakes and guillemots. Smaller numbers of many other seabirds are also found.

Harbour porpoises are common, and long-finned pilot whales live around the islands. Other whales, such as bottlenose, orcas and blue whales, may be seen seasonally. Only grey seals are found in the islands.

Svalbard Islands

Capital : Longyearbyen, 78° 13′N 15° 38′E
Population: 2,667

The Svalbard Archipelago is a remote group of islands only 1,300km from the North Pole. The islands, which never had an indigenous population, are 60 per cent covered by ice with more than 2,000 glaciers. The archipelago has an interesting history, as until 1920 it was 'terra nullius' or no man's land. The Svalbard Treaty of 9 February 1920 recognised Norwegian sovereignty over the islands, including Bornoya, which is somewhat remote from the main group. However, the treaty gave citizens of signatory countries the right to exploit mineral resources, and this was taken up by Russia, which maintains a small coal mining settlement on the island of Spitsbergen at Barentsburg, about 55km from Longyearbyen. A new cruise pier is proposed for Barentsburg.

The islands were first noted by the Dutch in the late sixteenth century, and by the early seventeenth century and through the eighteenth century were a centre for

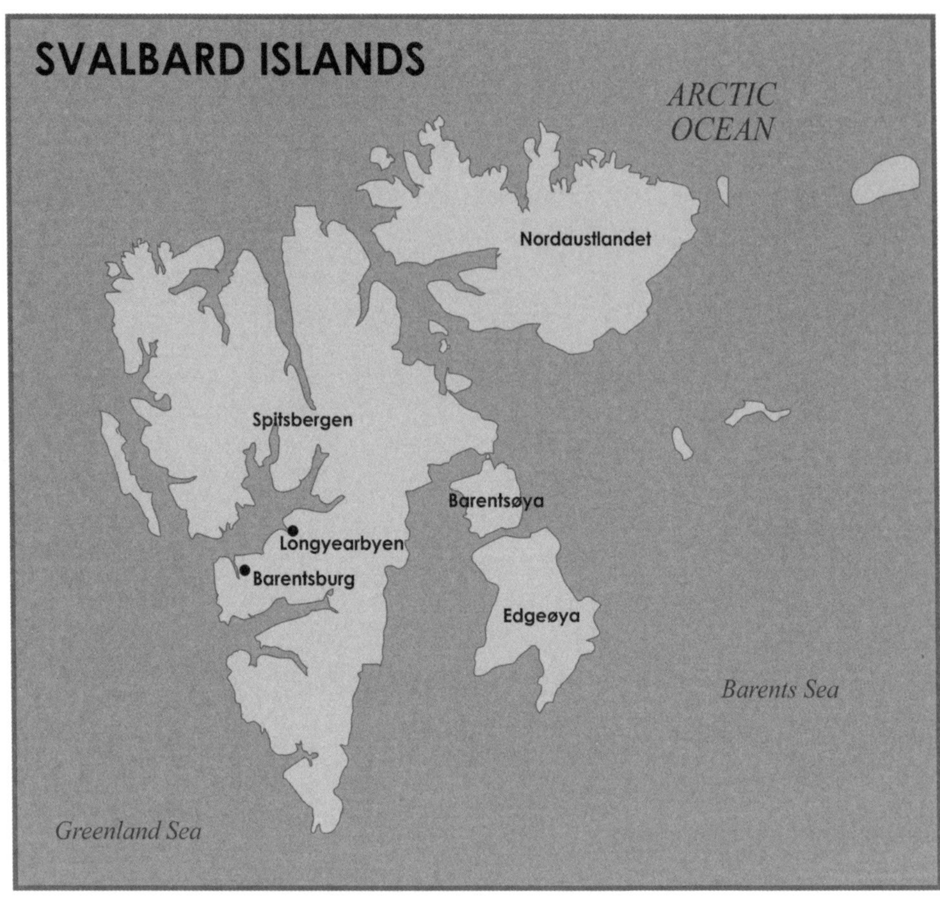

Map of the Svalbard Islands.

whaling. While about fifty whaling stations have been identified, Smeerenburg in the north-west has perhaps the largest collection of archaeological remains from this period. At its peak, there were more than 300 whalers.

Spitsbergen has been home to active coal mining for more than a century, and commercial mining got its start when the American entrepreneur John Munro Longyear visited Spitsbergen in 1901. During the visit, he came across prospectors with coal samples. He later bought the claims, set up the Arctic Coal Company and established a coal mine that started in 1906 at Longyear City. The mine did not do well during the First World War and was purchased by a Norwegian company in 1916, which continued mining and renamed the town Longyearbyen. The export of coal was discontinued in 2017 due to declining profitability, and just enough for local power generation is now mined. However, mining continues at Barentsburg.

Spitsbergen is also home to the Svalbard Global Seed Vault, which was completed in 2008 as a depositary for duplicate copies of seeds held by gene banks elsewhere. The intent by the Consultative Group on International Agricultural Research was to provide a secure location against the catastrophic loss of national seed holdings. At present, the just under 1 million seed packets represent about a third of the world's most important crop varieties. The vault has space for 4.5 million 500-seed packets.

Early Expedition Cruising

During the nineteenth century, the islands became the virtual preserve of the wealthy looking for adventure. They either arrived in their own yachts, or banded together to charter a ship. The first commercial cruise was offered by Henry Clodius, who chartered the *Pallas* in 1881 and took about thirty intrepid vacationers to Spitsbergen.[39] They had answered advertisements in hunting magazines, including *The Field*, promising polar bear, seal, walrus and reindeer hunting. The cruise was not successful as Clodius needed about twice the number of guests to cover costs, and those who did take the cruise felt cheated as they did not get the promised hunting and fishing. An essential part of this cruise and all subsequent visits was to get as far north as the ice would permit.

The Ocean Steam Yachting Company sent the *Ceylon* on three cruises, each with eighty people, in 1884, but then did not return to cruising in the north. The Orient

⬆ Svalbard Islands 'Land of Eternal Ice'. (David McEown, courtesy OneOcean Expeditions)

Steam Navigation Company began cruising in 1894 with the *Lusitania*. However, the true originator of expedition cruising to Spitsbergen is considered to be Wilhelm Bade, who organised his first cruise in 1891 with the *Amely*, and then went on to charter the *Admiral* in 1893, together with the purpose-built whaler *Gluckhauf*. Passengers could join the *Gluckhauf* for a whale hunt. Hunting and fishing were key offerings by all companies for the cruises to Spitsbergen, and as a result the local reindeer were almost hunted to extinction prior to the introduction of controls by Norway following the 1920 treaty. Bade catered to a less wealthy clientele, and his prices for a three-week cruise ranged from 800–1,800 marks. Bade was the quintessential tour leader. He arranged unique events for his cruises, was well liked by his guests and received a favourable mention in the Baedecker Guides of the period. He personally conducted tours until his death in 1903, when his son Alex took over his role until Bade cruise activity ceased in 1908.

An indication of the importance of hunting and fishing can be found in an extensive passage from Thomas Cook's *Excursionist and Tourist Advertiser* for 1 June 1888. In this the company announces that it has made arrangements with a whaler leaving Tromsø on 1 July for Spitsbergen for one or two gentlemen to accompany the trip to

⬆ P&O *Canberra* at Spitsbergen. (© P&O Heritage Collections, www.poheritage.com)

Icefjord for white fish. There was also the prospect of hunting for river horses, seals, white bear, reindeer, etc., excellent salmon fishing as well as enormous quantities of birds, including wild swans, geese and eider ducks. The price was £150 for one and £250 for two passengers.

Hamburg-Amerika Line (HAL) started its cruises with *Columbia* in 1893, and was present with one or more vessels each year until the First World War. Its Spitsbergen cruise itineraries also incorporated the Norwegian fjords, Nordkapp and Iceland. HAL's 1894 prices on the *Auguste Victoria* ranged from 450DM for servants to 2,500DM for a suite. The company had four ships and probably eight cruises in 1911, which was the peak pre-First World War season when nine ships visited on at least eighteen cruises.

Cie Generale Transatlantique offered annual cruises on its ships *Lafayette* and *Cuba* during the 1930s, the high point being to see how far into the pack ice they could proceed.

Because of proximity to Europe and the ability to incorporate a Spitsbergen cruise with Norwegian fjords and Nordkapp, the archipelago has continued to be a popular destination, particularly for large vessels. However, climate change has permitted some companies to establish week-long cruises within the islands, and in 2018 eighteen small expedition cruise ships made a total of 111 local cruises. Cruise statistics show that large ships rather than smaller expedition-style cruise ships dominate Spitsbergen arrivals, with the presence of such ships going back many years.

Wildlife

With an estimated population of 3,000 polar bears, the islands are home to more bears than people. The native reindeer population has recovered and stabilised since Norway introduced controls in 1925. Interestingly, it is understood that the unique Svalbard Reindeer bloodline continues in the Falkland Islands, by way of South Georgia. In the Svalbard Islands reindeer are suffering from the effects of climate change, and being forced to eat seaweed to survive. This is because winter rain creates an ice sheet on the snow that the animals cannot paw through with their hoofs to get at vegetation underneath.

Beluga whales are the most common but fin and minke may be seen, while humpback and blue whale sightings are becoming more frequent. Ringed, bearded and harbour seals are common. Walrus have made a comeback after being widely hunted by whalers and early adventurers.

Nordaustlandet and the islands to the east and south, including Bjørnøya, are designated as a nature reserve, while many of the coastal areas of Spitsbergen are designated as a national park.

🠉 Russian icebreaker *50 let Pobedy* en route to the North Pole. (Courtesy Robert Headland, Scott Polar Research Institute)

North Pole Cruises

The North Pole has long exerted a fascination for explorers, and while many attempts were made to reach the different northern poles[40] during the nineteenth and early twentieth centuries, they were mainly unsuccessful. William Parry's attempt in 1827 was perhaps the earliest, although he only made it as far as 82° 45'N.

An Austro-Hungarian expedition of 1872 was unsuccessful, but did find the Franz Josef archipelago east of Svalbard. Andrée's balloon expedition base at Danskoya in north-west Spitsbergen became part of Wilhelm Bade's cruise itinerary of 1896 with the *Erling Jarl*.

Some supposedly successful expeditions to be the first to reach the pole, such as those by Frederick Cook in 1908 and Robert Peary in 1909, as well as Richard Byrd's flight in 1926, have been challenged and their success is now considered doubtful based on log evidence.

However, the 1926 over-the-pole flight by Roald Amundsen in the dirigible *Norge* from Spitsbergen to Teller[41] in Alaska with a crew of sixteen succeeded. Amundsen had originally intended to fly the *Norge* to the North Pole from a base at Kings Bay, Spitsbergen, but was upstaged by Richard Byrd, who also flew out of Spitsbergen on 9 May using a Fokker Trimotor. The *Norge* left King's Bay (Ny Alesund) on 11 May and arrived in Teller on 14 May. King's Bay was also used as the base for the North Pole flight by the dirigible *Italia*, which crashed on its return on 23 May 1928.

It was not until 1968 that Richard Plaisted[42] made the first successful, and properly documented, overland trip in a skidoo, while the first ship to reach the pole was the Russian icebreaker *Arktika* on 17 August 1977.

In 1990, Quark Expeditions arranged a unique charter with the Murmansk Shipping Company (which managed the Russian icebreaker fleet) for a North Pole cruise on the nuclear icebreaker *Rossiya* with fifty selected and specially invited guests. This was successful and Quark then arranged a transpolar cruise from Murmansk to Providenyia on the Russian Pacific coast using the nuclear icebreaker *Sovetskiy Soyuz*.

Murmansk adapted three nuclear icebreakers to accommodate up to 100 cruise passengers plus staff and additional crew for housekeeping and catering. The ships were the *Sovetskiy Soyuz* (*Soviet Union*), *Yamal* (*End of Land*) and *50 let Pobedy* (*Fifty Years of Victory*). Since then Quark has arranged regular cruises using mainly *Yamal* and *50 let Pobedy*. In all there have been 109 North Pole cruises, which are listed in the Appendices. While Quark has been the lead operator, other companies have booked parties on board the icebreakers and undertake their own marketing. Cyprus-based Poseidon Expeditions entered the market in 2010, and since then has chartered its own voyages in *Yamal* and *50 let Pobedy*.

Due to the complexities of an embarkation in Murmansk, some of the cruises have turned around in Longyearbyen, Spitsbergen, despite the need to use helicopters to transfer passengers and baggage.

Nordkapp

Honningsvåg: 78° 13'N 15° 38'E

Access to the 307m sheer promontory off the northern coast on Norway is via the village of Honningsvåg. The headland is believed to have first been sighted by Hugh Willoughby during the Company of Merchant Adventurers to New Land's expedition in search of the Northeast Passage in 1553. The name North Cape was given by the ship's captain, Richard Chancellor. However, it was a visit by the priest Francesco Negri, who in 1664 gave the Cape a lasting description in *Viaggio Settentrionale*, an account of his travels to Scandinavia published in 1670.

Here he wrote:

> and now I have arrived at the North Cape, which is the outermost tip of Finnmark and more than that I have arrived at the very end of the earth, as from here to the pole there is no other land inhabited by human beings …[43]

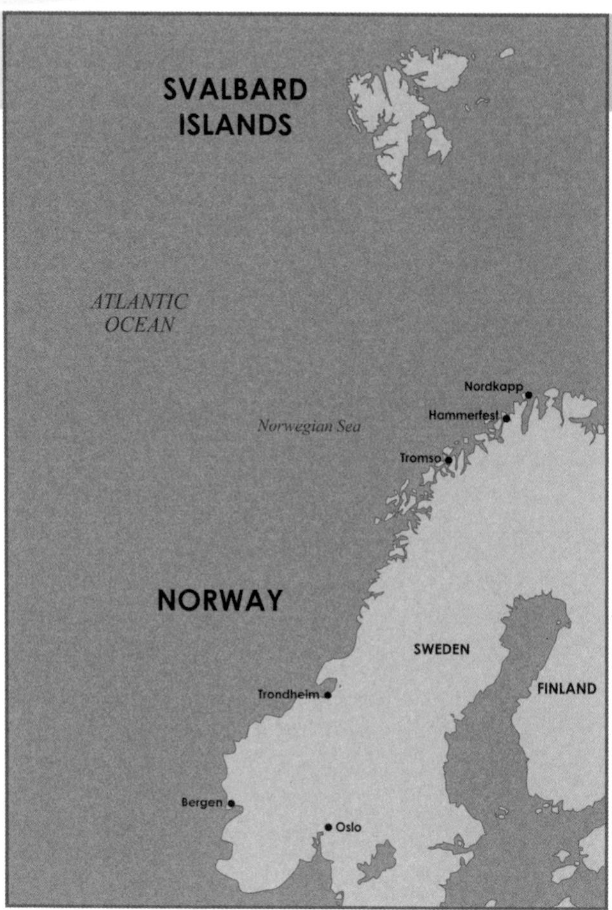

← Map of Norway showing the location of Nordkapp.

However, it was not until the Swedish/Norwegian King Oscar II visited the crag during his well-publicised[44] post-coronation cruise in 1873 that much notice was taken. He was accompanied on the cruise by several reporters, one of whom headed his article 'Land of the Midnight Sun',[45] and the phrase became universally adopted. Because Norway had installed telegraph lines in 1870 along the North Shore, news that the king had climbed to the top of the crag was widely broadcast, as was the fact that an accompanying ambassador had to be carried down, being unable to complete the ascent. It helped that the weather was excellent.

Kaiser Wilhelm took his yacht on annual cruises from 1878 to 1914 and even participated in a whale hunt in 1892. German shipping lines, including HAL, offered cruising on the Norwegian coast so that citizens could salute the Imperial Yacht *Hohenzollern II,* admire the scenery and see the midnight sun. In July 1898, passengers on the *Auguste Victoria,* en route back from Spitsbergen, met the Imperial yacht in Alesund. The Kaiser visited the cruise ship and passengers were invited to tour the yacht in groups of thirty to forty.

It is interesting to speculate whether the First World War would have occurred if the Kaiser had not taken his annual cruise in 1914. His diary entries suggest a concern about the fallout from Sarajevo that was not shared by his diplomatic corps. Assured that nothing would come of the incident, he sailed as usual, and apparently all his senior diplomatic staff also went on vacation at the same time. The Kaiser had to keep himself informed of developments by way of articles in Norwegian newspapers, and became sufficiently concerned that he cut his cruise short, but by then the situation was out of control.

Norway's post line steamers had provided a regular, but seasonal, service along the coast from Trondheim, and then Bergen to Hammerfest – an early version of the Hurtigruten ferry service. Year-round service was not started until 1893 by Richard With and his ship *Vesteraalen* under a four-year government contract. Seeing his success, the other companies (Berganske D/S and Nordenfjeldske D/S) that had offered seasonal service began upgrading their operations and also obtained mail contracts. The ships *Kong Harald* and *Neptun* appear regularly in Thomas Cook's publications with sailings from Bergen and Trondheim. The *Vega* and *Ragnald Jarl* offered sailings from Newcastle every Tuesday during the summer for fourteen-day cruises.

Thomas Cook intended to take advantage of these scheduled trips in offering an excursion to Nordkapp and the midnight sun in 1875. The tour started in London on 10 or 12 July, depending on the route selected by the excursionists, but all met up at the Streit Hotel in Hamburg before proceeding by rail to Kiel. A chartered steamer took the party to Copenhagen, where they boarded the SS *Dronningen* for Bergen. However, a misunderstanding over cabin bookings led to the company having to charter the *President Christie* to fulfil its obligations to the twenty-one excursionists. The tour had continued to Trondheim while negotiations were taking place and eventually the excursionists embarked at Christiansund for the trip north. Because of delays, the party would have been too late to see the midnight sun at Nordkapp, so the ship steamed north, and at 73° 22'N, the spectacle was observed, and the passengers returned home well satisfied. The tour, which included some options for additional destinations, cost £52 and returned to London on 25 August.

A Norwegian fjord cruise typically terminated with a visit to Nordkapp, but sometimes the itinerary was extended to Spitsbergen and these became very popular in the late nineteenth and early twentieth century. In 1893, the Hurtigruten Express Coastal Line ships went regularly to Horn Bay (Hornvika) and visitors then climbed a steep narrow path to the summit. A small champagne pavilion had been built in 1892, but was blown down; a stone structure was built later.

Norwegian coast and Nordkapp cruises continued to be popular during the 1920s and '30s and again after the Second World War. Hamburg-Sud offered fairly basic cruises to the midnight sun with the *Monte Cervantes.* The Nazi organisation Strength Through Joy provided classless cruises from 1934 to 1939.

⬆ *Marco Polo* at Svartisan Glacier on the Norwegian coast. (Courtesy Cruise and Maritime Voyages)

In the 1930s, Cunard took the *Carinthia* to the Fjords and North Cape as part of a cruise that included the Faroe Islands and Iceland. Commencing in 1951, the *Caronia* established a seventeen-year summer tradition of Norwegian coastwise cruises from New York on a very similar itinerary. When the ship arrived, at least on the 1951 cruise, crew members lugged coffee, tea and snacks to the plateau at the top of the crag. In 1952, there were 550 passengers on the cruise.

Hapag-Lloyd re-established its traditional northern cruises with the *Europa*[46] after its delivery in 1981, and the destination, anchored by the dramatic scenery of the Fjords, continues to the present day. The ship carried a spare lifeboat from the earlier *Europa* on its foredeck, and used it as a floating landing stage in Spitsbergen for beach landings. Also in the 1980s, the first *Albatross* called during her short cruising career.

Future cruise activity to the Norwegian fjords will be impacted by the government's action plan for green shipping. This calls for cruise ships on the Western Coast World Heritage Sites (Geirangerfjord and Nærøyfjord – an arm of Sognfjord), to be emission-free as soon as technologically possible, but no later than 2026. The Green Party in Norway has gone further, wanting to ban all fossil fuel ship activity by 2030.

Hurtigruten's move to install battery packs would enable some activity to be maintained by their ships, but at present capacity only allows about two hours' operation at low speed.

3

ARCTIC PASSAGES

The Northwest Passage

The Northwest Passage is perhaps best known for efforts to find a way through the Canadian Arctic from Atlantic to Pacific by British explorers. Exploration commenced with Martin Frobisher in 1576, culminating with Sir John Franklin and the *Erebus* and *Terror* in 1845.

Frobisher's efforts segued into a gold scam that saw 1,500 tons of worthless rock mined and hauled back to England in 1577 and 1578. Frobisher's voyages, though, did lead to further exploration of Arctic North America. These voyages materially expanded knowledge of the Arctic and eventually led to Franklin's unsuccessful expedition on which he disappeared. Between 1847 and 1859 there were thirty-two expeditions to find Franklin, or his remains. Of these expeditions, twenty were actual search parties and the remainder supply missions. The wreck of the *Erebus* was found in 2014, while the *Terror* wreck was found in 2016 courtesy of Inuit oral histories that had been ignored for decades.

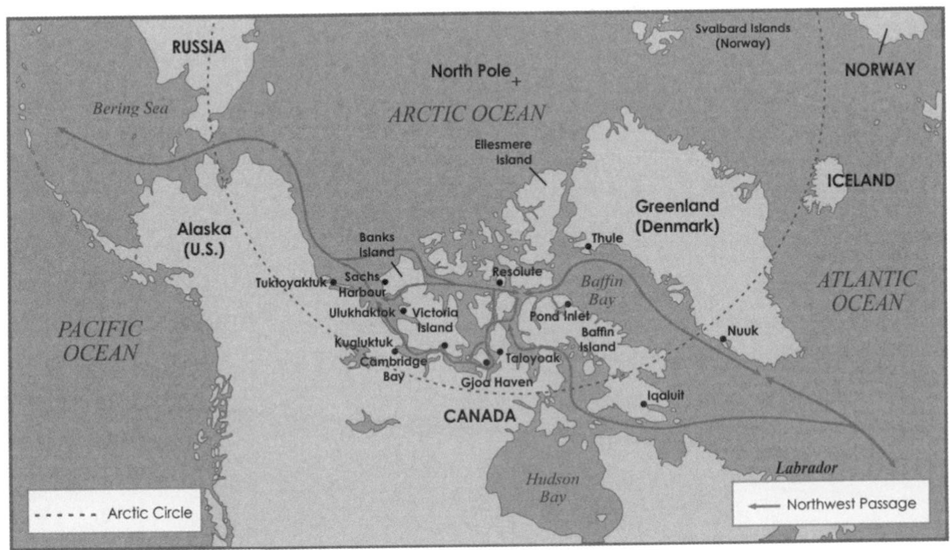

Map showing the different Northwest Passages.

To accomplish a true Northwest Passage, a ship must proceed from the Atlantic to Pacific Ocean, or vice versa, and the first successful one was by Roald Amundsen in the *Gjoa*, although it took him three years between 1903 and 1906 to accomplish it. Other transits by governmental and research vessels took place after Amundsen, although the tanker *Manhattan* in 1969 did not, technically, complete a transit as it turned around at Point Barrow.

A cruise company may advertise a passage, but the cruise actually remains in Canadian waters and does not proceed past Demarcation Point at the border between Canada and the USA. For example, the Marine Expeditions Northwest Passage cruise between 5–25 September 1995 in the *Marine Challenger,* aka *Livonia*, started at Søndre Strømfjord in Greenland, sailed up the coast to Ilullissat, crossed over the Davis Strait to Pond Inlet, then proceeded via Prince Leopold Island, Beechey Island, Resolute Bay, Holman (Ulukhaktok) to Sachs Harbour, before turning back to Cambridge Bay to disembark passengers. The cost, in Canadian dollars,[1] ranged from $5,895 to $7,495 plus port dues and taxes of $295. Airfare from Montreal was included.

⬆ The Northwest Passage. (David McEown, courtesy OneOcean Expeditions)

Calls by selected ships and years on Northwest Passage itineraries

MV *Kapitan Khlebnikov*	**MV *Hanseatic***
Westbound 19 August–19 September 2001	Eastbound 23 August–9 September 1998
Thule, Greenland	Herschel Island
Coburg Island	Smoking Hills
Grise Fjord	Holman
Tanqueray Fjord	Ross Point
Eureka	Cambridge Bay
Mokka Fjord	Jenny Lind Island
Radstock Bay	Arctic Bay
Beechey Island	Beechey Island
Resolute Bay	Resolute Bay
Bent Horn	Dundas Harbour
Smoking Hills	Nungavik
Walker Bay	Pond Inlet
Sachs Harbour	Sam Ford Fjord
Herschel Island	Umanaq, Greenland

Herschel Island was not the termination or originating location in these itineraries. It was the last and first place called at in the Canadian Arctic.

The first true passenger transit was by the 13m Dutch sloop *Williwaw* with Willy de Roos at the helm in 1977, then on 20 August 1984, the 2,398grt, 104-passenger *Lindblad Explorer* left St John's, Newfoundland, bound for a forty-three-day voyage to Yokohama through the Northwest Passage, thus accomplishing the first polar cruise ship transit. In 1985, the 3,153grt, 138-passenger *World Discoverer* became the first ship to transit the Northwest Passage in the opposite direction, completing a thirty-two-day, 6,295-mile voyage from Nome to Halifax for Society Expeditions. The *Lindblad Explorer* came back in 1988 as the *Society Explorer* with a west to east transit. There were no transits by cruise ships in 1989, 1990 and 1991, although some adventurers made it through, as they did in 2018 when ice prevented any cruise ship transits.

Regular expedition vessel transits have taken place each year since 1992, although typically only one or two transits took place in any given year. The *Kapitan Khlebnikov* holds the record for the number of transits (eighteen), including back-to-back trips in 1994, 2001 and 2005. A full list of cruises through the Northwest Passage is provided in the Appendices.

⬆ *Clipper Adventurer.* (Courtesy SunStone Ships)

Wildlife

What may be seen will depend, to a certain extent, on the Northwest Passage route taken by the ship. However, Eclipse Sound and Lancaster Sound are common points of entry or egress from the Passage, and these areas are rich in marine mammals and seabirds. A route that is not common for cruise ships, through Fury and Hecla, passes through major walrus areas at the head of Foxe Basin. In the west, the Mackenzie Delta area is a significant home for beluga whales, and other whales may be found in the Amundsen Gulf leading up to Dolphin and Union Strait. Banks Island is home to a major population of muskox. The island was also home to the 'Bankslanders', skilled Inuit trappers who focused on the Arctic fox, and made fortunes from the pelts during the 1920s.

The Northern Sea Route

The first attempt to find a sea route across the roof of Russia was made by Hugh Willoughby and Richard Chancellor in 1553. A three-ship expedition was sponsored by a group of London merchants as the Company of Merchant Adventurers to New Lands. They were not successful and Willoughby, together with his crew and the crew of a second ship, died when wintering. Chancellor, however, made it to the entrance of the Dvina River, from where he was invited to the court of Ivan the Terrible.

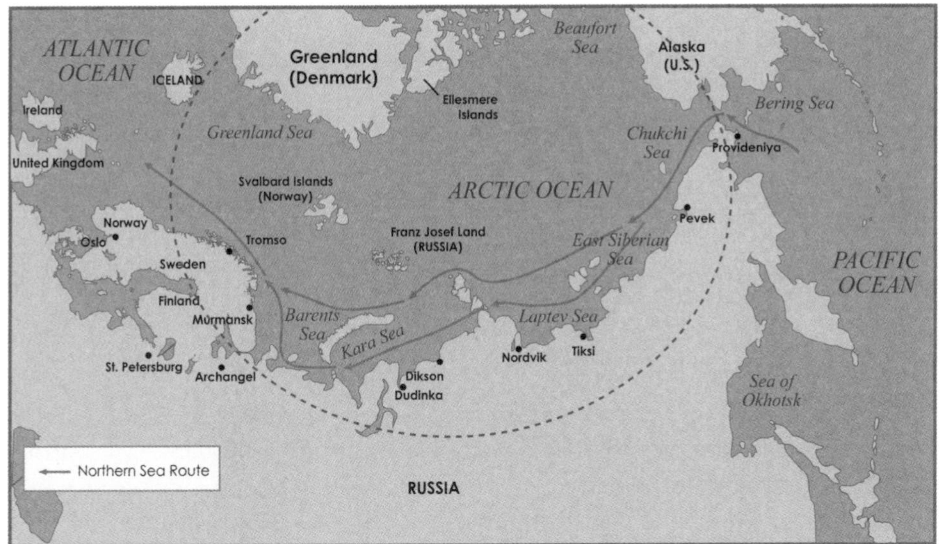

⬆ Map of the Northern Sea route of the Northeast Passage.

The czar welcomed the opportunity for a sea-trading route that avoided the Baltic Sea and the monopolistic Hanseatic League. Chancellor was able to negotiate a trading agreement that established the Muscovy Company, which was chartered in 1555 and survived until the Russian revolution of 1917. It had a monopoly on Arctic trade, and was directed by the English Privy Council in 1574 to issue a licence to Martin Frobisher for an exploratory voyage in search of the Northwest Passage. Perhaps fearing competition, it at first refused, but Frobisher had friends in court and a licence was eventually issued. Michael Lok, a director of the Muscovy Company, went on to organise Frobisher's expeditions to the north-west.

The first confirmed passage was made by the Swedish/Finnish scientist and explorer Adolf Erik Nordenskjold. Together with Louis Palander as captain of the *Vega*, they sailed from the Atlantic to the Pacific in 1878–79 (due to pack ice, he was forced to winter just a few days' sailing distance from Bering Strait). The Imperial Russian Navy icebreakers *Taymyr* and *Vaygach* made the second transit of the Northern Sea Route in 1914–15, then in 1940 the Russians facilitated a transit from the North Sea to the Pacific by the German raider *Komet*.

Polar Cruising

Although not a transit of the Northern Sea Route (NSR), the first Russian Arctic cruise was promoted by Intourist (the Soviet Union state tourist agency) on the icebreaker *Malgyin*[2] in 1931, to meet up with the airship *Graf Zeppelin* during its Arctic scientific trip between Archangel and Franz Josef Land. The tour was under the guidance of Professor V Yu. Vize, and included shore excursions to historic sites. The icebreaker also had on board Umberto Nobile, who had piloted the *Norge* in 1926 and the ill-fated *Italia* North Pole flight in 1928. He was advising the Russians on airship design and construction.

The *Graf Zeppelin* made an unusual sea landing using inflatable pontoons at Hooker Island in Franz Josef Land, and sacks of mail were exchanged (philatelists had contributed to the cost of the flight). However, the landing lasted less than an hour because the airship was drifting towards an ice floe and had to take off for safety.

Intourist had started promoting Arctic cruises on the *Malygin* in 1930 with box advertisements in the English press. The length of cruise wasn't given, but they started in Archangel and called at Franz Josef Land, Rudolf Island and Novaya Zemlya from £122.

⬆ *Kapitan Khlebnikov.* (Courtesy Quark Expedition)

The first cruise by a Western company was reportedly organised by Aurora Expeditions in 2011 with the *Akademik Shokalskiy*[3] between Murmansk and Anadyr. The company apparently arranged a follow-up cruise in 2012, but this is not recorded in the NSR traffic report. In 2014, the *Kapitan Khlebnikov* is reported to have undertaken back-to-back cruises, while the *Hanseatic* undertook a single cruise. Passenger numbers were not given. In 2015, the *Bremen* sailed from Murmansk to Provideniya with 137 passengers, while in 2016, the *Kapitan Khlebnikov* sailed from Anadyr to Murmansk with 120 passengers and the *Hanseatic* sailed in the opposite direction with 126 on board. The NSR traffic report does not give any passenger traffic for 2017, but it is separately reported that the *Akademik Shokalskiy* undertook a transit from Anadyr to Murmansk as well as a return voyage.

Wildlife

The northern shores of Russia are relatively shallow and have many major rivers, deltas and estuaries. There are also many offshore islands that are ideal for Arctic seabirds such as ivory, Sabine's and Ross's gulls and many marine species. Polar bears are found on Wrangel Island and Franz Josef Land is a major denning area. Walrus are frequently to be seen, as are other seals. As with the Canadian Arctic, bowhead and beluga whales as well as narwhal can be found.

While Franz Josef Land is seen as an attractive expedition cruise destination, access can be uncertain. In 2019, Hurtigruten approvals for two prearranged cruises were cancelled at the last minute due to purported Russian military exercises. In October 2019, it was announced that consideration is being given to a special customs zone for the islands with a checkpoint at Alexandria Island, so that ships do not have to clear at Murmansk. A new tourist facility has been built on Guker Island, and reportedly inaugurated by the *Silver Explorer* on its 2019 Northern Sea Route transit.

4

OPERATORS

The following lists for Arctic and Antarctic operators are taken from cruise resource material available in 2017 and 2018 and some operators and ships have changed during 2019.[1] The reader should be aware that many expedition operators might only charter[2] the ship that they use (that is, they pay the owner an amount for the ship and the operating crew), although they may embark their own staff and guides. This is why some ships appear more than once in the lists. Also, some companies advertise polar cruises, but simply book groups onto selected ships. These companies are not listed.

While some expedition operators will offer both Arctic and Antarctic programmes, many focus on a single location. Also, the Arctic is a massive region and some companies only offer cruises to a particular destination. By comparison, cruises to the Antarctic are almost all to the Antarctic Peninsula, a comparatively small region compared with the size of the continent.

Major cruise companies operating large ships are excluded. These companies usually offer a conventional itinerary with calls at ports where the ship can be docked as they are not set up for tendering. By comparison, an expedition cruise vessel may only use a dock for turnaround, and all other places on the itinerary are anchorages where guests can be safely ferried ashore by Zodiac for wildlife observation, scenic hiking or visits to remote historic sites.

Also excluded are operators of yachts and mega yachts, typically twenty-five passengers or fewer. In 2019 there were seventeen providing Antarctic cruises. It is not known how many operate in the Arctic region.

Arctic

Company	Ship(s)
Adventure Canada	*Clipper Adventurer, Ocean Endeavour*
Aurora Expeditions	*Polar Pioneer*
G Adventures	*Expedition*
Hapag Lloyd	*Bremen, Hanseatic*
Hurtigruten	*Fram, Spitsbergen*
Iceland Pro[3]	*Ocean Diamond*
Lindblad Expeditions	*National Geographic Explorer*

Oceanwide Expeditions	*Hondius, Plancius, Ortelius, Nordlicht*
OneOcean Expeditions	*Akademik Ioffe, Akademic Sergiy Vavilov*
Peregrine Expeditions	*Ocean Adventurer*
Plantours Kreuzfarhten	*Hamburg*
Polar Quest[4]	*Quest*
Ponant	*Le Boreal, Le Soleal*
Poseidon Expeditions	*Sea Spirit*
Quark (North Pole Cruises)	*50 let Pobedy*
Quark	*Ocean Adventurer, Ocean Nova*
Silversea Cruises	*Silver Cloud, Silver Explorer*

Antarctic

Company	Ship(s)
Abercrombie and Kent	*Le Lyrial*
Albatros Travel	*Ocean Atlantic*
Antarpply Expeditions	*Ushuaia*
Antarctica XXI SA	*Ocean Nova*
Aurora Expeditions	*Polar Pioneer*
Bark Europa	*Europa*
G Adventures	*Expedition*
Grand Circle Corporation	*Corinthian*
Hapag Lloyd	*Bremen, Hanseatic*
Heritage Expeditions	*Akademik Shokalskiy, Spirit of Enderby*
Hurtigruten	*Fram, Midnatsol*
Lindblad Expeditions	*National Geographic Explorer, National Geographic Orion*
Noble Caledonia	*Island Sky*
OneOcean Expeditions	*Akademik Ioffe, Akademic Sergiy Vavilov*
Oceanwide Expeditions	*Ortelius, Plancius*
Plantours Kreuzfarhten	*Hamburg*
Ponant	*Le Boreal, Le Lyrial, Le Soleal*
Polar Latitudes	*Hebridean Sky, Island Sky*
Quark Expeditions	*Island Sky, Ocean Diamond, Ocean Endeavour, Ocean Adventurer*
Poseidon Expeditions	*Sea Spirit*
Seabourn Cruise Lines	*Seabourne Quest*
Silversea Cruises	*Silver Cloud, Silver Explorer*
Zegrahm Expeditions	*Island Sky*

5

SAFETY

Cruise Ship Incidents in Polar Waters[1]

Commentators tend to make a big deal of the 2007 sinking of the *Explorer* in Antarctica when discussing safety of passenger ships in polar regions. However, an incident of much greater importance was the wrecking of the Argentine supply/tourist ship *Bahia Paraiso* when it grounded in January 1989. Not only did eighty-one passengers plus 234 Argentine military personnel and crew need to be evacuated, but the ship released an estimated $600m^3$ of petroleum products that had a long-term impact on wildlife in the vicinity. There have been other oil pollution reports in polar waters, but fortunately most have been minor, usually the result of oil leakage from stern tube bearings after propeller damage when contacting rocks, or the sea bottom. There was a diesel spill after a grounding by the *Nordkapp* in 2007.

Apart from these two incidents in the Antarctic, there have been no other wrecks of cruise ships in polar waters. The yacht *Berserk* sank in a storm in the Ross Sea in 2011 with the loss of three crew. On the whole, and considering that the ships go to out of the way locations in regions that are not well charted, and there is probably a desire to get as close to a landing beach as possible to minimise the Zodiac run, the record is actually very good. The Appendices provide a list of reported incidents from 1891 to date, but the following table offers an overview of incidents and cruise activity. Because of data quality, the Antarctic is the primary focus; Arctic incidents are provided solely for comparison as the total number of cruises into all north polar regions is not known with any reliability. This is partly because cruises may incorporate more than one polar destination. Incident data for the current five-year period is incomplete as only one Antarctic incident has been reported in the media. Two Arctic incidents in 2018 were widely reported, as was the 2019 *Viking Sky* incident.

In this table, a major incident is one where the ship is wrecked, or the damage is of such severity that passengers have to be rescued, or the cruise is frustrated and the ship has to return to port for repairs. Future cruises may, or may not, be affected. A minor incident is one where the ship was able to continue its itinerary, albeit with some delay. These include two known medical emergencies, both in the Antarctic.

Polar Cruise Ship Activity and Incidents

Period	Antarctic Cruises	Antarctic Major	Antarctic Minor	Arctic Major	Arctic Minor
1980–84	40*	0	0	0	0
1985–89	87	1	1	1	0
1990–94	233	0	3	0	1
1995–99	518	0	4	2	4
2000–04	707	1	6	1	0
2005–09	991	9	1	3	3
2010–14	801	4	2	1	2
2015–18	1,270	1	0	2	0

*author's estimate.

Ice Class

In the early years of polar navigation, ships were reinforced based on the whims of the owner and the advice of the shipyard. Typically, they were built to withstand crushing, rather than having features specific to ice breaking. Masters avoided the ice whenever they could, and it is interesting to note that the Hudson's Bay Company that sailed into Arctic waters for more than 300 years lost more ships to stranding on reefs, or as a result of foul weather, than through collisions with ice.[2] To prevent crushing, cargo ships had 'ice beams' that were positioned inside the holds to strengthen the ship. Even the *Nascopie*, although a strongly built iron-hulled ship, carried eighty-two portable ice beams that weighed 100 tons.

The ships that were seen as being suitable for ice navigation were often those from the Newfoundland sealing fleet; the *Panther*, for example, had an iron prow as well as a thick hull. One ship, Job Brothers' *Neptune*, reportedly had 8ft of wood in its bow area. A ship used in Spitsbergen sailings was reputedly sheathed with Australian iron bark, which, being exceptionally strong, was sometimes used to sheath boats heading into Arctic waters.

The Finns were the first to introduce ice class rules, in 1890, mainly for passenger ships operating in the winter season. The first rules that incorporated a fee structure for icebreaker assistance came into force in 1920, but the commonly referred to Baltic rules were not introduced until 1932. To make the rules more attractive ships received a discount on ice fees depending on their ice class. These rules had classes 1A, 1B and 1C, but 1A Super wasn't introduced until 1965. The initial 1A Super designation required costly ship features, and was not popular; requirements were reworked to make them more economic in 1971, when Finland and Sweden joined forces in introducing the Finnish Swedish rules. These new rules amended the old percentage on open water requirements to a more scientific basis, and power requirements were increased to ensure that ships could keep station in convoy with an icebreaker. Changes were made again in 1985 and the current rules date from 2010.

One of the problems with high ice class ships is that a bow shape suitable for use in ice is not efficient in open water. Research by Kvaerner Masa[3] suggested that if a ship went astern in ice it could make its way more readily than going ahead, because the propeller provided hull lubrication. However, it needed the development of podded propulsion systems to make what has become known as the Double Acting principle workable. Today many cargo ships have reinforced sterns and podded[4] propulsion for navigation in ice.

The biggest change in polar navigation came on 1 January 2017 when new ships needed to comply with the International Maritime Organisation Polar Code. This code, which was an initiative of Canada based on experience in Arctic waters, introduces new ice classes for ships and rules for operation in polar waters.

Until the Polar Code came into effect most ships designed to work in ice-infested waters complied with Finnish/Swedish regulations, which were generally adopted by the international classification societies. Canada's Arctic Shipping Pollution Prevention Regulations had some slightly different classes, but these could be related back to the Finnish Swedish rules except for ships with ice strengthening greater than 1A Super.

Ice Class Comparisons

According to Notations Used by Authorities[5] and Commonly Quoted by Expedition Cruise Companies

Authority	Lowest	>	>	>	Highest
Finnish/Swedish	1D	1C	1B	1A	1A Super
Bureau Veritas	1D	1C	1B	1A	1A Super
Det Norske Veritas	Ice C	Ice 1C	Ice 1B	Ice 1A	Ice 1A*
Germanischer Lloyd	E	E1	E2	E3	E4
Lloyd's Register	1D	1C	1B	1A	1AS
Russian Register[6]	L4	L3	L2	L1	UL

All of these notations now come under Category C of the Polar Code.

New ships intended for polar cruising are mainly being built to a PC6 Designation, which is roughly equivalent to the old 1A Super. The new Lindblad ships are being built to the higher designation of PC5, which permits year-round operation in polar waters with medium first-year ice that may have old ice inclusions.[7] The lower PC6 designation is only suitable for summer/autumn operation in medium first-year ice. However, most operators take ships into polar waters during the northern or southern hemisphere summer when ice is not usually present. Ponant's *Le Commandant Charcot* will have a PC2 designation, making it a true icebreaker.

6

REGULATIONS

All the destinations described in this book have regulations of some sort designed to control access to primary areas of interest. Some, but not all, also charge fees either on a per capita or a ship size basis, or both. There are two associations that provide guidance to their members as to protocols in polar areas. These are AECO, the Association of Arctic Expedition Cruise Operators in the north, and IAATO, the International Association of Antarctic Tour Operators in the south.

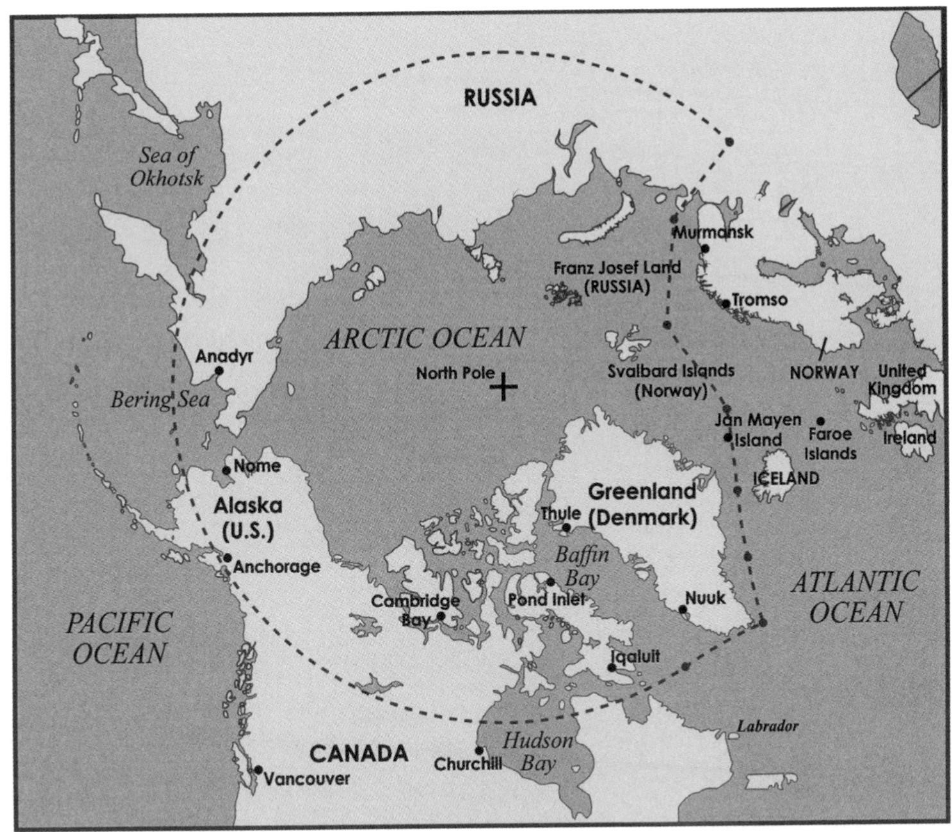

⬆ Northern boundary of the Polar Code.

The overarching regulation for all cruise ships in polar waters is now the International Maritime Organisation (IMO) Polar Code. The Code covers all water south of 60°S, and waters designated as shown in the map above in the north polar region. As will be seen, although generally considered polar destinations as they are north of 60°N, Iceland and the Faroe Islands are south of the limits. Much of the Norwegian coast is also north of 60°N, but outside the Polar Code region.

As of 1 January 2017, new ships needed to comply with the code, while existing ships were included after 1 January 2018, although compliance was not required until their first survey[1] after this date. All ships needed to meet Manning and Training requirements as of 1 July 2018. This latter requirement is key, as skill sets for managing a ship in first-year ice, such as the Baltic in winter, are not the same as managing a ship in places where multi-year ice may be present.[2] Also, training establishments must be able to provide appropriate courses, and the Nautical Institute in the UK is taking a lead in certifying organisations that offer training courses for seafarers to Polar Code standards.

Under the Polar Code, ships are divided into three categories. Category A includes ice classes[3] PC1 to PC5. Ponant's *Le Commandant Charcot* has a PC2 rating and will be the highest ice-classed cruise ship.

The next group is Category B, covering ships with PC6 and PC7 designation. These are ships suitable for summer/autumn operation in medium first-year ice in which there may be some older ice. Most new polar expedition ships are being built to PC6 requirements.

Category C ships include all those that have a Baltic Ice class down to unstrengthened vessels. Depending on their class, they can still operate in first-year ice but are considered only suitable for operation in open water in which different amounts of ice are present. For example, the Baltic Ice 1A, or Canada class B vessels, are considered suitable to navigate in waters with no more than 3/10ths ice present.

There are several IMO conventions that govern all ships, and particularly the design, construction and operation of cruise ships. The main ones are Safety of Life at Sea, known as SOLAS, Marine Pollution (MARPOL) and Standards of Training, Certification and Watchkeeping for Seafarers (STCW). The loss of the ferry *Estonia* in 1994 resulted in new subdivision and stability requirements being introduced for passenger ships with a capacity in excess of 400 berthed passengers. The *Costa Concordia* grounding and subsequent chaotic rescue of passengers and crew resulted in requirements that passengers be mustered prior to departure instead of the previous lax rule of 'within twenty-four hours'. This incident has also resulted in further tightening of subdivision and stability requirements, as of 1 January 2020, to try and ensure that ships are able to remain afloat long enough for safe evacuation. There is a safe return to port provision that was introduced by the IMO as of 1 July 2010 that applied to ships of 120m and greater.

A somewhat contentious component of the Polar Code is that life-saving equipment has to provide for a five-day survival period after an incident. However, independent studies of personal survivability have strongly suggested that, even with the best equipment and proper attention to survival suits, five days is not achievable.

As a part of MARPOL, on 1 August 2011 IMO introduced a ban on burning and carrying heavy fuel south of 60°S. This requirement hit larger cruise ships, as smaller expedition-style cruise ships tended to use Marine Diesel Oil (MDO), or Marine Gas Oil (MGO) for ship propulsion and power generation. The effect was quite noticeable in the cruise-only passenger numbers, which dropped from 15,700 in the 2009/10 season to 4,872 in 2011/12. Numbers stayed relatively low at +/-9,000 passengers until the 2017/18 season, when they increased to 14,440. While this suggests that cruise companies had found a way to manage the ship fuel restriction, it also reflects the response of cruise companies to ongoing efforts by the IMO to reduce worldwide sulphur dioxide emissions from ships.

Annex VI of MARPOL required ships to reduce the sulphur content of fuels (or equivalent in engine exhausts) from 4.5 per cent to 3.5 per cent in 2012, but then there has to be a major reduction to 0.5 per cent by 1 January 2020. An option taken by many cargo ship operators has been to install exhaust gas scrubbers to reduce sulphur in their engine emissions. This is not an easy solution for cruise ships because of the size and weight of the scrubbers, and many have opted instead to move to low-sulphur fuels such as MDO and MGO, or in some cases LNG.

There are also a number of, mainly coastal, Emission Control Areas that have introduced more stringent sulphur emission requirements. As cruise ships tend to spend more time in these areas than cargo ships, and it is easier to pass on the extra fuel cost through passenger fares, many cruise ships have been converted[4] to burn low sulphur fuels.

IAATO

The Antarctic Treaty[5] of June 1961 designated the continent as a 'natural resource dedicated to peace and science'. It has provisions similar to those found in the Svalbard Treaty of 1920 and contains an extensive Environmental Protocol to ensure protection of the Antarctic environment together with associated ecosystems. IAATO was established in 1991 by the seven tour operators active at the time to ensure that visits to Antarctica recognised and protected the unique nature of the region. Today there are 115 members. The original guidelines adopted by IAATO were as follows:

- To be knowledgeable of and abide by the Antarctic Conservation Act of 1978;
- To not enter areas designated as being of specific scientific interest or that need special protection;
- To operate only with qualified expedition staff of which at least 75 per cent must have previous Antarctic experience;
- To hire only Zodiac drivers with experience in polar regions (essential to safe operations);
- To educate passengers and crew and enforce the members' self-imposed Antarctica Visitor Guidelines;
- To assign one qualified naturalist staff member to accompany and supervise each group of maximum 20–25 passengers ashore;
- To cooperate with science stations and to not disturb sites of science research;
- To limit the number of passengers ashore;
- To follow the international MARPOL treaty guidelines regarding marine pollution.

The key current requirements for IAATO members landing passengers at Antarctic sites are:

- Passengers must be briefed regarding protocols at the site before landing
- Only one ship at a landing site at any one time
- No more than 100 passengers ashore at any time
- The guide to passenger ratio should be 1:20 or better
- No ships with over 500 passengers to undertake landings

During the IAATO 2019 Annual General Meeting, members unanimously agreed to a whale protection measure, whereby ships will limit speeds to 10 knots in certain areas and at specific times. Alternatively they will introduce whale strike mitigation measures including extra watch persons on the bridge. The measures will come into effect prior to the 2019/20 season. In order to avoid overcrowding and delays, scheduling has been undertaken by members since the early 2000s. In response to the extraordinary growth in cruise ship numbers this activity is being materially updated.

Members of the organisation also undertake pre- and post-visit activity reporting, and ensure Antarctic experience of staff and that they have contingency and emergency medical plans in place. Visitor guidelines in multiple languages are available on the internet.

ATCP

The Antarctic Treaties Consultative Parties is a separate organisation that represents the consultative parties to the Antarctic Treaty, and is the ultimate decision-maker regarding continental governance. A major activity is administering the CCAMLR, or the Convention on the Conservation of Antarctic Marine Living Resources. Of relevance to shipborne visits is an excellent series of thirty-five site-specific guidelines and descriptions developed with the assistance of IAATO. These can be found on the ATCP website, but are not obvious. Follow this guide to find them:

1. Go to this link: ats.aq/devAS/Ats/VisitorSiteGuidelines?lang=e
3. Click on Select Guideline
4. A pulldown list of sites will appear
5. Click on the one desired, e.g. Half Moon Island
6. Click on open
7. A description of the site will appear, including maps and photographs

CCAMLR

The Convention on the Conservation of Antarctic Marine Living Resources does not relate to tourism and cruise ship visits per se, but it is the main international mechanism for managing the fishery of the southern ocean, and through that governance ensuring the survival of penguins, seals, whales and avian life south of 60°S.

Prior to the entry into force of the convention in 1980, there was a virtual free-for-all in the regional fishery. As a consequence, krill[6] stocks were depleted (the 1981/82 krill take was 535,253 tonnes) and two types of southern fish, marbled rock cod and mackerel icefish, were effectively fished out. A benefit to fishery control was the collapse of the Soviet Union at the end of the 1980s as it had been the major operator of factory trawlers in the Southern Ocean. Today, the annual catch is managed on a science basis using extensive modelling to ensure adequate young krill for population reproduction as well as providing adequate resources for regional predator species. Catch monitoring also applies to fin fish and the most important is the Patagonian toothfish (aka Chilean sea bass).

The latest figure for krill catch was 2017 at close to 300,000 tonnes, although it had been much lower during the previous five years. Norway has consistently taken the highest quantity with more than 50 per cent of total catch. The fin fish catch in 2017 was about 12,000 tonnes, but there is an extensive illegal, unreported and unregulated (IUU) fishery in the region that was estimated at six times the regulated catch in the 1990s. However, proactive measures by the CCAMLR have materially reduced the

IUU fishery from 2003 onwards, although toothfish stocks in some areas are seriously depleted. At the end of its 2019 Annual Meeting, the CCAMLR was unable to obtain approval for either an Antarctic marine park, or a marine protected area for the Weddel Sea and Antarctic Peninsula. Both have been mooted for many years.

AECO

The Arctic does not have a treaty system similar to the Antarctic, although individual countries have their own requirements for cruise ships. AECO was founded in 2003 to represent the views of expedition cruise ship operators and promote environmentally responsible tourism in the Arctic. Its mandate covers all destinations north of 60°N. In many ways its approach is the same as IAATO – to ensure that members adhere to best practices, but with the added layer of protocols regarding interaction with indigenous peoples. A unique activity is an annual desktop search and rescue (SAR) exercise. The 2019 edition was in Reykjavik and attended by seventeen AECO members and SAR entities from Canada, Iceland, Greenland, Faroe Islands, Svalbard, mainland Norway and Sweden.

The organisation operates a voluntary scheduling system to avoid overcrowding, and has thirty full and five provisional members plus associates and affiliates. The current eight guidelines, together with an animated visitor guideline, are available on the internet. AECO members have undertaken not to burn heavy fuel in Arctic waters and also to minimise plastic waste.

National Regulations

Canada

There is an unbelievably complex process required for cruise ships to travel in the Canadian Arctic. Depending on the type of cruise and itinerary there could be as many as thirty-three permits needed.[7] To assist planning, Transport Canada has issued *Guidelines for Passenger Vessels Operating in the Canadian Arctic (TP13670)*. This comprehensive document indicates that ships must commence the approval process at least twenty-four months prior to the planned cruise. Requirements are slightly simpler if the ship is operated foreign to foreign, or foreign to Canada and vice versa; Canada to Canada cruises come under cabotage regulations and require additional permitting, as well as fees that are to be paid depending on the size and value of the ship and the duration of the Arctic programme.

Appendix 3 of the Transport Canada guidelines summarises requirements by jurisdiction, but does not include Nunavik. Any provincial requirements for Quebec, Ontario or Manitoba, which are of an Arctic nature, but south of 60°N, are not included either. The appendix shows that some relatively minor fees are payable for access to certain locations. Also, some applications need to be made in Inuktitut as well as English.

Greenland

The primary area of regulation in Greenland relates to the North-East Greenland National Park, which extends up the east coast from Scoresby Sound to the far north. The National Park was established in 1974, expanded in 1988 and covers 972,000 sq km. It is reputed to have about 40 per cent of the world's musk ox population. Unless climate change opens up the island's east coast in a significant way, this is unlikely to affect cruise ships except if visiting Scoresby Sound for shore excursions.

The most likely place to be visited by expedition cruise ships is the Ilulissat Icefjord World Heritage Site on the western side of Greenland, and a permit is required from the Ministry of Domestic Affairs. Compared to Canada, cruising in Greenland has been characterised by one operator as needing only five permits versus fifty for Canada and three for Norway.

Ships are required to pay a fee based on gross register tons and length of time in the coastal waters. Vessels carrying more than 250 passengers must also use the pilotage service unless it can be demonstrated that the bridge team has both the qualifications and experience for navigation in Greenland waters. Vessels need to report to GREENPOS every six hours.

A downloadable document *Cover Letter for Cruise Vessels* relates primarily to overland expeditions including, as with Svalbard regulations, that search and rescue insurance must be carried. The document does imply that application for a cruise itinerary should commence twelve weeks prior to arrival.

Faroe Islands

There are no specific regulations that relate to cruise ships other than typical requirements for ship arrival at an international port. Pilotage is compulsory if using a dock at Tórshavn, but not if the ship is anchoring. Tugs are available, but not compulsory.

Iceland

As with the Faroe Islands, regulations at Reykjavik are similar to any international port activity. Pilotage is compulsory for ships over 60m length.

Svalbard Islands

Regulations relate primarily to the nature reserve of Nordaustlandet and the islands to the east and south, including Bjørnøya. Tour operators are required to carry insurance to cover search and rescue as well as medical evacuation. The level is fixed by the governor and may be waived. The Norwegian Maritime Authority has introduced new safety regulations for the Svalbard Islands and surrounding waters from 1 January 2020. Apparently these will include that all people in open tenders wear full body suits with thermal protection and flotation devices. Also, that all vessels must comply with the Polar Code and SOLAS. Vessels that do not currently comply with the Code will have a five-year phase-in period. Most of the requirements will not affect existing expedition cruise ships as they already comply.[8]

Antarctic and South Shetland Islands

Tourism in the Antarctic region, and this includes South Shetland Islands, is governed by provisions laid out in the Antarctic Treaty System. Measures relating to flora and fauna were adopted in 1964. Specific conventions adopted in 1972 and 1980 protect seals and living resources. This latter provision affords protection to all sea life but especially krill, which is critical for the survival of all species dependent on the ocean.

South Georgia and South Sandwich Islands

South Georgia has strict biosecurity requirements in place and a number of places are off limits for landings. These include all whaling stations other than Grytviken. A list of permitted landing places is provided and some of these are identified on the South Georgia map.

Non-IAATO passenger ships are only permitted to visit under exceptional circumstances. Fees are charged based on vessel NRT,[9] number of passengers and length of stay. The booklet *Visiting South Georgia* (available online) contains comprehensive information on access and visit guidelines.

Falkland Islands

There is considerable concern regarding biosecurity and inadvertent importation of foreign materials. Cruise ships are required to ensure that passengers disembarking have clean footwear and that any bags do not carry foreign material. Harbour dues are payable on a ship's NRT depending on time in port. A passenger tax is charged that depends on whether a ship has called at a privately owned island and paid the owner for landing privileges. For example, if a 200-passenger capacity ship only called at Stanley, fees would be about £6,000, but if the ship had visited at least one island, the fees would be about £2,500 plus any fee paid to the island owner.

APPENDIX 1

PAST AND PRESENT POLAR CRUISE SHIPS

Shipping Companies and Ships on Polar Cruises Before the First World War (known ships and dates; not an exhaustive list)

Shipping Companies	**Flag**	**Ships Employed**	**Years Active**[1]
Albion Steamship Co.	Br	*Midnight Sun*	1888 onwards
Anchor Line	Br	*City of Rome*	1898
Cie Generale Transatlantique	Fr	*Ile-de-France*	1906, 1910
Berganske D/S	No	*Neptun, Vega*	1906–14
Co-Operative Cruising Company	Br	*Argonaut*	1895–1908
Dominion Line	Br	*Canada*	1898
Hamburg-Amerika Line	Ge	*Columbia, Auguste Victoria, Meteor, Koenig Wilhelm II, Blucher, Oceana, Cincinnati, Prinzessin Victoria Luise, Victoria Luise, Kronprincessin Cecile, Furst Bismark, Moltke*	1893–1914
Henderson Bros	Br	*Victoria*	1888 onwards
Nordenfjeldske D/S	No	*Kong Harald*	1908–14
Nordeutscher Lloyd[2]	Ge	*Grosser Kurfurst, Prinz Friedrich Wilhelm*	1908, 1910–13
North of Scotland, Orkney and Shetland Shipping Company	Br	*St Rognvald, St Sunniva*	1886–1908
Ocean Steam Yachting Company	Br	*Ceylon*	1884–96
Orient Steam Navigation	Br	*Lusitania, Mexico, Ophir, Garonne, Chimborazo, Cuzco*	1890–1904
Österreichischer Lloyd	Ge	*Thalia*	1909, 1910, 1913

Peninsula & Oriental Steam Navigation Co.	Br	*Vectis*[3]	1904–13
Polytechnic Touring Association	Br	*Ceylon*	1896–?
The Royal Mail Steam Packet Company	Br	*Avon, Arcadian*	1910–14
The Viking Cruise Company	Br	*The Viking*[4]	1908–14
Vesteralen D/S	No	*Andenaes, Lofoten*	1896–99 1911–14
Wilson Line	Br	*Domino et al*	1885–91
Independent Charterers			
Henry Clodius		*Pallas*	1881
Thomas Cook		*President Christie*	1875
Wilhelm and Alex Bade		*Amely, Admiral, Danzig, Stettin, Erling Jarle, Kong Harald, Herthe, Oihanna, Thalia, Andenaes*	1891–1907

Details of Selected Ships Active in Polar Cruising Pre-First World War

Ship	Year Built	Year Upg. or Cvtd	GRT	Passengers 1st, 2nd, 3rd	Crew	Dimensions metres Length × Breadth
Auguste Victoria	1889		7,661	400, 120x-x580s		144.8 × 18.9
Avon	1907	1919	11,073	300, 140, 1,200s		163.1 × 19.0
Blucher	1902		12,334	333, 169, 1,200s	252	167.5 × 18.9
Ceylon	1858	1866 1881	2,012	160		93.3 × 12.47
Columbia[5]	1893	1899	7,241	220, 120, 800		146.3 × 17.0
Cuzco	1871	1886	3,918	70, 85		117.1 × 12.6
Ile de France	1882		3,358	214 total		106.7 × 12.0
Kaiser Wilhelm II	1907		9,410	337, 86, 580s	219	149.48 × 16.48
Kong Harald	1890	1892	955	70		63.95 × 9.02
Oceana[6]	1891	1905	7,859	nd		161.85 × 16.7
Oihonna	1898		1,076	nd		61 × 9.5
Meteor	1904		3,718	220		105.5 × 13.5
Moltke	1902		12,335	333x169x0x1,600	252	167.5 × 18.9
Pallas	1879		502	100?		49.07 × 7.38
Prinzessin Victoria Luise[7]	1900		4,409	192	161	124.2 × 15.9
St Sunniva	1887		960	110		71.9 × 9.2

Vectis	1881	1892, 1904	5,013	150		140.2 × 13.4
Victoria	1872		3,358	nd		109.76 × 12.2
Victoria Luise	1900	1911[8]	16,703	487	536	208.5 × 20.4

Upg. = Upgraded, Cvtd = Converted, s = Steerage, nd = No Data
Where a single passenger number is given, the ship was one class, often advertised as 1st Class.

Shipping Companies and Ships on Polar Cruises During the Interwar Years (known ships and dates, not an exhaustive list)

Shipping Companies	Flag	Ships Employed	Years Active
Bergen Line	No	*Meteor, Stella Polaris, Venus*	1922–39
Blue Star Line	Br	*Arandora Star*	1929–39
British India Line	Br	*Neuralia*	1932, 1934
Cie Generale Transatlantique	Fr	*Lafayette, Cuba*	1931, 1937
Canadian Pacific	Br	*Montcalm, Montclare, Montrose Melita*	1930–39
Cie. Mar Belge	Be	*Albertville* (charter)	1931
Cunard Line	Br	*Franconia, Carmania, Lancastria*	1923–39
Hamburg-Amerika Line	Ge	*Reliance, Milwaukee*	1927–39
Hamburg South America Line	Ge	*Monte Cervantes, Monte Rosa*	1928–34
Kraft durch Freude	Ge	*Der Deutsche, Monte Sarmiento, Oceana, Robert Ley, Sierra Cordoba, Stuttgart, Wilhelm Gutsloff, Monte Rosa*	1934–39
Lamport and Holt	Br	*Vandyck, Voltaire*	
Nordenfjeldske D/S	No	*Prins Olaf*	1925–35
Nordeutscher Lloyd[9]	Ge	*Munchen, General von Steuben*	1925–39
Orient Lines	Br	*Orion, Orama, Orontes, Otranto, Orduna, Orford*	1929–39
P&O	Br	*Viceroy of India, Ranchi, Starthnaver, Strathaird*	1929–39
Royal Mail Line	Br	*Asturias, Atlantis, Avon*	1930–39
Swedish America Line	Sw	*Kungsholm*	1931
Wilson Line	Br	*Calypso, City of Nagpur, Eskimo*	1935–39
Northern Canada			
Alberta and Arctic Transportation Company	Br	*Distributor*	1922–24
Hudson's Bay Company	Br	*Mackenzie River, Distributor*	1922–41

Canadian Eastern Arctic			
Hudson's Bay Company	Br	*Nascopie*	1933–41
Antarctic			
British Government	No	*Fleurus* (charter)	1924–33
Argentine Government	Ar	*Pampa*	1933, 1937

Details of Selected Ships Active in Polar Cruising During the Interwar Years

Ship	Year Built	Year Upg. or Cvtd	GRT	Passengers 1st, 2nd, 3rd	Crew	Dimensions metres Length × Breadth
Arandora Star	1927	1929 1935	14,694	354		156.1 × 20.8
Asturias	1926		22,071	410, 232, 768		199.8 × 23.9
Asturias		1934	22,048	330, 220, 768		203.0 × 23.9
City of Nagpur	1922	1938	10,138	226, 92	190	149.5 × 18.0
Franconia[10]	1923	1930	20,158	221, 356, 1,266	414	190.0 × 22.3
Gelria[11]	1913	1928	13,868	233, 350, 704	330	170.7 × 20.0
General von Steuben[12]	1922	1930 1935	14,690	214, 358, 221 484 1st Class	356	167.8 × 19.8
Kungsholm	1928	1932	20,223	115, 490, 970	340	185.6 × 23.8
Lafayette[13]	1915	1919	12,220	583, 388, 108		171.6 × 19.5
Milwaukee[14]	1929	1935	16,699	270, 259, 428	335	175.1 × 22.1
Montclare[15]	1922	1928	16,314	542, 1,268	390	175.3 × 21.4
Monte Sarmiento[16]	1924		13,625	1,328, 1,142	280	159.7 × 20.1
Munchen	1922		13,325	171, 350, 558	356	167.8 × 19.8
Otranto[17]	1925	1933	20,032	572x0x1,114		200.6 × 22.9
Ranchi	1925	1931	16,738	308, 282	380	173.7 × 21.7
Reliance	1915	1922	19,582	290, 320, 400	480	187.4 × 21.9
Reliance		1934		500 1st Class		187.4 × 21.9
Reliance		1937	19,618	633, 186		187.4 × 21.9
Robert Ley	1939		27,288	1,774t	435	203.8 × 24.0
Stella Polaris	1927		5,020	32, 166	130	127.1 × 15.5
Venus	1931		5,406	182, 52		121.5 × 16.5
Viceroy of India	1929		19,648	415, 258	420	186.5 × 23.2
Wilhelm Gutsloff	1938		25,484	1,464t	426	208.5 × 23.6

Upg. = Upgrade or Refit, Cvtd = Converted, t = Tourist Class
Where a single passenger number is given, the ship was one class, often advertised as 1st Class, but sometimes Tourist, or Cabin class.

Shipping Companies and Ships on Polar Cruises During the Post-War Period (known ships and dates, not an exhaustive list and not after 1989)

Shipping Companies	Flag	Ships Employed	Years Active
Argentine Government	Ar	*Libertad, Rio Tunyan, Regina Prima*	1958–72
Chandris Lines	Gr	*Britanis*	1970–82
Chilean Government	Ch	*Navarino*	1959
Cie. Gen. Transatlantique	Fr	*France*	1960
Costa Armatori	It	*Enrico C, Eugenio C*	1974–76
Cunard Lines	Br	*Caronia*	1951–68
FANU	Ar	*Yapeyu*	1959
German Atlantic Line	Ge	*Hanseatic, Hamburg*	1967–73
Hapag-Lloyd	Ge	*Ariadne*	1958–60
Holland America Line	Ne	*Rotterdam*	1960
Lindblad Expeditions	CHA	*Lapataia, Navarino, Aquiles, Magga Dan*	1967–69
Lindblad Expeditions	No	*Lindblad Explorer*	1970–85
Nordeutscher Lloyd	Ge	*Berlin, Bremen*	1959–71
P&O	Br	*Canberra*	?
Society Expeditions	Pa	*World Discoverer*	1978–2000
Peter Dielmann	Ge	*Nordbrise*	?
Swedish Lloyd	Sw	*Gripsholm*	1957–
Ybarra & Company	Sp	*Cabo san Roque, Cabo san Vicente*	1973–75

CHA = Charters

Details of Selected Ships Active in Polar Cruising During the Post-War Period

Ship	Year Built	Year Upg. or Cvtd	GRT	Passengers 1st, 2nd, 3rd	Crew	Dimensions metres Length × Breadth
Ariadne	1951	1958	7,764	239	159	138.4 × 17.77
Berlin	1925	1949/55	18,600	98, 878t	nd	179.8 × 22.7
Bremen	1939	1959/66	32,336	216, 906t	540	212.4 × 26.8
Britanis	1931	1956/71	18,254	1,655	nd	192.6 × 24.2
Cabo san Roque	1957		14,491	241c, 582t	231	169.7 × 21.1
Cabo san Vicente	1959		14,569	241c, 582t	231	169.7 × 21.1
Canberra	1961		45,270	548, 1,650t	900	249.9 × 31.1

Caronia[18]	1948	1956/65	34,183	581, 351c	600	217.9 × 27.8
Enrico C	1951	1965	13,607	218, 980t[19]	nd	176.7 × 22.3
Europa	1953	1965	21,514	122, 721t	418	182.9 × 23.5
France	1962		66,348	407, 1,637t	1,200+	315.5 × 33.7
Gripsholm	1957		23,191	150, 692t	364	192.3 × 24.9
Hamburg	1969		22,022	652 one class	406	194.7 × 26.6
Hanseatic (1)	1930	1958	30,030	85, 1,167t	nd	205.2 × 25.5
Hanseatic (2)	1964	1964	25,388	148, 864	469	191.7 × 24.8
Libertad[20]	1950	1963/64	12,634	96 (400t)	145	161.5 × 21.7
Lindblad Explorer	1969	1972	2,398	104	54	76.2 × 14
Marco Polo	1965	many	22,080	848	356	176.28 × 23.55
Regina Prima	1939	1965	10,153	650 one class	nd	150.3 × 19.5
Rio Tunyan[21]	1951	1963/64	11,317	116 (372)	155	167.5 × 20.0
Rotterdam	1959		38,645	655, 801t	776	227.9 × 28.7
Yapeyu	1951		11,450	13, 740t	165	158.6 × 19.6

Upg. = Upgrade or Refit, Cvtd = Converted, c = Cabin Class, t = Tourist Class
Where a single passenger number is given, the ship was one class, often advertised as 1st Class, but sometimes Tourist, or Cabin class. Many post-war ships operated as two class only, first either tourist, or cabin class. Figure in brackets are author's estimates.

Large Soviet Passenger Vessels Used in Polar Cruising

Name	Other Names	Built	GRT	Pax	Crew	Dimensions metre Length × Breadth	Notes
Alexandr Pushkin	*Marco Polo*[22]	1965	22,080	848	356	176.28 × 23.55	Operating
Baltika		1940	7,494	437		135.7 × 18.34	Scrapped
Fedor Dostoevsky	*Astor*[23]	1987	20,704	650	300	176.25 × 22.6	Operating
Maxim Gorkiy	*Hamburg*	1968	25,022	788	340	194.72 × 26.57	Scrap 2004
Mikhail Kalnin[24]		1958	4,871	250?		122.15 × 16	Scrap 1994

Russian Research and Small Passenger Vessels used for Polar Expedition Cruising

Original Name	Other names	Built	GRT	Years Used
Akademik Ioffe		1989	6,450	1994–2017
Akademik Sergey Vavilov		1988	6,450	1993–2000, 2003–17
Akademik Boris Petrov		1984	2,318	1992, 96, 2000–08, 11, 13, 15, 16, 17
Akademik Shokalskiy		1982	1,764	1995–2008, 11, 13, 15, 16, 17
Akademik Shuleykin	*Polar Pioneer* (O)	1983	1,753	1997, 98, 99, 2001–17
Professor Khromov	*Spirit of Enderby*[25] (O)	1983	1,759	1995, 96, 97, 2006–17
Professor Multanovsky		1983	1,753	1995–2000
Professor Molchanov		1982	1,753	1992–2009
Aleksey Marysheev		1990	1,729	2005–08
Grigory Mikheev		1990	1,729	2000–08
Arnold Veymer	*Livonia*	1984	1,753	1991–96
Kapitan Dranitsyn		1980	12,919	1995, 96, 98, 99, 2000, 07
Kapitan Khlebnikov		1981	12,288	1992–2008, 10, 16
Alla Tarasova[26]	*Ocean Adventurer* (O)	1975	4,376	1994–2001, 04, 05, 06, 2008–17
Lyubov Orlova[27]		1976	4,251	2001, 04, 2006–10
Maria Yermalova[28]		1973	4,251	2001
Konstantin Chernenko	*Ocean Atlantic* (O)	1985	12,798	2017
Konstantin Simonov	*Ocean Endeavour* (O)	1982	12,907	2015, 16, 17
Maria Svetaeva	*Ortelius* (O)	1980	4,575	2005, 07, 08, 2010–17
Olga Sadoskaya		1977	4,250	1997
Antonina Nedzhanova		1978	4,250	1989

(O) Indicates ship is operating under this name at present.
Antarctic deployment by the second year of the season. Thus 1993/94 entered as '94.

Polar Expedition Cruise Ships Past and Present[29]

Name	Previous Name	Built	Refit	Gross	Dimensions LOA × B ×d	Pax[30]	Crew Staff	SR	Ice	Notes
Akademik Ioffe		1989	2002/11	6,450	117.17 × 18.2 × 5.9	92/ 110	46/65	48	1A	Withdrawn due to contract dispute
Akademik Sergey Vavilov		1988	2003/ 12/16	6,450	117.17 × 18.2 × 5.9	92/ 110	46/65	48	1A	Withdrawn due to contract dispute
Akademik Boris Petrov		1984		2,318	73.06 × 14.7 × 4.5	42	32		Y	Now Russian research
Akademik Shokalskiy		1982	1998	1,764	71.06 × 12.82 × 4.5	48/ 54	30	24	1D	
Aleksey Maryshev		1990	1998	1,729	64.9 × 12.8 × ?	46		23	1D	Laid up 2010
Alexander von Humboldt[31]	*Minerva*	1996	2012	12,892	133 × 203 × 5.8	350	160			Currently laid up
Antarctic Dream	*Piloto Pardo*	1959	1998/ 2004	2180	83 × 11.9 × 4.6	80	43		1A	Last position in Red Sea, September 2019
Bremen	*Frontier Spirit*	1990	93/06	6,752	111.5 × 17 × 4.8	164	94/100	82	E4	
Caledonian Sky	*Renaissance VI*	1991	01/12	4,200	90.6 × 15.3 × 4.2	114	74	57	Y	
Clipper Adventurer	*Alla Tarasova*	1975	Note[32]	5,750	100.58 × 16.3 × 4.72	122	84/72	61	1A	
Corinthian[33]	*Clelia II*	1990	2001/ 09/15	4,077	88.3 × 15.3 × 4.5	98	55		1D	
Europa		1911	1994	310	39.8 × 7.45 × 3.8	40	24			Three-mast barque

Abbreviations: LOA = Length over all, B = Beam, d = Draft; Pax = Passengers, lower berth: SR. = Staterooms; Ice, Y = Yes, but degree not known; E3, E4 = Germanischer Lloyd, 1A, 1B, 1C, 1D, Lloyds Class; L3, UL Russian Register; IB = Ice Breaker. N = No Ice Class

Name	Previous Name	Built	RF	Gross	Dimensions LOA × B ×d	Pax	Crew	SR	Ice	Notes
Expedition	*Ålandsfärjan*	1972	2008/09/15	6,334	105 × 18.9 × 4.71	134	69	67	1B	Built as a ferry
Explorer	*Lindblad Explorer*	1969		2,398	76.2 × 14 × 4.3	104	54		1A	Sank 2007 Antarctic
Fram		2006	2017	12,700	114 × 202 × 5.0	318	75	124	1B	
Fridjof Nansen		2019		20,889	140 × 23.6 × 5.3	530	151	265	PC6	
Greg Mortimer		2019		7,400	104.4 × 18.2 × 5.3	120	56	60	1A	
Grigoriy Mikheev		1990	1998	1,729	64.9 × 12.8 × ?	46		23	1D	
Hamburg	*cColumbus*	1997	2012	15,067	144.1 × 21.5 × 5.15	400	170	197	No	Great Lakes Fitted
HANSEATIC Inspiration		2019		15,540	138 × 22 × 5.75	199/230	170	120	PC6	Great Lakes Fitted
HANSEATIC Nature		2019		15,540	138 × 22 × 5.75	199/230	170	120	PC6	
Hebridean Sky[34]	*Sea Explorer*	1991	2014/ 2016	4,200	90.36 × 15.3 × 4.2	120	70	59	1C	
Hondius		2019		5,590	107.6 × 17.6 × 5.3	176	72	83	PC6	
Illiria		1962		3,745	103.8 × 15 × 5.02	209				Believe scrapped
Island Sky[35]		1992	2010/ 2014	4,200	90.36 × 15.3 × 4.2	120	70	59	1C	
Kapitan Dranitsyn		1980	1990	12,919	129.02 × 26.5 × 8.5	106	60	53	I/B	Charter only via Poseidon
Kapitan Khlebnikov[36]		1981	1992	12,288	129.1 × 26.4 × 8.5	108	70	54	I/B	
L'Austral		2009		10,700	142.1 × 18 × 4.8	264	136	132	1C	
Le Boreal		2009		10,700	142.1 × 18 × 4.8	264	136	132	1C	
Le Bougainville		2019		10,700	142.1 × 18 × 4.8	264	136	132	1C	
Le Champlain		2018		10,700	142.1 × 18 × 4.8	264	136	132	1C	

Name	Previous Name	Built	RF	Gross	Dimensions LOA × B ×d	Pax	Crew	SR	Ice	Notes
Le Dumont d'Urville		2019		10,700	142.1 × 18 × 4.8	264	136	132	1C	
Le Laperouse		2018		9,900	131 × 18 × 4.8	184	110	92	1C	
Le Levant		1998	2012	3,504	100 × 14 × 3.5	90	60	45	N	Now *Clio*
Le Lyrial		2015		10,700	142.1 × 18 × 4.8	264	140	132	1C	
Le Soleal		2013		10,700	142.1 × 18 × 4.8	264	136	132	1C	
Lindblad Explorer		1969		2,398	76.2 × 14 × 4.3	104	54		1A	Sank 2007
Livonia	*Arnold Veymer*	1984	1991	1,753	71.06 × 12.82 × 4.5	52	23	26	Y	Now HSwNS *Trosso*
Lyubov Orlova[37]		1976	2006	4,251	100.58 × 16.24 × 4.72	110	70	53	L3	Sank 2013
Magellan Explorer		2019		4,900	90.7 × 16.2 × 4.3	70/100	60		PC6	
Marco Polo	*Aleksandr Pushkin*	1965	Note[38]	22,080	176.3 × 23.6 × 8.2	848	356		1C	See text for history
Maria Yermalova		1973		4,251	100.58 × 16.3 × 4.72	122	72	61	1A	
Midnatsol		2003		16,140	135.7 × 21.6 × ?	500	109	278	1C	
Minerva		1996	2003/12	12,892	135.1 × 16.6	350	160		1D	Laid up
Nat. Geo. Endeavour	*Endeavour*	1966	1983, 2001	3,132	89.2 × 14 × ?	112	64	56	1C	Scrapped 2017
Nat. Geo. Explorer	*Midnatsol II*	1982	08/15	6,471	112 × 16.5 × 4.74	146	96	81	1A	
Nat. Geo. Orion	*Orion*	2003	2010	4,000	103 × 14.25 × 3.82	102	75	53	E3	
Ocean Atlantic	*Konstantin Chernenko*	1985	2010/16	12,798	137.61 × 21.01 × 5.6	198	140	99	1B	
Ocean Adventurer	*Sea Adventurer*	1975	Many	5,750	100.58 × 16.3 × 4.72	132	84/72	61	1A	
Ocean Diamond	*Le Diamant*	1974	86/11	8,282	124.19 × 16.03 ×	366		189	1D	

Name	Previous Name	Built	RF	Gross	Dimensions LOA × B ×d	Pax	Crew	SR	Ice	Notes
Ocean Endeavour[39]	*Kristina Katerina*	1982	See note	12,907	137.61 × 12.01 × 5.6	199	124	100	1B	
Ocean Nova	*Sarpik Ittuk*	1992	2002/06	2,183	72.8 × 11.1 × 3.7	96	38	38	1A	
Orion		2003		3,984	102.7 × 14.25 × 3.8	106	75	53	E3	
Ortelius	*Marina Svetaeva*	1980	2012/17	4,575	90.95 × 17.2 × 5.4	100/116	56	53	LI	
Plancius	HNLMS *Tydeman*	1976	2009	3,175	90.2 × 14.4 × 4.7	116	46	53	1D	
Polar Circle		1990		5,129	91 × 17.9 × 6.5	95		35	IB	Scrap 2016
Polar Pioneer	*Akademik Shuleykin*	1982	2000	1,753	71.06 × 12.82 × 4.5	54	23	26	1D	Now New Zealand coastal
Polar Prince[40]	*Humphrey Gilbert*	1958	2009	2,153	72.5 × 14.7 × 5				1B	Now charter research
Polar Star	*Njord*	1969	2000	4,998	86.5 × 21.2 × 6.2	96	35	46	1B	Possibly scrap
Polaris[41]	*Shearwater*	1968	2000/05	2,907	70.52 × 15.54 × 4.2	76	36	38	1A	Now internal Russian service
Prince Albert II	*World Discoverer*[42]	1989	2008	6,130	108 × 15.6 × 4.38	132	111	66	1A	
Professor Multanovskiy		1983	1990/1996	1,753	71.06 × 12.82 × 4.5	48/52	30	24	1D	Now Russian research
Professor Molchanov		1982	1990/1996	1,753	71.06 × 12.82 × 4.5	48/52	30	24	1D	
Quest	*Sea Endurance*	1992	05/18	1,211	49.65 × 11.1 × 3.4	53		26	1B	
RCGS Resolute	*Hanseatic*	1993	1997/09/11/15	8,378	122.8 × 18 × 4.9	184	125	92	E4	
Rembrandt van Rijn	*Enno Doedens Star*	1924	1933/51/93	307	44.83 × 6.65 × 2.8	33	12		?	Three-mast schooner

Name	Previous Name	Built	RF	Gross	Dimensions LOA × B ×d	Pax	Crew	SR	Ice	Notes
Roald Amundsen		2019		20,889	140x23.6x5.3	530	151	265	PC6	
Scenic Eclipse		2019		16,500	166 × 22	228	182	114	PC6	
Sea Adventurer	*Clipper Adventurer*	1975	many	5,750	100.58 × 16.3 × 4.72	132	84/72	61	1A	
Sea Endurance	*Saqqit Ittuk*	1992	05/18	1,211	49.65 × 11.1 × 3.4	53		26	1B	
Sea Spirit	*Spirit of Oceanus*	1991	2010/ 2017	4,200	90.36 × 15.3 × 4.2	120	70	59	1C	Built as *Renaissance V*
Seabourn Quest		2011	13/18	32,346	198.15 × 25.6 × 6.5	450	335	225	No	
Shearwater	*Disko*	1968	2000/05	2,907	70.52 × 15.54 × 4.2	76	36	38	1A	
Silver Cloud[43]		1994	2013	16,800	157 × 22 × ?	260	208	148	1C	
Silver Explorer	*Prince Albert II*	1989	2008	6,130	108 × 15.6 × 4.38	132	111	66	1A	
Society Explorer	*Lindblad Explorer*	1969		2,398	76.2 × 14 × 4.3	104	54		1A	Sank 2007
Spirit of Enderby[44]	*Professor Khromov*	1983	2004	1,759	71.06 × 12.8 × 4.5	48	30	24	1D	
Spitsbergen[45]	*Atlantida*	2009	2015	7,025	97.58 × 18 × 5.3	280/290	70	106	1C	
The World[46]		2002	2016	43,524	196.35 × 29.8 × 6.7	200	280	165	1C	
Ushuaia	*Malcolm Baldridge*	1970	1990	2,963	84.73 × 15.41 × 5.48	84	40	46	Y	
World Discoverer		1975	1996	3,724	87.51 × 15.1 × 4.4	137	75/80	76	1A	Wrecked 2000, Solomon Isl.
World Explorer		2019		9,300	126 × 19 × 4.7	176	125		1B	

Polar Cruise Ships on Order for Delivery in 2019 and Later

Company/ Ship Name	Yard	Yard #	Dely	GRT	Pax	Ice
Ponant						
Le Bellot	Vard		2020	10,000	184	1C
Le Bougainville	Vard	850	2019	10,000	184	1C
Le Dumont d'Urville	Vard	851	2019	10,000	184	1C
Le Jacques Cartier	Vard		2020	10,000	184	1C
Le Commandant Charcot	Vard	887	2021	30,000	270	PC2
Hapag Lloyd						
HANSEATIC Inspiration	Vard	871	2019	15,650	199/230	PC6
HANSEATIC Nature	Vard	870	2019	15,650	199/230	PC6
HANSEATIC Spirit	Vard		2020	15,650	199/230	PC6
Hurtigruten						
Fridjoft Nansen	Kleven Verft	401	2020	20,889	530/600	PC6
Roald Amundsen	Kleven Verft	400	2019	20,889	530/600	PC6
Crystal Yacht Expedition						
Crystal Endeavour I	MV Werften		2020	19,800	200	PC6
Crystal Endeavour II	MV Werften		2020	19,800	200	PC6
Crystal Endeavour III	MV Werften		2021	19,800	200	PC6
Scenic Luxury Cruises and Tours						
Scenic Eclipse	Ulajnik	530	2019	17,085	228	PC6
Scenic Eclipse II	Ulajnik		2020	17,085	228	PC6
Oceanwide Expeditions						
Hondius	Brodosplit	484	2019	5,590	180/196	PC6
Janssonius	Brodosplit		2021	5,590	180/196	PC6
Mystic Cruises and Atlas Ocean Voyages						
World Explorer	Westsea, Viana	?	2019	9,300	176/200	1B
World Voyager	Westsea, Viana	?	2020	9,300	176/200	1B
World Navigator	Westsea, Viana	?	2021	9,300	176/200	1B
World Traveller	Westsea, Viana	?	2022	9,300	176/200	1B
World Seeker	Westsea, Viana	?	2022	9,300	176/200	1B
World Adventurer	Westsea, Viana	?	2023	9,300	176/200	1B
World Discoverer						
Quark Expeditions						
Ultramarine	Brodosplit	487	2020	13,000	200	PC6

Minke/Antarctica XX1						
Magellan Explorer	ASEANAV Chile		2019	4,900	70/100	PC6
Norwegian Yacht Voyages						
M/Y Caroline	Metalships Vigo		2022	16,500	220	PC6
#2	Metalships Vigo		2023	16,500	220	PC6
#3	Metalships Vigo		2025	16,500	220	PC6
#4	Metalships Vigo		2027	16,500	220	PC6
Lindblad Expeditions						
Nat. Geo. Endurance	Gdynia/Ulstein	312	2020	12,300	126	PC5
Nat. Geo Resolution	Gdynia/Ulstein		2021	12,300	126	PC5
Aurora Expeditions						
Greg Mortimer	China Merchants		2019	8,000	160/190	PC6
Sylvia Earle	China Merchants		2021	8,000	160/190	PC6
Sunstone Ships[47]						
Ocean Victory	China Merchants		2020	8,000	160/190	PC6
Ocean Explorer	China Merchants		2021	8,000	160/190	PC6
Ocean Odyssey	China Merchants		2022	8,000	160/190	PC6
Ocean Discoverer	China Merchants		2022	8,000	160/190	PC6
Ocean Albatros	China Merchants		2022	8,000	160/190	PC6
Seabourn Cruise Line						
Seabourn Venture	Mariotti/Damen		2021	23,000	264	PC6
#2	Mariotti/Damen		2022	23,000	264	PC6
Viking Ocean						
Viking Octantis	Vard	906	2022	30,150	378	PC6
Viking Polaris	Vard	908	2022	30,150	378	PC6
	Vard		2022	nd	378	PC6
	Vard		2023	nd	378	PC6
Seadream Yacht Club						
Seadream Innovation	Damen		2021	15,300	220	PC6
Vodohod						
	Helsinki		2021	nd	148	PC6
	Helsinki		2022	nd	148	PC6
REV Ocean[48]						
	Vard		2020	17,440	30/60	PC6

Pax = Passengers Polar/Maximum; Ice = Ice Class where indicated
(excludes expedition ships known to be destined for warm water cruising, e.g. Ritz Carlton Yachts)

APPENDIX 2

CRUISE PASSENGER ACTIVITY AT MAJOR POLAR DESTINATIONS

Cruise Ships and other Passenger Ship Activities in the Canadian Arctic 1989-2018

Primarily from NORDREG reports, not cruise brochures

Year	Ships	Cruises	NWP	Adv.	MegY	Year	Ships	Cruises[1]	NWP	Adv.	MegY
1989	1	3	0	2	-	2004	8	17	1	7	-
1990	2	4	0	2	-	2005*	7	16/5	1	8	1
1991	2	4	0	1	-	2006*	11	25/7	2	6	0
1992	2	2	2	1	-	2007*	11	26/7	3	5	0
1993	5	8	2	3	-	2008*	12	28/8	1	7	0
1994	4	4	2	4	1	2009*	9	20/8	2	11	1
1995	7	14	1	4	-	2010*	12	19/4	2	10	3
1996	4	6	2	1	-	2011	6	10	2	16	5
1997	5	7	2	0	-	2012	6	11	2	24	3
1998	8	13	2	1	-	2013	9	16	3	24	4
1999	8	17	1	3	-	2014	9	16	2	28	3
2000	6	13	2	3	-	2015	11	19	2	20	3
2001	5	8	1	5	1	2016	11	22	3	17	5
2002	6	11	2	2	-	2017	14	19	4	28	4
2003	5	11	2	8	-	2018	13	21	0[2]	16	1

Ships = Number of cruise ships cruising in the eastern Arctic. Excludes ships undertaking a Northwest Passage unless they also undertook one or more cruises prior to, or following, the NWP.

Cruises = Number of cruises they made. Author's estimate based on a combination of number of cruise days, logical turnaround community together with call repetition after the turnaround. Some 'cruises' are very short and may only include one or two places. For example in 1998 and 2002 the *Albatross*, and in 2009 the *Maxim Gorkiy*, made a single call at Pangnirtung, possibly as part of a transatlantic voyage.

NWP = Northwest Passage. These are also counted in ships and in cruises as having undertaken one cruise.
Adv. = Adventurer. Small vessels, typically under 30m length. Includes boats cruising the eastern Arctic and undertaking a NWP.
MegY = Mega yachts. Vessels over 30m in length. Includes boats cruising the eastern Arctic and undertaking a NWP. Prior to 2005 it is difficult to determine small vessel lengths.

*Cruise North Expeditions operating with support from the Makivik Corporation and the Province of Quebec used the *Ushaia* in 2005 and *Lyubov Orlova* in 2006–10 with a cruise programme based out of Kuujjuaq in Nunavik. Turnarounds were also undertaken in other locations, such as Churchill, Iqaluit and Nanisivik. Number of cruises, figure to the right of, e.g. 26/8. The programme collapsed in 2010 because of problems with the operator of the *Lyubov Orlova*. The ship was under arrest in St John's in 2010–13. It broke away from a scrap tow and is believed to have sunk off Ireland in 2013.

Estimated numbers of Cruise Passengers in the Canadian Arctic

Year	2015	2016	2017	2018	2019
Passengers	3,018	3,993	3,667	3,925	4,890

Antarctic Cruise Calls and Passenger Numbers[3]

Season	Pax Not Landed	Number of Ships[4]	Number of Cruises	Pax Landed	Number of Ships	Number of Cruises	Yachts[5]	Yacht Cruises
2000/01	0	0	0	12,109	18	118	15	20
2001/02	2,029	1	2	11,588	16	111	20	30
2002/03	2,424	3	3	13,571	20	128	25	33
2003/04	4,939	3	5	27,537	25	158	4	6
2004/05	5,024	4	5	22,736	27	190	5	9
2005/06	4,632	3	4	25,191	31	224	8	14
2006/07	6,930	5	6	29,028	37	249	12	21
2007/08	13,015	7	11	32,794	39	264	12	23
2008/09	10,702	5	8	26,883	31	251	14	27
2009/10	15,720	9	12	20,922	29	202	13	26
2010/11	14,373	7	10	19,065	23	219	15	26
2011/12	4,872	4	5	21,421	24	200	12	27
2012/13	9,070	4	7	24,930	24	227	15	36
2013/14	9,670	4	8	27,374	28	224	19	51
2014/15	9,459	4	7	26,812	24	220	13	32
2015/16	8,109	4	7	29,960	27	239	16	39
2016/17	8,528	5	9	36,103	31	279	15	35
2017/18	14,440	3	10	43,110	32	305	20	55
2018/19	10,889	4	7	45,070	31	304	17	52
2019/20[6]	16,681	6	11	54,139	39	337		

Pax = Passengers

The following table provides cruise numbers and ships for earlier years, and is derived from a number of sources, including IAATO papers. However, the data should be treated with caution as there are significant problems with the 1999/00 season that may have also occurred with accounting in other years. Section 2.3 of *Overview of Antarctic Tourism 2000* issued by IAATO gives 15,559 passenger visits for 1999/00, and section 2.4 lists twenty ships. In section 7.2 a table by a researcher at the US National Science Foundation gives 14,623 visitors with twenty-one ships. This number is slightly different from the most widely quoted numbers given in the table.

Conversations with Patrick Shaw, ex-VP Operations for Marine Expeditions, and Geoff Green, founder and President of Students on Ice, but in 1999/2000 an expedition leader for Marine Expeditions, has suggested a resolution to the passenger numbers quoted by Bauer for the *Aegean I* (912) and *Ocean Explorer I* (889). The *Aegean I* appears to have undertaken two visits, one over the millennium from Ushuaia and one about 6 January 2000 with its round-the-world passengers. The passenger count on the *Ocean Explorer I* was probably about 500. The figure of 889 is likely the maximum count with all berths filled, although IAATO quotes a lower number.

Early Antarctic Cruise Passenger Numbers[7]

Season	Pax Nos.	Year	Pax Nos.	Year[8]	PT Pax Nos	ENZ Pax Nos	ENZ Ships	ENZ Trips
1933	~42	1970/71	943	1980/81	855	756		
1937	~42	1971/72	984	1981/82	1,441[9]	960		
1957/58	194	1972/73	1,175	1982/83	719	707	2	7
1958/59	344	1973/74	1,876	1983/84	834	732	2	8
		1974/75	3,644	1984/85	544	506+	2	6+[10]
1965/66	58	1975/76	1,890	1985/86	631	552	2	5
1966/67	94	1976/77	1,068	1986/87	1,797	1,714	4	16
1967/68	147	1977/78	845	1987/88	2,782	2,751	5	24
1968/69	1,312	1978/79	1,048	1988/89	3,146	3,097	5	30
1969/70	972	1979/80	855	1989/90	2,460	2,277	5	21

Pax = Passengers, PT = Polar Tourism, ENZ = Enzenbacher[11]

1990s Cruise Passengers Numbers[12]

Season	Passengers Landed	Passengers Not Landed	Operator Numbers	Ships	Trips
1990/91	4,698		6	8	35
1991/92	6,317			10	53
1992/93	6,983[13]		10	12	59
1993/94	7,957		9	11	65
1994/95	8,098		9	14	93

1995/96	9,212		10	15	113
1996/97	7,323		11	13	104
1997/98	9,473		12	13	92
1998/99	9,857[14]		15	15	116
1999/00	13,887[15]	936	17	21	154

South Georgia Cruise Ship and Yacht Traffic[16]

Season	Ship Numbers	Ship Visits	Passenger Numbers[17]	Yacht Numbers	Yacht Visits
1991/92		11	954		
1992/93		6	nd		
1993/94		13	nd		
1994/95		18	nd		
1995/96		19	nd		
1996/97		23	nd		
1997/98		25	nd		
1998/99		29	2,180		
1999/00		34	2,704		
2000/01		27	2,100		
2001/02		33[18]	2,385	16	
2002/03		45	3,606	4	
2003/04		42	3,584	nd	
2004/05		40	3,765	18	
2005/06		49	5,463	28	
2006/07	21	51	5,214	11	14
2007/08	29	64	8,068	18	22
2008/09	28	70	7,700	22	25
2009/10	22	63	7,214	18	21
2010/11	22	46	5,354	13	18
2011/12	18	51	5,831	4	7
2012/13	22	51	5,792	11	16
2013/14	23	55	7,024	14	18
2014/15	22	65	8,142	16	21
2015/16	23	68	8,787	16	22
2016/17	23	68	8,946	6	8
2017/18[19]	24	68	10,109	16	28
2018/19	nd	73	10,351	14	nd

nd = no data

Falkland Island Cruise Visitors

Year	Number of Expedition Ships	Number[20] of Calls	Number of Large Ships	Number of Calls	Passengers[21]
1995/96					3,940
1996/97					7,008
1997/98					19,523
1998/99					19,638
1999/00					22,370
2000/01					22,125
2001/02					27,230
2002/03					27,461
2003/04					36,691
2004/05					37,880
2005/06					45,229
2006/07					51,282
2007/08					62,203
2008/09					62,488
2009/10					48,359
2010/11					40,542
2011/12					35,159
2012/13					29,553
2013/14					39,688
2014/15					43,437
2015/16					59,476
2016/17					55,633
2017/18[22]	25	76	9	25	57,496
2018/19[23]	29	76	13	38	62,505

1970s Tourist Passengers Visiting the Falkland Islands by Cruise Ship[24]

Year	1970	1971	1972	1973	1974	1975
Numbers	146	419	1,620	3,189	3,999	6,201

Cruise Visitors to Greenland[25]

Year	Numbers of Ships[26]	Numbers of Cruises	Cruise Tourists	Air Arrivals for Cruises
1991	2	4		
1992	4	5		
1993	3	5		
1994	3	5		
1995	7	15		
1996	6	7		
1997	3	7		
1998	6	10		
1999	9	13		
2000	7	11		
2001	5	9		
2002	4	10		
2003	14		9,993	
2004	24		15,654	
2005	25		16,446	
2009	28		22,051	
2007	35		23,506	
2008	39	105	28,891	
2009		79	26,976	
2010		85	30,271	
2011		65	29,826	
2012		72	23,399	
2013		88	21,496	
2014		89	20,214	
2015		84	25,049	6,148[27]
2016		104	24,244	
2017[28]		101	38,182	
2018		110	45,739	

Iceland Cruise Calls[29]

Year	Reykjavik Cruise Calls	Passenger Numbers	Cruise ships Embarking	Arriving by Air for Embarkation	Akureyri Calls[30]	Passenger Numbers
2001	49	27,574			28	
2002	50	30,077			35	
2003	58	31,264			44	
2004	70	44,630			53	
2005	77	54,795			56	
2006	74	55,223			54	
2007	76	53,529			59	
2008	83	59,308			55	
2009	80	68,867			58	47,597
2010	74	70,133			56	55,734
2011	67	62,673			55	49,475
2012	81	91,954	7	1,167	63	66,383
2013	80	92,412	8	1,897	63	71,338
2014	91	104,816	12	2,876	79	72,651
2015	108	100,141	30	5,210	86	82,268
2016	114	98,676	35	8,416	93	85,432
2017	135	128,275	50	7,551	124	115,565
2018	152	144,658		9,708		

Faroe Island Cruise Calls and Passenger Numbers[31]

Year	Tórshavn, All Cruise Calls	Tórshavn Expedition Ship Calls	Tórshavn Passengers	Runavik[32] Cruise Calls	Klaksvik Cruise Calls
1994	17		6,415		
1995	16		5,253		
1996	24		10,546		
1997	19		8,544		
1998	25		12,141		
1999	25	4	8,869		
2000	26	6	10,835		
2001	27	4	13,240		
2002	23	5	10,568		

2003	34	13[33]	12,014		
2004	42	11	19,875		
2005	36	6	20,776	5	
2006	41	8	24,154		
2007	42	10	28,923	3	
2008	39	9	27,745	6	
2009	48	7	29,050	1	
2010[34]	48	13	31,262	1	
2011	41	7	26,233	1	
2012	47	12	23,604	1	
2013	47	8	30,840		
2014	44	5	32,602	1	
2015	63	10	42,695	4	
2016	39	3	22,533	3	
2017	45	8	30,713		4
2018	46	8	30,000	7	6
2019	58	12		2	4

Nordkapp Cruise Numbers[35]

Year	Ship Calls	Passenger Numbers
1956[36]		7,000
2010	97	98,170
2011	80	87,505
2012	110	121,054
2013	98	121,189
2014	103	121,782
2015	94	110,900
2016	102	112,840
2017	96	124,746
2018	104	133,000

Svalbard Cruise Numbers Interpreted[37]

Year	Passengers Direct Calls	Number of Ships	Passengers By Air for Cruises	Numbers of Local cruises	Passengers on Local Cruises
1997	15,437	24			
1998	17,463	21			
1999	17,763	31			
2000	16,404	29			
2001	20,069	25	5,000	14	nd
2002	16,892	22		14	nd
2003	19,736	28		16	nd
2004	21,206	28		17	nd
2005	29,004	34		18	5,536
2006	28,787	29		20	6,121
2007	32,781	30		22	7,475
2008	28,697	28	14,000	24	10,040
2009	29,813	24		19	8,459
2010	26,528	25		23	8,920
2011	24,187	21		20	9,706
2012	42,363	28		35	9,277
2013	36,257	27		24	10,530
2014	35,154	23	12,000	35	12,519
2015	30,829	14		30	14,408
2016	35,522	17		39	16,723
2017	42,839	17		37	17,523
2018	45,900	15		59	21,000

nd = no data

APPENDIX 3

SHIPS THAT HAVE CARRIED TOURISTS TO THE NORTH POLE[1]

(Adapted by the author from a list of all North Pole voyages from Robert Headland Scott Polar Research Institute.)

TPV	Name	Captain	Date of Arrival	Flag
	Rossiya[1]	Anatoly Lamehov	8 August 1990	Soviet Union
Y	*Sovetskiy Soyuz*[1]	Anatoly Gorshkovskiy[1]	4 August 1991	Soviet Union
	Sovetskiy Soyuz[2]	Anatoly Gorshkovskiy[2]	13 July 1992	Russia
	Sovetskiy Soyuz[3]	Anatoly Gorshkovskiy[3]	23 August 1992	Russia
	Yamal[1]	Andrey Smirnov[1]	21 July 1993	Russia
	Yamal[2]	Andrey Smirnov[2]	8 August 1993	Russia
	Yamal[3]	Andrey Smirnov[3]	30 August 1993	Russia
	Yamal[4]	Andrey Smirnov[4]	21 July 1994	Russia
	Kapitan Dranitsyn	Viktor Terekhov	21 July 1994	Russia
	Yamal[5]	Andrey Smirnov[5]	5 August 1994	Russia
	Yamal[6]	Andrey Smirnov[6]	21 August 1994	Russia
	Yamal[7]	Andrey Smirnov[7]	12 July 1995	Russia
	Yamal[8]	Andrey Smirnov[8]	28 July 1995	Russia
	Yamal[9]	Andrey Smirnov[9]	12 July 1996	Russia
Y	*Yamal*[10]	Andrey Smirnov[10]	27 July 1996	Russia
Y	*Yamal*[11]	Andrey Smirnov[11]	14 August 1996	Russia
	Sovetskiy Soyuz[4]	Stanislav Shmidt[1]	12 July 1997	Russia
	Sovetskiy Soyuz[5]	Stanislav Shmidt[2]	25 July 1997	Russia
	Sovetskiy Soyuz[6]	Yevgeniy Bannikov[1]	10 July 1998	Russia
	Sovetskiy Soyuz[7]	Yevgeniy Bannikov[2]	23 July 1998	Russia
	Yamal[12]	Stanislav Rumiantsev[1]	25 July 1999	Russia
	Yamal[13]	Aleksandr Lembrik[1]	29 July 2000	Russia
	Yamal[14]	Aleksandr Lembrik[2]	11 August 2000	Russia

	Yamal[15]	Aleksandr Lembrik[3]	12 July 2001	Russia
	Yamal[16]	Aleksandr Lembrik[4]	24 July 2001	Russia
	Yamal[17]	Aleksandr Lembrik[5]	5 August 2001	Russia
	Yamal[18]	Aleksandr Lembrik[6]	23 August 2001	Russia
	Yamal[19]	Aleksandr Lembrik[7]	11 July 2002	Russia
	Yamal[20]	Aleksandr Lembrik[8]	24 July 2002	Russia
	Yamal[21]	Aleksandr Lembrik[9]	12 August 2002	Russia
	Yamal[22]	Aleksandr Lembrik[10]	25 August 2002	Russia
	Yamal[23]	Stanislav Rumiantsev[2]	25 July 2003	Russia
	Yamal[24]	Stanislav Rumiantsev[3]	10 August 2003	Russia
	Yamal[25]	Stanislav Rumiantsev[4]	24 August 2003	Russia
	Yamal[26]	Aleksandr Lembrik[11]	8 July 2004	Russia
	Yamal[27]	Aleksandr Lembrik[12]	21 July 2004	Russia
	Yamal[28]	Aleksandr Lembrik[13]	7 August 2004	Russia
	Yamal[29]	Aleksandr Lembrik[14]	28 August 2004	Russia
	Yamal[30]	Aleksandr Lembrik[15]	11 September 2004	Russia
	Yamal[31]	Stanislav Rumiantsev[5]	7 July 2005	Russia
	Yamal[32]	Stanislav Rumiantsev[6]	20 July 2005	Russia
	Yamal[33]	Stanislav Rumiantsev[7]	7 August 2005	Russia
	Yamal[34]	Stanislav Rumiantsev[8]	19 August 2005	Russia
	Yamal[35]	Stanislav Rumiantsev[9]	1 September 2005	Russia
	Yamal[36]	Aleksandr Lembrik[16]	8 July 2006	Russia
	Yamal[37]	Aleksandr Lembrik[17]	19 July 2006	Russia
	Yamal[38]	Aleksandr Lembrik[18]	7 August 2006	Russia
	Yamal[39]	Aleksandr Lembrik[19]	18 August 2006	Russia
	Yamal[40]	Stanislav Rumiantsev[10]	2 July 2007	Russia
	Yamal[41]	Stanislav Rumiantsev[11]	14 July 2007	Russia
	Yamal[42]	Stanislav Rumiantsev[12]	27 July 2007	Russia
	Yamal[43]	Stanislav Rumiantsev[13]	11 August 2007	Russia
	Yamal[44]	Stanislav Rumiantsev[14]	23 August 2007	Russia
	50 let Pobedy[1]	Valentin Davydyants[1]	29 June 2008	Russia
	50 let Pobedy[2]	Valentin Davydyants[2]	12 July 2008	Russia
	50 let Pobedy[3]	Valentin Davydyants[3]	25 July 2008	Russia
	Yamal[45]	Aleksandr Lembrik[20]	28 July 2008	Russia
	Yamal[46]	Aleksandr Lembrik[21]	8 August 2008	Russia
	50 let Pobedy[4]	Dmitriy Lobusov[2]	15 July 2009	Russia
	50 let Pobedy[5]	Dmitriy Lobusov[3]	28 July 2009	Russia

	50 let Pobedy[6]	Valentin Davydyants[4]	14 July 2010	Russia
	50 let Pobedy[7]	Valentin Davydyants[5]	28 July 2010	Russia
	50 let Pobedy[8]	Valentin Davydyants[6]	10 August 2010	Russia
	50 let Pobedy[9]	Dmitriy Lobusov[4]	1 July 2011	Russia
	50 let Pobedy[10]	Dmitriy Lobusov[5]	17 July 2011	Russia
	50 let Pobedy[11]	Dmitriy Lobusov[6]	28 July 2011	Russia
	50 let Pobedy[12]	Dmitriy Lobusov[7]	9 August 2011	Russia
	50 let Pobedy[13]	Valentin Davydyants[7]	1 July 2012	Russia
	50 let Pobedy[14]	Valentin Davydyants[8]	12 July 2012	Russia
	50 let Pobedy[15]	Valentin Davydyants[9]	25 July 2012	Russia
	50 let Pobedy[16]	Valentin Davydyants[10]	4 August 2012	Russia
	50 let Pobedy[17]	Dmitriy Lobusov[8]	25 June 2013	Russia
	50 let Pobedy[18]	Dmitriy Lobusov[9]	5 July 2013	Russia
	50 let Pobedy[19]	Dmitriy Lobusov[10]	16 July 2013	Russia
	50 let Pobedy[20]	Dmitriy Lobusov[11]	30 July 2013	Russia
	50 let Pobedy[22]	Valentin Davydyants[12]	25 June 2014	Russia
	50 let Pobedy[23]	Valentin Davydyants[13]	6 July 2014	Russia
	50 let Pobedy[24]	Valentin Davydyants[14]	20 July 2014	Russia
	50 let Pobedy[25]	Valentin Davydyants[15]	31 July 2014	Russia
	50 let Pobedy[26]	Valentin Davydyants[16]	11 August 2014	Russia
	50 let Pobedy[27]	Dmitriy Lobusov[12]	9 June 2015	Russia
	50 let Pobedy[28]	Dmitriy Lobusov[13]	21 June 2015	Russia
	50 let Pobedy[29]	Dmitriy Lobusov[14]	2 July 2015	Russia
	50 let Pobedy[30]	Dmitriy Lobusov[15]	14 July 2015	Russia
	50 let Pobedy[31]	Dmitriy Lobusov[16]	25 July 2015	Russia
	50 let Pobedy[32]	Dmitriy Lobusov[17]	5August 2015	Russia
	50 let Pobedy[33]	Dmitriy Lobusov[18]	16 August 2015	Russia
	50 let Pobedy[34]	Oleg Shchapin[2]	20 June 2016	Russia
	50 let Pobedy[35]	Oleg Shchapin[3]	3 July 2016	Russia
	50 let Pobedy[36]	Oleg Shchapin[4]	16 July 2016	Russia
	50 let Pobedy[37]	Oleg Shchapin[5]	27 July 2016	Russia
	50 let Pobedy[38]	Oleg Shchapin[6]	7 August 2016	Russia
	50 let Pobedy[39]	Dmitriy Lobusov[19]	19 June 2017	Russia
	50 let Pobedy[40]	Dmitriy Lobusov[20]	30 June 2017	Russia
	50 let Pobedy[41]	Dmitriy Lobusov[21]	15 July 2017	Russia
	50 let Pobedy[42]	Dmitriy Lobusov[22]	25 July 2017	Russia
	50 let Pobedy[43]	Dmitriy Lobusov[23]	5 August 2017	Russia

	50 let Pobedy[44]	Dmitriy Lobusov[24]	17 August 2017	Russia
	50 let Pobedy[45]	Oleg Shchapin[7]	20 June 2018	Russia
	50 let Pobedy[46]	Oleg Shchapin[8]	30 June 2018	Russia
	50 let Pobedy[47]	Oleg Shchapin[9]	13 July 2018	Russia
	50 let Pobedy[48]	Oleg Shchapin[10]	25 July 2018	Russia
	50 let Pobedy[49]	Oleg Shchapin[11]	4 August 2018	Russia
	50 let Pobedy[50]	Dmitriy Lobusov[25]	19 June **2019**	Russia
	50 let Pobedy[51]	Dmitriy Lobusov[26]	29 June 2019	Russia
	50 let Pobedy[52]	Dmitriy Lobusov[27]	13 July 2019	Russia
	50 let Pobedy[53]	Dmitriy Lobusov[28]	24 July 2019	Russia
	50 let Pobedy[54]	Dmitriy Lobusov[29]	3 August 2019	Russia
	50 let Pobedy[55]	Dmitriy Lobusov[30]	17 August 2019	Russia

TPV indicates a trans-polar voyage that crossed from the Atlantic Ocean to the Pacific Ocean, or vice versa, via the North Pole.

Superscript numbers are total and cumulative numbers of ship voyages, commands.

On 21 August 2019, the Norwegian icebreaker *Svalbard* reached the North Pole, but she was not carrying passengers. It had been intended that Norway's new icebreaker *Kronprinse Haakon* would make the first Norwegian North Pole voyage but, owing to exceptionally thick ice that even *50 let Pobedy* had difficulties with, this was abandoned around 84° 40'N. Five voyages of *50 let Pobedy* later, and after reports that ice conditions were much more favourable, *Svalbard* was in a position to take advantage of the easier ice and performed Norway's first North Pole voyage. She carried Coastguard and scientific staff.

APPENDIX 4

PASSENGER SHIPS THAT HAVE UNDERTAKEN A NORTHWEST PASSAGE

Name	Years when a Passage was Undertaken and Direction
Bremen	2003W, 06W, 07E, 08W, 09W, 11E, 13E, 17E, 19W
Crystal Serenity	2016E, 17E
Frontier Spirit	1992W, 93W
Hanseatic	1994W, 96E, 97W, 98E, 00W, 02E, 07W, 09E, 10W, 11E,12E, 13W
Kapitan Dranitsyn	1996E, 99W, 00W
Kapitan Khlebnikov	1992E, 93E, 94E&W, 95E, 97E, 98E, 01E&W, 02E, 03E, 04E, 05E&W, 06E, 07E, 10E, 16W
Lindblad Explorer	1984W
L'Austral	2014W, 16W, 19W
Le Boreal	2015W, 17E, 17W, 19W
Le Soleal	2013W, 15W
Polar Prince	2017W
Roald Amundsen	2019W
Silver Explorer	2014W
Society Explorer	1988E
The World	2012E, 19W
World Discoverer	1985E

West means that the ship was heading from the Atlantic to the Pacific Ocean, while east is vice versa.

Some ships set out on a NWP but were unable to complete the trip due to ice conditions. In 1986, the *World Discoverer* met heavy ice in Peel Sound and had to turn back at the western end of Bellot Strait, even though it had icebreaker support. In September 1991, the *Frontier Spirit*, heading east, had to turn back at Point Barrow because of heavy ice. In 2018, *Le Boreal* waited off Fort Ross for several days in the hope of making it through Bellot Strait on its proposed transit. *Le Soleal* was also scheduled, but was unable to make a transit because of ice conditions.

Other cruises are planned as 'technical' transits, i.e. they do not meet the criteria of a full ocean-to-ocean voyage, but travel through most of the NWP. Turnarounds have been at, or planned for, Kugluktuk or Cambridge Bay in the western Arctic. In 2014, the *National Geographic Explorer* had to turn back in Peel Sound and undertake the turnaround in Resolute Bay due to heavy ice. The *Akademik Ioffe* was more successful in 2012 and achieved a turnaround in Kugluktuk.

APPENDIX 5

PASSENGER FARE CURRENCIES AND PRESENT-DAY EQUIVALENTS

Chapter 1 covers the different periods of polar cruising and includes different passenger fares and currencies[1] as well as there being obvious value changes[2] to the present day.

Before the First World War, the currency for German ships and cruises would have been in goldmarks as the country still adhered to the gold standard for currency. Typically these were worth about US$.25, or one shilling in sterling. Thus the top end suites on the *Victoria Luise* for the twenty-eight-day 1912 northern cruise, which sold for 6,000 marks, would have been about US$1,500 or £300. The lowest cost berths at 700 marks would have cost US$175 or £35.

Germany dropped the gold standard at the beginning of the First World War and after the war introduced the 'papermark'. The country suffered from hyperinflation from 1920 to 1924, when the Reichmark was introduced, again pegged to the value of gold; this stabilised the currency at 4.2 Reichmark per US Dollar. The Deutschmark was introduced in 1948. From 1919 to 1920 the papermark exchange rate was about 8 to the US Dollar. The value steadily declined and by the start of 1922 the rate was about 100/US$, but by the end of the year it was 2,000/US$.

For British Flag ships, passage fees were quoted in pounds sterling or guineas, which were 21 shillings, i.e. one pound and one shilling. From the 1880s through to the 1930s the value of the pound sterling was about US$5, except for a blip in the 1920s when it declined to about US$3. During the 1930s it was more stable than the French Franc, declining very little in value through to 1939. For the 1950s and '60s the rate was US$2.85 and then fell to about $2.3 in the 1970s and '80s.

The French Franc lost considerable value relative to the US Dollar during the 1930s. In 1934 the exchange rate was 15FF/US$, by 1939 the rate had declined to 39.84FF.

The following table offers a very broad guideline to changes in value from 1875 to the present day.

Approximate multipliers for prices to the present day

1875	1885	1900	1912	1920	1925	1935	1950	1960	1970	1980	1990	2000
23	28	30	25	13	15	17	10	9	7	3	2	1.5

APPENDIX 6

KNOWN CRUISE SHIP INCIDENTS IN POLAR WATERS

In a recent article, the Norwegian Maritime Authority noted that there had been twenty-four groundings in Svalbard since 1993. The following list has only four reported groundings in Svalbard, although there were four others on the Norwegian coast.

1891: *Chimborozo* struck and grounded on a rock in Toft Sund. Passengers evacuated on seven boats and the ship's steam launch. The ship was able to get off on the rising tide, and the passengers re-embarked some hours later after taking shelter in a farmhouse.

1906: *Ile de France* grounded on rock at the entrance to Raudfjorden, Spitsbergen. A total of 150 passengers evacuated, but re-embarked after the ship was towed off on the next high tide by the Dutch cruiser *Friesland*.

1928: *Monte Cervantes* with 1,800 passengers hit a growler (small iceberg) en route to Svalbard from the North Cape. The pumps could not cope and the passengers were put ashore[1] at Spitsbergen. The Soviet icebreaker *Krasnin* assisted, but it took five days to repair the hull and enable the ship to return to Germany.

1934: *Monte Rosa* grounded in the Faroe Islands. Refloated the next day.

1967: Twenty-six passengers from the *Lapataia* were stranded overnight at Half Moon Island after the weather prevented their return to the ship.

1968: The second cruise of the *Navarino* had to be abandoned after the ship had steering gear failure.

Magga Dan went aground off Hut Point at McMurdo Sound. Eventually it freed itself, but it also suffered engine problems.

1969: Seventy passengers from the *Aquiles* were stranded overnight at Palmer Station after weather conditions prevented their return to the ship.

1971: *Lindblad Explorer* grounded in Gerlache Strait. The passengers were rescued by the *Piloto Pardo* and *Yelcho*, Chilean Navy. Ship towed off by Soviet tug *Uragan*.

1972: *Lindblad Explorer* aground in Admiralty Bay, South Shetland. Passengers taken off by Chilean ships, and ship towed off by German salvage tug *Arctis* to Buenos Aires. The ship was then taken to Kristiansand, Norway, for repair.
1973: Unidentified damage to the *Libertad*.
1979: *Lindblad Explorer* aground off Wiencke Island, South Shetlands. Seventy-four passengers and thirty-four crew taken off by Chilean icebreaker *Piloto Pardo*. Captain and twenty-one crew waited for a tow to Ushuaia by Soviet tug *Uragan*.
1985: A passenger on the *Lindblad Explorer* needed urgent medical attention during an Antarctic cruise. Assistance provided from Faraday Station.

Hapag-Lloyd's *Europa* grounded off the coast of Greenland in August. It took three days to get the ship off.
1989: *Maxim Gorkiy* hit an ice floe in fog near Spitsbergen. The ship started sinking and 575 passengers were rescued by the Norwegian Coast Guard Vessel *Sonja* and taken to Longyearbyen. The ship was stabilised and was able to sail to Germany for repair.

Bahia Paraiso Argentine resupply/tourist ship was wrecked when it grounded after leaving Palmer Station. An estimated 600m^3 of petroleum products was spilled. There are different reports about numbers on board, but it is likely there were 234 Argentine military and crew plus 89 passengers on board. The passengers, and some military, were taken to King George Island by the *Illyria* and the *Society Explorer.*
1990: A passenger on *World Discoverer* with a suspected fracture taken to a British Antarctic Survey station for an X-ray.
1991: *World Discoverer* grounded on an uncharted rock approaching Cape Evans, Ross Island.

Pomaire (ex *Aquiles*) grounded in Jones Sound.
1993: *Alla Tarasova*, ice damage, Frobisher Bay, 500–900mm hole in bulbous bow.
1996: *Hanseatic* with 149 passengers and 100 crew grounded on a shoal in the Simpson Strait.[2] Eventually freed by tug *Edgar Kotakak* and Canadian Coast Guard survey ship *Nahidik*. Passengers and some crew transferred to *Kapitan Dranitsyn*,[3] chartered by Hapag-Lloyd.

Kapitan Dranitsyn, pollution, Cambridge Bay, Canadian Arctic.

Professor Multanovskiy grounded on rocks near Penguin Island.
1997: *Hanseatic*, ice damage, Coronation Gulf, Canadian Arctic.

Hanseatic aground on sand bank near Spitsbergen. Passengers evacuated, but no damage to ship.

Professor Khromov grounded on uncharted rock in Neumayer Channel.

Akademik Sergeiy Vavilov, oil spill in Pieneau/Havgaard area.
1998: *Alla Tarasova*, ice damage, Frobisher Bay.
1999: *Le Levant* mechanical problems, Hudson Strait.

Clipper Adventurer, ice damage to two of five port propeller blades while at anchor near Seymour Island.

Hanseatic, starboard propeller damaged in Paradise Harbour.

2000: *Clipper Adventurer* beset in Martha Strait. Freed by an Argentine icebreaker.

Akademik Sergeiy Vavilov, collision with humpback whale in Dallmann Bay.

2001: *Vistamar*, port propeller damaged manoeuvring in Hope Bay. Gland oil leakage

National Geographic Endeavour hit by a rogue wave in the Drake Passage that smashed the bridge windows and took out navigation and communication equipment. Escorted to Ushuaia by a Chilean Navy tug.

2002: *Clipper Odyssey* with 106 passengers and 76 crew aground on St Matthew Island in the Bering Sea. Crew shifted all water aft and were able to get the ship off using the stern anchor. No damage or pollution.

Clipper Adventurer, strong winds grounded ship on sand bar at Deception Island, South Shetlands. Freed by a Chilean icebreaker. Minor damage, no pollution.

Professor Multanovskiy nudged iceberg and damaged port bow bulwark (Antarctic).

Explorer generator/alternator problems (Antarctic).

2003: *Marco Polo* blown aground on Half Moon Island due high winds and mechanical problems. Ship returned to Ushuaia for hull repairs.

Mona Lisa[4] hit rocks near Spitsbergen damaging both propellers and hull. Total of 690 passengers evacuated.

2005: *Hanseatic* aground near island of Lurøy (66° 25'N) off Norwegian coast. Ship sailed to Bodø and passengers repatriated.

2006: *Lyublov Orlova* with 150 passengers and crew grounded Whalers Bay, Deception Island. Ship freed after eight hours with assistance of a Spanish vessel and returned to Ushuaia.

Clipper Adventurer had ice damage to a propeller, completed the cruise on one engine and then sailed to Belfast for repairs.

2007: *Fram* had a power outage and drifted into an ice wall at Brown's Bluff. Lifeboat damaged and railing bent. Subsequent cruise cancelled.

Nordkapp hit bottom in Neptune's Bellows, Deception Island, due to navigation error. Sustained 25m gash in hull and 757 litres of diesel spilled. Total of 294 passengers transferred to *Nordnorge* and taken to Ushuaia. Rest of ship's season cancelled.

Explorer hit ice and sank in Bransfield Strait, 100 passengers and 54 crew rescued by *Nordnorge*, which was nearby.

Aleksei Maryshev, twenty-three passengers injured, two seriously, by a wave of ice and water washed onto the deck by a calving glacier in Svalbard Islands.

Disko II with fifty-two passengers, two tour guides and eighteen crew grounded near Qeqertarsuaq in Greenland. Passengers and guides evacuated pending evaluation of the damage.

2008: *Fram*, oil spill Sisimiut, Greenland.

Antarctic Dream with 130 persons on board aground east of Spitsbergen. Took six hours to release the ship, which then continued on its itinerary.

Ushuaia with eighty-nine passengers and thirty-three crew ran aground in the Wilhelmina Bay, South Shetlands. Fuel tank punctured and some leakage of diesel fuel. The eighty-four passengers were transferred to the Chilean Navy ship *Achiles* and taken to King George Island for repatriation to Ushuaia. The *Antarctic Dream* was nearby and stood by the ship until the *Achiles* arrived. The *Ushuaia* spent forty days in dry dock after the event.

Lyublov Orlova, four cruises cancelled over 2008/09 season due to mechanical problems (Antarctic).

2009: *Prince Albert II* damaged by heavy seas in the Drake Passage.

Clelia II damaged a propeller during a grounding at Petermann Island, South Shetlands. *Corinthian II* was nearby and rendered assistance. A new propeller was needed and the balance of the Antarctic programme was cancelled.

Ocean Nova, with sixty-four passengers and forty-one crew, blown onto rocks in Marguerite Bay by a sudden squall while engines were shut down for maintenance. Ship unable to free itself and passengers transferred to *Clipper Adventurer* for return to Ushuaia. Estimated that three days of repairs needed, so following cruise cancelled, and passengers rebooked on *Polar Star.*

Richard With, carrying 153 passengers on board, ran aground just off the dock at Trondheim, Norway. Some propeller damage and leaks from a shaft seal.

2010: *Clelia II* partially disabled by heavy seas in the Drake Passage. *National Geographic Explorer* was nearby and rendered assistance. The following cruise had to be cancelled.

Clipper Adventurer grounded on a sea mount in the Coronation Gulf. A total of 128 passengers transferred to Canadian Coast Guard icebreaker *Amundsen* and taken to Kugluktuk. Subsequent cruises cancelled.

Le Boreal had mechanical issues, which caused the cancellation of an Abercrombie and Kent Antarctic cruise.

2011: *Polar Star* with eighty passengers and thirty-five crew grounded at Detaille Island, South Shetlands. After inspection by divers from the Polish research station at Arctowski on King George Island, passengers disembarked and returned to Ushuaia mainly on *Marina Svetaeva*, and *Ushuaia.*

Sea Spirit grounded at Whalers Bay, Deception Island. Freed at high water.

Yacht *Berserk* sank in a storm with the loss of three lives in the Ross Sea area.

2012: *Expedition* grounded in Ispiten, Nordaustlandet, Svalbard Islands. Ship freed itself and continued on itinerary.

2013: *Kong Harald* with 258 passengers grounded on rocks off Trollfjord, Norway. Ship continued to Svolvaer and passengers disembarked.

Marco Polo with 1,117 passengers[5] touched bottom at Sortland, Norway, ballast tank damaged.

Orion had cooling water system problems (Antarctic).

Akademik Shokalskiy trapped by ice east of the French Antarctic base at Dumont d'Urville. The Chinese icebreaker *Xue Long* and the Australian resupply vessel *Aurora Australis* responded. Helicopters from the *Xue Long* (which had also become trapped) airlifted the fifty-two passengers to the *Aurora Australis*. The Russian crew of twenty-two remained on board. The two trapped vessels were able to break free on 8 January 2014.

2015: *Ocean Endeavour* damaged by ice off South Shetlands with 167 passengers on board. Next sailing cancelled.

2018: *Akademik Ioffe* grounded in Western Gulf of Boothia. The *Akademik Sergei Vavilov* was nearby and took passengers to Kugaaruk. Vessel sailed to Quebec for repairs.

2019: *Viking Sky*[6] with more than 1,300 passengers and crew suffered engine failure off the Norwegian coast in storm conditions and came within 100m of grounding. A total of 497 passengers were taken off by helicopter to Molde, where the ship eventually sailed after managing to restart one engine. The ship is diesel/electric propulsion and a faulty policy regarding lubricating oil tank levels, combined with the stormy weather, resulted in the engines shutting down. Helicopters were requested because the captain deemed the weather too rough to launch lifeboats.

NOTES

Introduction

1 Climate change is extending the season into October and April.

2 Until the First World War, immigration to the United States (mainly via the North Atlantic) was close to 1 million per annum with a peak of 1.3 million in 1907. Numbers fell off after the US imposed quotas after 1921, and averaged about 400,000 during the 1920s. They never reached these numbers again, ranging from 200,000 to 300,000 per annum from after the Second World War to 1969.

3 Venice is a classic example of this problem, although the decision by Dublin to limit cruise calls is based on allocation of dock space, rather than an over-tourism.

4 The *Prinzessin Victoria Luise* was an all-suite ship. Each stateroom had a living room, bedroom and an en suite bathroom. The two Regal suites had en suite toilets, but facilities for other passengers were elsewhere.

5 As delivered. Reduced to 155 after the 1954 refit. Staterooms were increased in size, and 'almost all' had en suite facilities.

6 IAATO has two categories of ships that undertake landings: 13–200 and 201–500 passengers.

7 Reports consistently note that the *Ocean Princess* carried 480 passengers on Antarctic visits, and called for three seasons commencing with 1990/91. Technically, accommodation with all lower berths filled was 587, although the ship had twenty-eight cabins with a third Pullman berth and two four-berth cabins. The lowest passenger deck, the Capri Deck, was all inside cabins. If all of these were closed off except for three better two-berth cabins and two single cabins, the capacity would have been 475.

Chapter 1

1 On 22 December 1863, the *Foam* arrived in Stanley, Falkland Islands, 'sent out for use of the Colonial Government'. On 26 January 1864 it undertook its first voyage as the islands mail ship and continued to provide a roughly monthly sailing between Montevideo and Stanley until 25 December 1872. Its role appears to have been taken over by the 110grt schooner *Black Hawk*, which arrived in Stanley from London in November of that year. Reportedly *Foam* was purchased by the owner of Carcass Island and was in service until wrecked in the 1950s.

2 She was a 411-ton Norwegian brig-rigged vessel that ran together with a similar ship called the *Michael Krohn*. The pair were based in Bergen and competitors of the Bergen Line. During the 1850s she traded as far south as Hamburg and apparently also to Hull in the UK. She even made an emigrant voyage from Hamburg to New York, with eighty-eight passengers, in June 1852. By 1875, however, when Thomas Cook used the *President Christie*, this pair were regulars on the Bergen–Vadsø run, calling at sixty-six posts en route to northern Norway. Wilhelm Frimann Koren Christie was President of Norway's first Storting (supreme legislature) in 1814, and founded the Bergen Museum in 1825.

3 An unofficial award for the fastest transatlantic crossing. Because of different conditions, such as the Gulf Stream, the award was made both east and west bound. The *Deutschland* held both east and west awards at a little over 23 knots. The last true ocean liner to receive the award was the SS *United States* in 1952, at 34.51 knots west and 35.59 knots east.
4 Built in 1858 and purchased from P&O by J. Clark in 1881 for conversion to a cruise ship to undertake a round-the-world cruise, which it accomplished. The *Ceylon* undertook three cruises in 1884 to the Mediterranean, Atlantic Isles and northern latitudes.
5 Built 1877, 810grt.
6 One pound and one shilling.
7 Travel was offered in two segments as the route was split by the rapids at Fort Smith (NT). Passengers took one boat to Fort Fitzgerald and were then ferried by automobile or motor coach the 16 miles to Fort Smith to embark on the second boat.
8 The American travel writer Fullerton Waldo took a trip in 1922 and noted that the rail fare was $18.25.
9 Although the *Grahame* was built in 1882 at Fort Chipewyan, it is typical of riverboats on both the upper and lower portions of the Mackenzie Route. Their design did not change over the years.
10 The official reason was to prevent spreading diseases to the Inuit.
11 On charter to the British Government from the Tonsberg Whaling Company for four trips per year between Stanley, Grytviken and, when necessary, to the whaling base at Deception Bay.
12 Laid down in 1915, and delivered as the *Limburgia* to Royal Holland Line in 1916. Sold to United American Line in 1922; renamed *Reliance* and sold again to Hamburg-Amerika in 1926. After 1928 cruising exclusively. Refitted and modernised in 1937.
13 Built 1922. Gutted by fire in New York 1930, rebuilt as *General von Steuben.*
14 *Monte Sarmiento, Monte Olivia, Monte Cervantes, Monte Pascoal, Monte Rosa.*
15 Strength Through Joy.
16 Later part of the KdF fleet.
17 *Robert Ley, Wilhelm Gutsloff, Stuttgart, Der Deutsche, Sierra Cordoba, Oceana, Monte Sarmiento, Monte Rosa.*
18 The 'large' yacht *Victoria and Albert* had been considered too unwieldy for many royal voyages.
19 Pre-1931 US$4.86, after 1931 US$3.49.
20 380 first class, 259 second class, 700 third class.
21 These cabins only had cold running water. All others had hot and cold. However, most were outside.
22 Probably a golf game of the period.
23 Named after Bibby Line, who came up with the idea. These were inside cabins that, by way of a corridor past the adjoining outside cabin, provided a porthole.
24 British Overseas Airways Corporation. This had been the pre-war Imperial Airways service.
25 A Pan American World Airways Stratocruiser landed at McMurdo Sound on 15 October 1957.
26 Pan American introduced a Boeing 707 service three weeks later.
27 These are ships that survived the war and became available for passenger service.
28 Rationing in Britain did not end until 1954.
29 Operated on Bergen to Newcastle (UK) services 119 first class, 384 tourist.
30 Wrecked and burned on an uncharted reef off Mustique in 1971.
31 Built 1950 as *Provence* for SGTM. Sold 1965 to Costa Lines and refitted. Cruising only after 1972.
32 Built 1966, very similar to P&O *Canberra*. Mediterranean and Spain to South America service (27 knots service speed) and cruising.
33 Reference material states 700 passengers, but both Ushuaia and the *Falkland Islands Gazette* give 989, mainly Brazilians.
34 Capacity for forty first-class and sixty tourist-class passengers.
35 There is little information about the *Navarino*. A Chilean Navy website states that the ship was built in Scotland and had an all-riveted hull. Accommodation was twenty-five first class, seventy-five second class, 150 third class, and a suggestion of 800 steerage, but the note is truncated.

36 Although mainly engaged in the southern European emigrant service to Argentina, Uruguay and Brazil, these sister ships also offered South American tourist cruises. Accommodation was 241 cabin class and 582 tourist class, with five cargo holds.
37 Other sources state four cruises by the *Cabo san Roque* and one by the *Cabo san Vicente.*
38 Sunk during the Falklands War.
39 Fermented mare's milk.
40 Lindblad notes in *Passport to Anywhere* that the *Navarino* could carry sixty-six passengers, but he limited numbers to forty-six for greater comfort.
41 Lindblad had brought in Norwegian investors to help finance the ship.
42 There were problems en route. The generators had to be replaced in Southampton and main engine problems in the South Atlantic required a five-day diversion to Dakar for repairs.
43 There are some differences between the report of the call in Stanley in the *Falkland Islands Review* and as recalled by Lars-Eric Lindblad in *Passport to Anywhere.*
44 As reported in the 1983 Sealift After Action Report: there were no incidents and icebreaker support was not required. The Sealift Report noted that this was the third time the ship had cruised in Canadian Arctic waters.
45 One of the founding partners of Quark in 1990.
46 Delivered in December 1973 as the *BEWA Discoverer*, the ordering company went into bankruptcy before the ship was finished.
47 Society Expeditions undertook a $1.5 million refit of the ship following acquisition.
48 *Hansa* rebuilt as *Sovetsky Sojus* and the *Berlin* as *Admiral Nakhimov.*
49 As was common with Soviet vessels at the time, there was strict class segregation with the first- and second-class passengers having quite separate facilities from third class, who were in four-, six- and eight-berth cabins.
50 One of the Ivan Franko class. Lost in February 1986 after hitting a reef in Milford Sound, New Zealand.
51 Launched as *Vyacheslav Molotov* in 1940. On a trip back from Cuba in 1973 with 'Technical Advisors', there were 232 passengers on board.
52 Refits 1991/93/2006/08/09/14/15.
53 The ship was built as the 2,661grt passenger/cargo *Tjaldur* in 1953. Acquired by Chilean interests in 1968 and renamed *Aquiles*. It became the *Pomaire* when purchased by Marinsular in 1990.
54 Later a founding partner of Quark in 1990.
55 Delivered as the *BEWA Discoverer,* but the company that placed the order went bankrupt before delivery. The ship was acquired by Adventure Cruises from the shipyard.
56 Acquired by Hanseatic Tours and renamed *Hanseatic* on a two-year bareboat charter. Hanseatic was purchased by Hapag-Lloyd in 1997. As of 2019 the ship has been taken on long-term charter from Hapag-Lloyd by OneOcean of Squamish, BC, and renamed RCGS *Resolute*.
57 In 1992 purchased by the UK Government and named HMS *Endurance*. In 2009, an error during routine maintenance led to serious flooding and the ship was laid up. It was scrapped in 2016.
58 Sixty-seven passengers, 1,489grt.
59 180 passengers, 8,282grt.
60 264 passengers, 10,944grt.
61 180 passengers, about 10,000grt. Named after prominent French explorers.
62 Artemis is controlled by the wealthy Pinault family, who also own Christie's Auction House and the Château Latour winery.
63 Some sources say that the company was established by The Makivik Corporation, which retained Dugald Wells to run it.
64 134 passengers, 6,334grt.
65 Hapag-Lloyd maintained an old tradition in accommodation by providing thirty-two single cabins, although these did have Pullman berths as well. Earlier ships, as was common at the time, were designed to accommodate the large number of single people who travelled. Ships today focus on couples and twin-berth cabins, to the detriment of singles wishing to cruise.

66 48 passengers, 1,759grt.
67 464 passengers, 11,285grt.
68 280 passengers, 12,700grt.
69 632 passengers, 16,150grt.
70 150 passengers, 2,191grt operating Norwegian coast and Spitsbergen.
71 243 passengers, 7,344grt.
72 530 passengers, 20,889grt.
73 History from various sources, including a prospectus filing with the SEC on 16 September 2015. It is reported that the German bank DVB's Cruise Ferry Master Fund holds 60 per cent of Lindblad Expeditions.
74 The '*Marine*' names were for marketing purposes. Name changes appeared to have been sporadic and seasonal. The *Professor Multanovsky* was *Marine Explorer* during the 1995/96 Antarctic season, but changed to *Marine Intrepid* for the next season.
75 There is confusion about the operator. Marine Expeditions advertised a round-the-world cruise on the *Ocean Majesty*, but substituted the *Aegean I* probably after their chosen vessel grounded in September 1999 and may not have been available for a 20 November departure. However, it may also be that passenger numbers were low and the larger ship would have been too costly as it could carry 620 passengers.
76 See Appendix 2.
77 The ship was built in 1944 and retained its original steam turbine machinery.
78 176 passengers, 5,590grt.
79 116 passengers, 3,034grt.
80 100 passengers, 4,575grt.
81 Some information from an interview with Andrew Prossin reported in *BC Business News*, 16 August 2017.
82 105 passengers, 3,500grt.
83 Personal communication with the author in 2011.
84 132 passengers, 6,130grt.
85 296 passengers, 16,800grt.
86 Author's definition.
87 This is the latest known refit, or refurbishment date. If a ship is not known to have been refitted then it is included under its date of construction.
88 Based on its *Ocean Nova* charters, this number probably includes staff.
89 The third new vessel appears uncertain. It was not mentioned in an October 2019 press release about the makeover of the yard.
90 Tier III marine diesel engines meet significantly reduced NOx limits imposed by MARPOL Annex VI.
91 Victory Cruise Lines was owned by Sunstone and operated the *Victory I & II*, which focused on the Great Lakes market. Victory was recently purchased by American Queen Steamboat Company, which has a focus on America river cruising. It will operate the *Ocean Victory* in Alaska during the summer. It will go on charter to Albatros for the Antarctic.
92 Vantage is a river cruise operator and initial itineraries only include the Arctic as a polar destination.

Chapter 2

1 Pacific Coast was purchased by 'Admiral Line' in 1916 and the combined companies traded until 1936 as Pacific Steamship Company.
2 As delivered had accommodation for 200 first class and 1,050 third class.
3 360.5'x40.4', 3,431grt. Extensively rebuilt and re-engined in 1887 and rebuilt and modernised in 1891.
4 It is reported that the US Naval Attaché, together with his wife and family, were on board. However, they disembarked at Ushuaia concerned about the capabilities of the crew for the voyage. It was completed successfully.

5 Elsewhere reported as eighty-four passengers.
6 The Peso to US$ exchange rate at this time changed monthly.
7 Although mainly engaged in the southern European emigrant service to Argentina, Uruguay and Brazil, these sister ships also offered South American tourist cruises. Accommodation was 241 cabin class and 582 tourist class, with five cargo holds.
8 Elsewhere underreported as 700 passengers. The *Enrico C* called at the Falkland Islands in 1974, and again in 1975 with a reported 912 passengers. Thus higher passenger numbers are credible. After its 1965 refit, the ship was reconfigured for 218 first-class and 980 tourist-class passengers.
9 The Japanese took 333 Minke whales in the 2018/19 season.
10 From www.penguins.cl. Census data approximately to 2016. Other sources suggest different breeding populations.
11 Small populations on many islands.
12 Additional populations in Chile and Argentina.
13 Additional populations in Chile and Argentina.
14 Otherwise known as Islas Orcadas del Sur.
15 Historic naturally occurring deposits by seabirds and bats. High in nitrogen, phosphorus and potassium, it made an excellent fertiliser.
16 The ship was later retired to the Falkland Islands in 1884, where she was used as a coal hulk. Recovered by Sir Jack Hayward in 1970, she is now a museum ship in Bristol, UK.
17 Otherwise known as Islas Malvinas, the English appellation has been used throughout.
18 *Orcoma*, 11,500grt was delivered in 1908.
19 The call of 22 January is described as the third visit by the ship, but we have not found earlier references to it at Stanley. The call of 13 February was on a charter to the Argentine DNT, and the captain refused to fly the Falklands flag. Local persons were upset at the discourtesy and closed their stores. Apparently there was a further call, when the ship again refused to fly the Falklands flag. Entry was refused and the ship sailed without landing any passengers. Reports regarding calls in the Antarctic suggest that there were six visits in all.
20 Information taken from the Shipping News in the *Falkland Islands Monthly Review*, various dates.
21 Anecdotal information suggests the rails had arrived by 1919, but the track bed and the trestle over the Christine River were so poor that 'end of steel' was for all practical purposes several miles short of Waterways until 1922. That year Jean Godsell reported that ten American tourists made it to Aklavik.
22 The American travel writer Fullerton Waldo took a trip in 1922 and noted that the rail fare was $18.25.
23 Peter G. Newman, *Merchant Princes*, p.237.
24 Other sources say 1908 and the boat was reportedly updated in 1923.
25 103ft LOA, 23ft beam, 4ft 6in draft ten cabins.
26 SS *Montreal*. Built by Blohm & Voss, Hamburg, in 1906 as the *Konig Freidrich August* (475.8ft × 55.4ft, twin-screw 15 knots) for the Hamburg-Amerika Line. She was ceded to Britain in 1919 as war reparations. In November 1920 she was purchased by Canadian Pacific and refitted with accommodation for 332 cabin-class and 990 third-class passengers, and renamed *Montreal*. Again refitted, in 1923, to accommodate 229 cabin- and 240 third-class passengers.
27 A sovereignty assertion exercise that took place each season in the Eastern Arctic, commencing in 1922.
28 In 1933 the southern terminus port was St John's, NL.
29 The number of tourists given in HBC summary reports are often different to numbers derived from the passenger lists. These are from the passenger lists, except for 1941. In 1934, the then Governor of the Company, Sir Ashley Cooper; his wife; and an entourage that included his piper took all tourist berths from Montreal.
30 Note that references to places in Greenland in cruise itineraries are not, necessarily, the turnaround location. They are the places that the ship advised to NORDREG as its last or first call in Greenland.

31 Canada's national passenger rail carrier.
32 Information partially derived from Canada's Arctic Marine Atlas, www.oceansnorth.org.
33 Summer visitors should not expect to see a white fox. During the summer, the foxes have a straggly greyish-brown coat. It only changes its colour in the winter to the brilliant white fur that was so popular during the first half of the twentieth century.
34 Sold 1992. Operated as a cruise ship in the Baltic as the *Ovik Saga*. Later scrapped.
35 Operated as the *Shearwater* 2000–01. Currently *Polaris* under Russian register.
36 Personal communication from Bjarne Rasmussen, author of *Danish Polar Shipping 1915–2015*.
37 Length 49.65m, breadth 11.1m and draft 3.4m. After lengthening, 72.8m and 3.7m draft. All had Ice 1A hulls.
38 Reports for 1985, 1993 and 1998 provided by Bjarne Rasmussen.
39 In England, the cruise was advertised at £20 per person from Tromsø to Spitsbergen and return for 2–3 weeks.
40 Magnetic, Geographic and Pole of Inaccessibility.
41 Originally the flight was to end at Nome, but bad weather required the crew to cut it short at Teller.
42 Reportedly, Sir Wally Herbert made the first trip on foot in April 1969, travelling from Barrow to Svalbard.
43 There are slightly different translations; here is another: 'Here I stand at the North Cape, the outermost point of Finnmark. I could even say that this is the end of the entire world, as no point farther north is inhabited by people. My thirst for knowledge is now sated, and I will return to Denmark and – God willing – to the land of my birth.'
44 A US senator was also present and he gave an enthusiastic report on his return to America.
45 There is no sunset or dawn at Nordkapp between mid May and the end of July, just the midnight sun.
46 Hapag-Lloyd has had six ships with the name *Europa*, dating back to 1891; this one was number five.

Chapter 3

1 For example, in 2019, *Hanseatic* moved to OneOcean as RCGS *Resolute*, and OneOcean's *Akademik Ioffe* and *Akademik Sergey Vavilov* were withdrawn by their Russian owners.
2 The US$ to Can$ exchange rate on 14 September 1995 was 1.3701.
3 Ex-Reid steamship *Bruce*, built 1912 for the run from Sydney (NS) to Channel Port aux Basques (NL), was sold along with many other icebreaking Newfoundland ships to the Russians in 1915.
4 Reportedly fifty passengers, ten staff and twenty-three crew. Although the trip was noted in the NSR traffic record as being in ballast.

Chapter 4

1 For example, in 2019, *Hanseatic* moved to OneOcean as *RCGS Resolute*, and OneOcean's *Akademik Ioffe* and *Akademik Sergey Vavilov* were withdrawn by their Russian owners. A number of new operators will also be involved in polar cruising from 2020 onwards.
2 An alternative type of charter is called a bareboat, where only the ship is rented, and the operator provides its own crew and staff.
3 Iceland circumnavigation cruises with occasional cruises to south-west Greenland.
4 Primarily small ship cruises on the Norwegian coast and Svalbard archipelago. Antarctic cruises as groups with other operators.

Chapter 5

1 The incidents recorded have been drawn from many sources. To the extent possible, duplicates have been eliminated. These may not be a complete record. Sources have included: *Cruise Tourism in Polar Regions: Promoting Environmental and Social Sustainability*, editors Michael Luck and Patrick T. Maher, author Emma J. Stewart; *Exploring the Last Continent: An Introduction to Antarctica*, ed. Daniela Liggett, Bryan Storey et al.; and www.cruisejunkie.com.

2 Seven out of twenty-four wrecked were known to be due to ice.

3 At the time Kvaerner Masa was a major Finnish shipbuilder with its own research and model testing facilities.

4 Now very common on cruise ships. The pods are usually electric drives suspended from the stern of the ship with the ability to turn freely.

5 There are twelve members of the International Association of Classification Societies.

6 The Russian register has different notations depending on the year the rules were issued. These are the notations for 1995 and appear to best fit the expedition ships listed in Polar Expedition Cruise Ships Past and Present in the Appendices.

7 Old ice, or multi-year ice, is very hard. By comparison, first-year ice is relatively soft.

Chapter 6

1 All ships are examined at regular intervals by a Classification Society, and must at all times be 'in class', which means they are safe to operate. The surveys here are either the first intermediate or renewal surveys after the code came into force. A renewal survey occurs every five years, and become more exhaustive over time.

2 The loss of the *Explorer* in 2007 was mainly due to the lack of experience by the master with multi-year ice, although he had considerable experience with first-year ice in the Baltic.

3 The ice class designations were developed by the International Association of Classification Societies.

4 Engines designed to run on heavy fuel cannot safely use lighter fuels for extended periods of time. The engines, fuel and lubrication systems have to be converted if MDO or MGO are to be used at all times. This can be an expensive operation, and figures in the evaluation of using scrubbers as a means of reducing engine emission sulphur dioxide content.

5 The ninth edition of the *Handbook of the Antarctic Treaty System*, published in the USA in 2012, is available from the IAATO website.

6 Essentially a very small shrimp.

7 Reportedly the *Crystal Serenity* needed about 100 permits.

8 On 9 December, the Norwegian Government announced that it is considering restricting ship sizes, as well as banning the carriage and use of heavy fuel for cruise ships visiting Spitsbergen. Svalbard currently bans the use and carriage of heavy fuel in Marine Reserves and Nature Park areas.

8 Net register tonnage, a measure of the ship's size.

Appendix 1

1 In 1901 only Hamburg-Amerika offered cruises with the *Auguste Victoria*.

2 Reportedly ran Arctic cruises from 1890, presumably to Nordkapp.

3 May have cruised to the Fjords from 1892 on. Did not visit Spitsbergen in 1909.

4 The company's first ship was the Royal Mail Steam Packet Company *La Plata*. Scrapped in 1913, she was replaced by *Atrato* from the same company and put into service in 1913.

5 At the requirement of Kaiser Wilhelm, all pre-First World War German passenger ships were built with a view to conversion to auxiliary cruisers in time of war. The *Columbia* was sold to

Spain in 1889 and converted to the auxiliary cruiser *Rapido,* repurchased by Hamburg-Amerika in 1899 for line service, then sold to the Russians in 1904 for conversion to the auxiliary cruiser *Terek*. Britain's Admiralty had a similar requirement, although it was optional whether companies wished to construct to their armed merchant cruiser standards. These had certain subdivision requirements as well as the position of the engine room and boilers. In some years a small allowance was paid to companies.

6 Ex-Union Line *Scot*, rebuilt by Hamburg-Amerika as a cruise ship.

7 Wrecked Jamaica 1906.

8 During the conversion, the engines were down rated from 37,800IHP to 15,000IHP. The ship could still achieve 17 knots. Some sources suggest it was re-engined.

9 Reportedly ran Arctic cruises from 1890, presumably to Nordkapp, but may have included Spitsbergen.

10 Passenger accommodation altered in 1930/31. The figures in the table are as delivered.

11 As delivered 250 first, 230 second, 140 third and 900 steerage.

12 After the 1935 conversion first class only.

13 As built, accommodation included steerage. The table gives accommodation following the 1919 refit.

14 Accommodation was cabin, tourist and third.

15 Accommodation was cabin and third.

16 Accommodation was tourist and steerage.

17 In 1933 the third class became tourist class.

18 The 1956 refit reduced first class to 500, with 330 tourist class.

19 Following 1965 refit.

20 Delivered as *17 de Octobre*. Name changed after the fall of the Peron Government in 1955. After 1963/64 refit 400 one class.

21 Launched as *Evita*. Name changed after the fall of the Peron Government in 1955. After 1963/64 refit 372 one class.

22 Refits 1991/93/2006/08/09/14/15.

23 Refits 1997/2009/10/12/14.

24 In 1959 took a group of Soviet and Polish scientists to the Antarctic.

25 To be replaced by *Greg Mortimer* for 2019/20 Antarctic season.

26 Renamed *Clipper Adventurer* 1997, *Sea Adventurer* 2002. Refits 1997, 1999 ($13 million and new main engines), 2002, 2017.

27 Sank off Ireland 2013.

28 Broken up, unknown date.

29 Passenger count, wherever possible, is based on lower berths. If known maximum berth numbers given.

30 Passenger numbers for polar cruising, particularly Antarctica, may be limited to 200 people.

31 There is a sail training vessel of the same name. From 2003 chartered to Abercrombie and Kent, December to April, as *Explorer II* and sailed with 198 passengers. During May to November chartered to Phoenix Reisen as *Alexander von Humboldt*.

32 Refits 1997, 1999 ($13 million and new main engines), 2002, 2017. See also *Sea Adventurer* and *Ocean Adventurer.*

33 Launched as *Renaissance IV*. The first four *Renaissance* small cruise ships were slightly different dimensions and capacity than the second group of four ships.

34 Built as *Renaissance VII.*

35 Built as *Renaissance VIII.*

36 Initially reported retired from passenger service in 2012 and returned to icebreaker escort duty on the NSR. However, in expedition cruise service in 2016.

37 Arrested in St John's, NL, in 2010, the ship was eventually presumed sunk off the coast of Ireland in 2013 during a scrap tow. Crew numbers on board in St John's reported to be fifty-one. This number may have excluded officers.

38 Refits 1991/93/2006/08/09/14/15.
39 Delivered as *Konstantin Simonov*. Refits 1988/2001/10/14.
40 A single trip in 2017 with a special purpose passenger ship certificate for Canada's C3. Passengers were invited guests for specific voyage legs.
41 Charter to G.A.P. Adventures in 2007.
42 Note this a different cruise ship to the one given in this table as having cruised the Canadian Arctic and wrecked at the Solomon Islands.
43 Ice strengthened 2017.
44 To be replaced by *Greg Mortimer* from the 2019/20 Antarctic season.
45 Doubler plates added to hull.
46 The *World* is owned by its residents. It is not a cruise ship per se and does not take cruise bookings.
47 Sunstone has ordered ten ships in this class.
48 Essentially an ocean science research mega yacht for up to thirty passengers and/or sixty scientists with crew/staff to maximum complement of ninety.

Appendix 2

1 Cruise numbers include those made by Cruise North.
2 Ice conditions were very bad and no cruise ships were able to make a transit. Two adventurers did make it through.
3 Author's compilation of data from IAATO. He has removed air figures from the total. Passengers not landed are cruise only on large ships. Passengers landed are from smaller ships and include passengers on yachts.
4 Until 2004, IAATO indicated which ships did not land passengers. From 2005 onwards, numbers are interpreted by the author based on size, reported cruise staff and previous activity.
5 Data collection methodology changed after the 2002 season. Numbers for 2003, 2004 and 2005 will be inaccurate. From 2006 onwards they may be reasonably accurate. Passenger numbers are included in the landed figure. Bark *Europa* is included under cruise ships, not yachts.
6 Author's estimate based partially on IAATO projections and web information. Cruise numbers estimated based on 2018/19 load factors.
7 From *Polar Tourism: Tourism in the Arctic and Antarctic Regions*, ed. Colin Michael Hale, Margaret E. Johnston, John Wiley & Sons. 1995; and *A Policy for Antarctic Tourism: Conflict or Cooperation*, Debra J. Enzenbacher Thesis, 1991.
8 After the 1979/80 season numbers include yachts where known.
9 Includes some fly-cruise passengers.
10 Enzenbacher only has one ship in Antarctica this season. However, Headland has two, but no cruise numbers. We have confirmed with the South Georgia BAS that two ships did call that season.
11 Enzenbacher numbers in Thesis Table 2.2 agree with those from Polar Tourism. However, Thesis Table 2.3 numbers for passengers do not agree with table 2.2. The figures in the ENZ columns are derived by the author from Thesis Table 2.1, which lists ship visits and passenger numbers. Some adjustments have been made regarding these for the *Lindblad Explorer/Society Explorer*. We believe a passenger complement of 110 is not possible, and for these entries have used 100.
12 1992/93 onwards mainly from *Prospects for Polar Tourism*, ed. J.M. Snyder, B. Stonehouse, CABI International, 2007. However, 1990/91 and 1991/92 numbers from footnote 1, IAATO figures for 1992/93 are 6,704 passengers landed and 13,687 in 1999/00.
13 Polar Tourism gives 7,037 passengers, but *Tourism in the Antarctic*, Thomas G. Bauer, gives 6,577 with minor variances in some other years. IAATO figures are 6,704 with the same number of ships and operators. Evidence suggests there were thirteen ships present that season. *Vistamar* may have been omitted.

14 Bauer gives 9,934 passengers.
15 This number may be high, given concerns regarding numbers of passengers on two large ships that appear to have been incorporated into the data.
16 From *Prospects for Polar Tourism* up to 1997/98, then from Annual Tourism and Visitor Reports provided by the government officer for South Georgia.
17 Numbers are for passengers advised to be on board the ships, not numbers landed. They do not include numbers attributable to yachts.
18 *Prospects for Polar Tourism* states forty-two visits. We have used the numbers advised by the visitor reports.
19 Cruise ship numbers exclude four yachts with fourteen visits. These have been added to the yachts. For 2018/19, four mega yachts have been transferred to the yacht numbers. Data for both years is less detailed than before.
20 Number of calls is the number of times the ships visited the Falkland Islands, not the number of places visited. In 2016/17, the Statistics Report states that there were 190 places visited, of which 35 per cent were Stanley. The author's figures for 2017/18 suggest 230 places visited with 40 per cent being Stanley. All large ships only visited Stanley.
21 From Falkland Islands Statistics Report 2017.
22 Vessel calls from author's analysis of 2017/18 Cruise Ship Schedule. One expedition ship call did not take place and another was cancelled due to weather. The twenty-five expedition cruise ships also undertook 250 cruises in the Antarctic and of the larger ships, two called eight times at Stanley and also undertook nine cruises into the Antarctic. Three expedition cruise ships were involved in turnarounds with 604 passengers arriving for embarkation on eight cruises, while 397 passengers disembarked from six cruises. Numbers are taken from the passenger counts in Antarctic statistics.
23 Subject weather and other cancellations.
24 From *Falkland Island Monthly Review*, August–September 1975.
25 From Greenland Tourism Report 2016, and http://tourismstat.gl/?lang=en. Ships and calls prior to 2003 author estimates from Canadian NORDREG data. This is incomplete as it consists mainly of ships turning around in Greenland before or after a Canadian cruise or Northwest Passage.
26 2003–08 from AMSA 2009. Source given as Greenland Tourism.
27 From 'Tourism Strategy 2016–2019', Visit Greenland. This document states that these were passengers departing Greenland by air from cruises and 16,242 passengers departed Greenland by ship for a total cruise passenger number of 22,390. However, unless this is a definition error, a certain number of passengers must have also arrived in Greenland by air for cruises. In 2015 there were five cruises to Canada that only embarked passengers while there were twelve cruises that both embarked and disembarked passengers in Greenland. At 80 per cent occupancy, this would mean about 2,000 passengers embarked, while about 1,500 disembarked to take flights out of Greenland. Other cruise operators may have had similar turnaround activities.
28 2017 and 2018 data as revised August 2019. 2015 and 2016 data still under revision.
29 Reykjavik numbers provided by Faxaflóahafnir. Because the figures include Reykjavik and three other small ports, ship arrivals and passenger numbers may be slightly overstated. However, figures for 2015, 2016 and 2017 are correct. Akureyri passenger numbers are taken from its 2018 port manual. This does not give ships numbers, which come from a file provided by the port director.
30 An analysis of 2018 cruise calls for Reykjavik and Akureyri shows that most, if not all, ships calling at Akureyri had also called at Reykjavik.
31 Data for Tórshavn provided by the Port of Tórshavn. Data for Runavik and Klaksvik from web sources.
32 A comparison of cruise ship arrivals at Tórshavn and Runavik suggests that operators choose a single port of call for a Faroe Islands visit.

33 Includes five calls by *Professor Molchanov*.
34 Four expedition-size cruise ships made two calls each.
35 Data provided by Cruise Northern Norway and Svalbard (CNNS). Earlier data is apparently not available. Published numbers attributed to SAS Hotels appear to be for all visitors, not just cruise ships.
36 Prior to construction of the road.
37 As supplied by the Governor's Office. The Port of Longyearbyen provides a time series from 2006, but the passenger and ship numbers, while of the same order of magnitude, are different and cannot be reconciled. The numbers probably depend on how ships are counted. From an analysis of 2018 cruise calls, nineteen generally large ships made twenty-nine cruise calls. Another eighteen smaller ships made thirty-six inbound and outbound calls to position themselves in the archipelago, followed by 111 short cruises, which were mainly of seven days. One ship made two early season calls, and two inbound and outbound cruises that sandwiched a four-cruise local programme, each of seven days.

Appendix 3

1 All ships listed are nuclear powered except *Kapitan Dranitsyn*, which has diesel-electric propulsion.

Appendix 5

1 Information from different Wikipedia articles about currencies and exchange rates.
2 From a combination of Bank of Canada Inflation calculator from 1914 onwards and a US Consumer Price index calculator by the Federal Reserve Bank of Minneapolis.

Appendix 6

1 No information is provided on how this many people were accommodated.
2 See Canadian Transportation Safety Board Report M96H0016.
3 The *Kapitan Dranitsyn* had been on a three-day promotional charter to Molson Breweries and had just disembarked 147 passengers at Resolute. The ship substituted for the *Hanseatic* for its next cruise.
4 An identical incident recorded for 2005 is considered to be a duplicate.
5 This seems an unlikely number of passengers for a ship of 820-passenger capacity, more likely the number is for passengers and crew.
6 This incident is now subject to a class action suit against the cruise company.

BIBLIOGRAPHY

General

Cruise: Identity, Design and Culture, Peter Quartermaine and Bruce Peter, Laurence King Publishing, 2006.

Cruise Ships: An Evolution in Design, Philip Dawson, Conway Maritime Press, 2000.

Cruise Tourism in Polar Regions: Promoting Environmental and Social Sustainability, eds Michael Luck and Patrick T. Maher, Emma J. Stewart, Author, Earthscan, 2016.

Full Steam Ahead: A Golden Age of Cruising, Boris Danzer Kanthof, Scriptum Editions, 2013.

Polar Tourism: Tourism in the Arctic and Antarctic Regions, eds Colin Michael Hale and Margaret E. Johnston, John Wiley & Sons, 1995.

Polar Tourism: An Environmental Perspective, Bernard Stonehouse and John Snyder, Channel View Publications, 2010.

Prospects for Polar Tourism, John Snyder and Bernard Stonehouse, CABI International, 2007.

Research Themes for Tourism, ed. Peter Robinsoin, Sine Heilman, Peter U.C. Dieke, Cabi International, 2011.

The British Newspaper Archive, www.britishnewspaperarchive.co.uk.

The Captain's Table, Sarah Edington, National Maritime Museum, 2005.

The Tourism Imaginary and Pilgrimages to the Edges of the World, eds Nieves Herrero and Sharon R. Roseman, Channel View Publications, 2015.

Thomas Cook: 150 years of Popular Tourism, Piers Brandon, Necker and Warburg, 1991.

To the Polar Sunrise, K. Westcott Jones, Museum Press, 1957.

Tourist Third Cabin, Lorraine Coons and Alexander Varias, Palgrave Macmillan, 2003.

Ship Information

A Hundred Year History of the P&O: 1837–1937, Boyd Cable, Nicolson and Watson, 1937.

A Pictorial Encyclopedia of Ocean Liners 1860–1994, William H Miller Jr, Dover, 1995.

Cabin Class Rivals, Donald L. Williams and Richard P. De Kerbrech, The History Press, 2015.

'Caronia 1951 Voyages Index', *RMS* Caronia *Timeline*, www.caronia2.info/voyages51.php.

Cruise Industry News, www.cruiseindustrynewswire.com.

Fabulous Interiors of the Great Ocean Liners in Historic Photographs, William H. Miller, Dover, 1984.

Fakta om Fartyg [Facts about Ships] www.faktaomfartyg.se (website is very comprehensive, but in Swedish).

Great Passenger Ships of the World (six volumes), Arnold Kludas, Patrick Stephens, 1972–1986.

Great Passenger Ships 1920–1930, William H. Miller, The History Press, 2014.

Great Passenger Ships 1930–1940, William H. Miller, The History Press, 2015.

Great Passenger Ships 1950–1960, William H. Miller, The History Press, 2016.

Liners and Cruise Ships: Some Notable Smaller Vessels, Anthony Cooke, Carmania Press, 1996.

Nedcruise [Dutch Cruise Site], www.nedcruise.info.

North Star to Southern Cross, John H. Maber, T. Stephenson & Sons, 1967.

Picture History of the French Line, William H. Miller, Dover, 1997.

The British Cruise Ship, Ian Collard, Amberley Press, 2013.
The Fred Olsen Line and its Passenger Ships, Anthony Cooke, Carmania Press, 2007.
The Story of P&O: Revised Edition, David and Stephen Howarth, Weidenfeld and Nicolson, 1996.
The Wilson Line, Arthur G. Credland, Tempus Publishing, 2000.
Waterline: Images from the Golden Age of Cruising, John Graves, National Maritime Museum, 2004.

Antarctic

A Chronology of Antarctic Exploration, R.K. Headland, Bernard Quaritch, 2009.
A Policy for Antarctic Tourism: Conflict or Cooperation, Debra Jean Enzenbacher, Scott Polar Research Institute, Thesis for Master of Philosophy on Polar studies, June 1991.
Exploring the Last Continent: An Introduction to Antarctica, ed. Daniela Liggett, Bryan Storey et al., Springer, 2015.
Tourism in the Antarctic: Opportunities, Constraints and Future Prospects, Thomas G. Bauer, The Haworth Hospitality Press, 2001.
Tourism at Antarctic Arctowski Station 1991–1997: Policies for Better Management, Polish Polar Research Paper, 1997.
Cruise Travel online archive, December 1991 and September 1992, www.cruiseindustrynews.com/
South Georgia Association website, www.southgeoorgiaassociation.org, historic Antarctic information up to 2008, but last tourist cruise entry 2000/01 season.
Ushuaia, Argentina, 50 Anos Comopuerto de Entrada Maritima al Continente Antarctico, Marie Jensen y Maria Elena Daverio, from www.histarmar.com.ar/InfHistorica-8/Ushuaia-Jansen/Ushuaia-PuertaALaAntartida.pdf

Alaska

Pacific Coastal Liners, Gordon Newell and Joe Williamson, Bonanza, 1958.
Empress to the Orient, W. Kaye Lamb, Vancouver Maritime Museum, 1991.

Canada

Arctic Cargo: A History of Marine Transportation in Canada's North, Christopher Wright, 2016.
Canada's Arctic: A Guide to Adventure Through the Northwest Passage, Captain Ken Burton, Pacific Maritime Press, 2018.
Down the Mackenzie, Fullerton Waldo, The MacMillan Company, 1925.
I Was No Lady, Jean Godsell, Ryerson Press, 1961.
HBCA File A105/31. Western Arctic passenger numbers from a handwritten document headed: 'see letter CCP#126 of 31/1/33 with accompanying report'. [This appears to be an ongoing exchange with Furness Withy (a British shipping company) regarding an analysis of HBC's operations. However, the passenger numbers and accompanying revenue figures do not appear to correspond. The report was not found.]
The Beaver Magazine articles:
'Trading into Hudson Bay', R.H.H. McCauley about the Governor's trip from Montreal to Churchill.
'Down North by River Steamer', J.C. MacDonald, June 1934.
'Edmonton to Aklavik 1920', Catharine Hoare, June 1938.
'By Sternwheeler to the Arctic', Josephine Robertson, June 1941.
Gertrude Perrin Fonds, www.gov.mb.ca/rearview/perrin/summercruise.html

Thirty Years of Northwest Passage Cruises, 22 September 2014. Posting by Kevin Griffin on Cybercruise Newsletter.

The Maximum of Mishap: Adventurous Tourists and the State in the Northwest Territories, 1926-1948, Tina Adcock. muse.jhu.edu/article/619052/pdf

1983 Sealift After Action Report by Canadian Coast Guard.

NORDREG Reports 1974–2019.

NWP Transits List from R.K. Headland, Scott Polar Research Institute, Cambridge.

TP 13670E Guidelines for the Operation of Passenger Vessels in Canadian Arctic Waters.

Spitsbergen

Greetings from Spitsbergen: Tourists at the Eternal Ice 1827–1914, John T. Reilly, Akademika AS, 2009.

The Commencement of Regular Arctic Cruise Ship Tourism: Wilhelm Bade and the 'Nordische Hochseefischerei Gesellschaft' of 1892/1893, Klaus Barthelmess (web download courtesy Sandra Walser).

Polar Cruising

Letters from High Latitudes, Being an account of a voyage in the Schooner Yacht 'Foam' 85 OM to Iceland, Jan Mayan and Spitsbergen in 1856, Lord Dufferin, Ticknor and Fields, Boston. Retrieved online from www.biodiversitylibrary.org/bibliography/2085#/summary

Polar Hayes: The life and Contributions of Isaac Israel Hayes MD, Douglas W. Wamsley, American Philosophical Society, 2009.

The Arctic Regions, William Bradford, published 1873, facsimile edition 2013, ed. Michael Lapides, David R. Godine and New Bedford Whaling Museum.

Harpers Weekly, Supplements 7, 14, 21 January 1871, articles written by Isaac Hayes, microfilm courtesy of Memorial University, NL.

The Lindblad Model

Passport to Anywhere, Lars-Eric Lindblad, with John G. Fuller, Times Books, 1983.

Obituary of Lars-Eric Lindblad in the *Independent* newspaper, 16 and 20 January 1994, accessed online.

Falkland Islands

Jane Cameron National Archives online resources, including the *Shipping Register, Shipping News, Falkland Islands Magazine, Falkland Islands Monthly Review.*

A Falklands Diary: Winds of Change in a Distant Colony, Jean Austin, The Radcliffe Press, 2009.

INDEXES

References followed by a 'd' indicate deck plans. References followed by a 'p' indicate pictures.

People

Ships

Companies and Organisations

General

ACKNOWLEDGEMENTS

As will be seen from the bibliography, this book has drawn on a wide range of sources. However, its development would not have been possible without the input from many people. The staff at Digby Library in Nova Scotia dug deep into Canada's library system to find essential reference material. Paul Smith, the Archivist at Thomas Cook, spent much time scouring the *Excursionist* for references to polar cruising. Bob Headland kindly provided an up-to-date list of North Pole cruises, advice regarding visits to the Antarctic, as well as some great photographs.

Bjarne Rasmussen, a Danish maritime historian, was very helpful regarding Greenland's cruise history, while Guillarmo C. Berger, President Fundacion Histamar (the Argentine Maritime History Group) together with its members offered interesting information about the early days of Antarctic travel. Also relative to Antarctica, Amanda Lynnes MCIPR, IAATO's Head of Communication and Environment, and Lisa Kelley, Director of Operations and Government Affairs, patiently put up with numerous emails, and provided much help relative to the organisation and its data.

Relative to penguin species and numbers, Mike Bingham was very helpful. James Frost, President of Marinova, who in a previous position had dealings with Marine Expeditions, provided his archival material on the company. Mike Louagie and Philippe Holtof helped open doors as well as providing industry contacts. The book benefits from a series of excellent maps produced by Courtney Everhart, who also pieced together some of the deck plans and photographs and improved others.

The many original photographs and ephemera in the book would not have been possible without significant input from many archival resources. These include Astrid Drew, the Archivist at the Steamship Historical Society of America; Beth Ellis, Curator, Digital Collections & Web Editor for the P&O Heritage Collection; Fabian Kneule, Archivist at H&C Stader GmbH, which administers the Hapag-Lloyd AG photo archive; and Kristy Aleksich at OneOcean Expeditions, who rifled their imagery files to provide the excellent wildlife and location photographs that appear.

Jamie Inglis and Sandra Still at the Aberdeen Museum did their best to find the *St Sunniva* deck plan, but it remains somewhere in storage. Racheal Crowie, Marketing Officer at Falkland Islands Tourism, was able to provide some excellent photographs illustrating the remarkable wildlife of this southern archipelago. Andrea Barlow, Director at the Falkland Islands Museum and Natural Trust, also helped with local contacts. Camilla Nissan at Knud E. Hansen found details of the *Lindblad Explorer* as well as suggesting the source of the photograph of this important little cruise ship.

Some visitor and ship call data was easy to find through books and in online resources, but much could only be acquired through direct communication with people including Steve Gough in South Georgia; Annfinn Hjelm, Head of Sales and Marketing at Tórshavn, Faroe Islands; Mads Lumholt, Senior Consultant, Market Research in Greenland; Petur Olafson, port director at Akureyri; and Erna Kristiansdottir, Market Quality Manager at Faxafloahafnir in Iceland. Erna also provided an introduction to Guojon Fridrickson, who kindly provided the two historic cruise photographs for Iceland

As noted earlier, the book has benefited enormously from Kevin Griffin's files and knowledge gleaned from many years in the cruise industry. Both Philip Dawson and Bob Headland kindly offered comments on the text after reading early drafts for their forewords. Andrew Kendrick, P.Eng. Vice President Operations at Vard Marine Inc. and someone who has been involved in the development of the Polar Code from its inception, advised about international regulatory issues, and Rasmus Nygard at Knud E. Hansen also helped here, but any errors are my responsibility.